MW01291591

Bruce Smith is the harde[...] case to date. No other jou[...] in peering into the nooks and crannies of this fascinating and alluring cold case.

Marty Andrade, DB Cooper Blogger

The most in-depth investigation published. Bruce has left no stone unturned as he retraces the steps in the investigation and discovers facts and suspects that have not been reported until now. I highly recommend this book.

Pat Forman, co-author of
The Legend of DB Cooper: Death by Natural Causes

If you want one book that gives you the most info about the case, get this one."

Boeing 377, parachute expert at the
2011 DB Cooper Symposium

Fascinating!!! This is a very thorough book on the Cooper mystery. Every avenue is explored. It also gives insights into a sub-culture which has evolved over time regarding the case. There are a lot of devoted and passionate people desperately seeking answers to what in all probability will be a case which is never solved.

Donald T Joyner, Amazon reviewer

This is the best book so far on the DB Cooper Case. Bruce describes many areas and suspects of the case and does not let the FBI get away without saying anything.

Michele Shaw, former landlady of
DB Cooper suspect, Sheridan Peterson

If someone were about to attend a DB Cooper conference, this is the best book to read to get a good overview of the case and review all of the current suspects. In fact, I'd say it is the ONLY book that does that.

Mark Bennett,
DB Cooper researcher, Seattle

Jam-packed with details and wonderfully obscure information about one of the most puzzling and colorful episodes in aviation history—if you're into mysteries, skyjackings, money trails, FBI lore and local legends, this is the book for you!

Cate Montana, author of
Unearthing Venus: My Search for the Woman Within

Bruce Smith is a tenacious investigative reporter. He was able to accomplish some things on the D.B. Cooper case that no one else could. He has his own style and he's his own guy, working alone like a maverick gumshoe reporter from a bygone era.

Galen Cook, Attorney and
noted DB Cooper researcher

DB Cooper and the FBI

A Case Study of America's Only
Unsolved Skyjacking

2nd Edition

Bruce A. Smith

Eatonville, Washington

To get in touch with the author:
brucesmith at rainierconnect dot com is best.

"I don't have a grudge against your airline, Miss,
I just have a grudge."

DB Cooper

Table of Contents

Introduction
DB Cooper and the FBI's
Investigation

The DB Cooper skyjacking is one of America's most perplexing true-crime mysteries. In 1971, the man known as DB Cooper hijacked a Northwest Orient airliner, and after exchanging the passengers for $200,000 he parachuted into the night skies north of Portland, Oregon.

He has never been seen since. We also don't know who Cooper was or if he survived, and nothing has ever been found of the skyjacking—no parachutes, no body or clothes, nor any of the money except for $5,800 that a young boy found eight years later buried on a Columbia River beach. Adding to the intrigue, no one knows how the money got there, or when.

The DB Cooper case is the only unsolved skyjacking in the history of the United States. Nevertheless, hundreds of FBI agents have hunted for Cooper along with scores of local police, and their investigation has been termed "Norjak," an amalgam of Northwest Orient Airlines hijacking.

Besides being a whodunit, the Norjak investigation also gives us a view into the workings of the Federal Bureau of Investigation, and shows us that the FBI is a closed shop—the Bureau only tells us what they want us to know and only when they want us to know it.

Thus, determining the facts beyond the headlines and cursory press releases has been difficult. Currently, the FBI has clammed-up on Norjak, which makes the federal investigation a mystery as well. This dynamic is troubling since it is increasingly evident from the work of open-sourced sleuths that the Norjak investigation is flawed. Arguably, it has been compromised or even corrupted, possibly sabotaged by political pressures.

Most damning is the FBI's loss of its most valuable piece of evidence: the eight cigarettes butts Cooper left on the plane, which contains his dried saliva and is the ideal substance to reveal the skyjacker's DNA. Worse, the butts were not secured in the evidence locker at the FBI's Seattle office, which is the "Office of Origin" for Norjak and should have been the repository for such important artifacts. Rather, they were stored in Las Vegas due to a bureaucratic turf battle. Worst though, the cigarette butts went missing only after their true value was realized. Adding to this disaster, the documentation of these findings is also missing.

Similarly, a Norjak FBI agent, Jeremy Blauser, vanished shortly after his assignment to the case in 2006. Since he was based in Los Angeles, this raises the question if a second, "shadow" investigation was being conducted alongside the official one in Seattle.

But perhaps the most disturbing aspect of the pursuit of DB Cooper is the murder of the FBI's parachute expert, Earl J. Cossey. Cossey was a key figure in assessing Cooper's skydiving abilities for the FBI, but over the years Cossey told plenty of lies and half-truths to the public. Now, many aficionados of the case wonder if he was killed because his deceitfulness puts the FBI in an unfavorable light.

Further, the red warning flags flying over the FBI's investigation are many. Besides a missing cop and a dead consultant, they include seemingly minor aspects of the case, such as the Bureau's inability to pinpoint Cooper's exact landing area. Also, basic police procedures were not followed seemingly, such as not establishing road blocks in Cooper's suspected landing zone. Yet, to evaluate the actions of the FBI it is necessary to fully understand the skyjacking.

Cooper's actions were straightforward.

The day before Thanksgiving, DB Cooper commandeered Flight 305, a NWO 727 inbound to Seattle. He used a bomb in a briefcase for persuasion, and at Seattle-Tacoma International Airport (Sea-Tac) he released the thirty-six passengers in exchange for $200,000 and four parachutes. After refueling, Cooper ordered the pilots to fly to Mexico, and forty-five minutes later he jumped into the chilly November rains of southwestern Washington with his money in a sack tied around his waist. Since nothing substantive of the crime has ever been found and the skyjacker's identity is still unknown, it is as if DB Cooper came from nowhere and returned there when he jumped.

The hijacking has amazed the world because it was history's most daring act of skypiracy. Hundreds of airplanes had been skyjacked prior, but they all had been political and no one had done it strictly for the money. More dramatically, no one had jumped out of the plane on their getaway.

Thousands of journalists and armchair sleuths have sought to solve the Norjak puzzle, seeking at least an inkling of who DB Cooper was. Author Geoffrey Gray calls it "The Hunt for DB Cooper," and that's a worthy title. The search is primal, visceral and impassioned. One researcher told me that he puts himself to sleep at night thinking about the hijacking, and I frequently write in the wee hours myself. In fact, spittle flies across the room whenever my fellow investigators and I discuss the case. Culturally, millions champion DB Cooper as a man who beat the system—a master criminal who perpetrated a mind-boggling crime, completely outsmarting "Da Man."

For its part, the FBI has investigated over 1,100 suspects, and officially the case is still open, although it's "inactive" according to the Bureau's public information officer in Seattle, Ayn Dietrich-Williams.

The night of the skyjacking every FBI agent in the Seattle office, over thirty men, were deployed on the case securing the grounds of Sea-Tac, interviewing the passengers, or managing the actual hijacking via radio through the Seattle Center FAA tower. Several hours later, two-hundred FBI agents and local police awaited Cooper's plane in Reno when it landed for a refueling.

Because of a tactical decision to deploy agents at the Seattle and Portland airports seeking evidence about Cooper, the FBI out-sourced the actual ground search to local county sheriff's departments. This effort was apparently fragmented and slow to develop since the feds weren't certain where to look for Cooper. Simply, the FBI and NWO struggled to determine the most likely landing zones because the flight path and time of Cooper's jump was uncertain.

The ground team tasked with combing the lands eventually identified as the optimum choice for Cooper's LZ—Ariel and Amboy, Washington—was composed of deputies from the Clark County Sheriff's Office. However, they didn't begin their surveillance until Friday afternoon, giving Cooper a 40-hour head start over his pursuers. More troubling, the ground team only covered about 10 percent of their assigned area before the FBI canceled their search on Monday, November 29, 1971.

However, the FBI did launch a partial aerial search over the Ariel-Amboy area, known as LZ-A, immediately following the hijacking. But again the attempt was hampered, this time by the fog, rain and clouds so typical of the Pacific Northwest. After a massive, one-day surveillance of the entire flight path from Seattle to Reno on the 29th, all aerial operations over LZ-A were terminated.

Nevertheless, the FBI resumed its ground search in LZ-A four months later in March 1972, when hundreds of soldiers and dozens of FBI agents returned to the fields and woodlands around Ariel. They searched for eighteen days in March and another eighteen in April, 1972, but they found nothing pertaining to the skyjacking.

As a youth, I'd been aware of Cooper's iconic status in American folklore but I'd never paid him much attention. In 1971, I was living in New York and attending college, and DB Cooper's exploits paled in comparison to my efforts to get into medical school. After relocating to Washington, though, I became reacquainted with the story while covering a local air show for the Pierce County (WA) *Dispatch* newspaper.

In August of 2008, while perusing dozens of vintage aircraft gathered at Thun Field in Puyallup, Washington, I was elated to see a beautifully restored Fairchild 24. It is a single-winged plane from the 1930s and was the "Rolls-Royce" of private airplanes for its day. I loved building model airplanes when I was a kid, and the first balsa wood job I made was a Fairchild. Now, for the first time I was seeing one for real.

Sensing my appreciation, the owner, Ron Forman, came over and we started talking. But after a few minutes in the broiling sun Ron suggested we retreat to the shade under the Fairchild's starboard wing. We camped in his lawn chairs, drank ice-cold cokes, and schmoozed.

After a few minutes I saw a book on the ground next to his chair titled, *DB Cooper*... something... *Legend*... something... *Death*.

"Are you into DB Cooper, Ron?" I asked.

"Heck, yeah!" he replied. "My wife and I just wrote that book!"

For the rest of the afternoon Ron regaled me with his story. "Besides the Fairchild, my wife and I have a Cessna 140, and for years we'd fly on the weekends with a few other 140 pilots here at Thun Field. One of the pilots, Barb Dayton, confessed to being DB Cooper during one of our coffee breaks when we were arguing about the Cooper skyjacking. Our book is about her life and how she did the skyjacking."

"*Barb?* I thought DB Cooper was a guy!" I roared.

"Yeah, he was, and Barb also told us that she was the first person in Washington State to get a sex-change operation. Before 1969 she was *Bobby* Dayton."

So right at the beginning I knew the DB Cooper story was going to be a wild ride.

As Ron continued, I learned that Barb/Bobby was a skydiver and an exceptionally skilled pilot. In addition, she was an explosives expert and daredevil, and had worked aboard ammunition ships in the 1960s before her "gender-reassignment surgery," sailing between San Francisco and Saigon. There, Bobby had killed a Viet Cong sapper with his bare hands during a late night sneak attack. Bobby had also fought in WW II with indigenous head-hunters in the jungles of Borneo against the Japanese. Bobby had even been chased by a grizzly in the Yukon while panning for gold.

Wow, what a story, I thought, and Ron and I spent the rest of the day talking Barb and Cooper. From what I gleaned about her, it seems she did the skyjacking to prove to herself that she still had *cajones.*

"Barb would tell us all these incredible stories that we only half-believed," said Ron. "But when she died in 2002, my wife and

I started checking everything out and it all proved true—except the DB Cooper confession, which we haven't confirmed yet. For that we need a DNA analysis from the FBI, but they won't give it to us. The won't even return our phone calls or emails—not a single one!"

I found such resistance troubling. *Doesn't the FBI want to hear a confession from DB Cooper?*

So, I decided to see what was wrong with the Bureau. Plus, I wanted to learn more about the remarkable Ms. Dayton. Ron educated me on the basics of Norjak, arming me with contact information for many of the individuals involved with the case.

But I encountered some of the same obstacles Ron had. Ralph Himmelsbach, former FBI agent and chief skyjacking investigator in Portland where the hijacking started, refused to discuss the case with me unless I paid him $600. After years of being stymied, however, I spoke with Ralph briefly in 2011 when I simply drove up to his house and begged a few questions.

More unyielding was Himmelsbach's counterpart in Seattle, Norjak case agent Ron Nichols—and the fellow in charge of the case when the money was found—who has been non-responsive to my phone calls, emails, and letters.

But I did speak with one Norjak official, Special Agent Larry Carr, the Cooper case agent from 2007–2009. My twenty-minute interview was memorable because he bullied me throughout our conversation, but I did receive plenty of valuable information.

Organizationally, I have also been rebuffed. The Bureau has denied me access to all files and evidence, although it has opened at least a few of its doors to other private citizens, such as Geoffrey Gray, Tom Kaye, and Galen Cook. The current case agent, Curtis Eng, declines to discuss the case with me in any form.

Also troubling, the FBI has never sent an agent to attend any professional Norjak gatherings, such as the DB Cooper Symposium in Portland in 2011, or the 2013 "COOPER" Symposium in Tacoma, hosted by the Washington State Historical Museum.

As a newsreporter, I have long known that law enforcement is leery of the media. In effect, the police merely view us as a way to distribute their side of the story to the public, and they rarely discuss complex cases with journalists. But in Norjak, they have stonewalled me while cherry-picking the voices they prefer, such as the aforementioned Geoffrey Gray, an A-list writer with New York magazine. This practice is possibly illegal since it runs counter to the Equal Access doctrine. It also raises the possibility of a *quid pro quo*—if you want access to the FBI's files then you'd better write copy that is favorable to the Bureau.

Adding to that concern, I have learned in my newspaper work that the central mission of law enforcement is not to catch criminals or fight crime—if that was the case then half of our country's cops would be camped on Wall Street. Rather, the primary purpose of the police is to protect the interests of the powerful, and in my view that dynamic is displayed in its full glory in Norjak, although what those interests are remain hidden.

But the silence and spin are the same as other major cases I've covered, such as the murders of Brian and Beverly Mauck near Seattle in 2007 that had negative ramifications for Mitt Romney's presidential aspirations, as both the cops and the family conspired to misdirect my investigative reporting.

But in Norjak, not only has the FBI withheld critical information from most journalists, it has withheld evidence among its own agents and between field offices. At times, it even appears that no one is in charge of the DB Cooper case, and it is mostly an "every-man-for-himself" type of operation. Part of that is due to the nature of how J Edgar Hoover had structured his FBI in the 1970s.

Allegedly, Hoover gave field agents cash bonuses for solving high-profile cases, which motivated investigators to become very competitive, and thus, highly selective with whom they shared information. In addition, case agents were given a lot of administrative leeway and ran their investigations like a fiefdom, a practice that continues to this day. This compartmentalization extended to how field offices interacted with each other, and as a result, the Bureau struggled to solve complex cases that involve multiple jurisdictions. This dynamic still exists in the current era, as we saw in the 9-11 attacks when the FBI had trouble "connecting the dots."

In Norjak, three main FBI offices shared investigatory responsibilities: **Portland**, where the skyjacking began and some of the ransom money was later found; **Seattle**, where the ransom exchange took place and the on-going skyjacking was managed; and **Las Vegas**, which supplied the agents for the evidence retrieval in Reno and where it was stored.

Later, as the dozen or so Cooper copycats began hijacking airplanes, other jurisdictions became involved in the Cooper investigation, particularly the **Salt Lake City** field office when Richard McCoy hijacked his airplane in April 1972. Thus, a fourth major player landed solidly into the Norjak mix.

In addition the case is huge, filling rooms with documents. So it is understandable that the record-keeping is untidy. But the Norjak information seems so disorganized, contradictory, or confusing that Cooper case agents appear befuddled. Larry Carr, who relished speaking publicly about Cooper, routinely presented a haphazard view of the role of Earl Cossey played in the FBI's investigation.

Further, it seems that Norjak investigators have not read many of the documents in the case files, and rely mostly on anecdotal narratives passed down from case agent to case agent, much like tribal lore being exchanged between chieftains. Additionally, Cooper case agents are rotated every few years, further eroding case management continuity. Further, young agents don't have any personal knowledge of Norjak and they stumble in their efforts to identify principals in the case. The mess is so complete these days the FBI reportedly has to ask journalists for the phone numbers of witnesses to the skyjacking. With such a muddle it is not surprising there are rumors of a cover-up engineered by Big Money and Big Power.

Welcome to one of America's greatest true-crime mysteries. Has there been a cover-up? Has the FBI's investigation been squashed by powerful sources claiming "national security" concerns or other geopolitical influences? Or is the FBI just sloppy, overwhelmed, or unlucky? Or could Cooper have outsmarted the FBI, and the feds just don't want the public to know? Perhaps Mother Nature simply stuffed Cooper into a tiny hole somewhere in the wilds of Washington along with his parachutes, the money, and a bomb in a briefcase, and no one has found him yet?

Even though this book is about the FBI as much as it is DB Cooper, I don't solve the case or prove a conspiracy. I just offer my findings of who said what and why. It's also my effort through truth-telling to deliver a measure of justice to the incompetent, the hubristic, and the power-hungry. So, follow me through the details of this astounding crime and come to your own conclusions.

Chapter 1

Skyjacking Begins

Just before 2 pm on Wednesday November 24, 1971 a middle-aged man approached the Northwest Orient Airlines counter in the Portland, Oregon airport. The day was the busy travel time before the Thanksgiving holiday and the gentleman bought a one-way ticket to Seattle. The total cost, including tax, was twenty dollars. He paid in cash.

The NWO ticket agent, Dennis Lysne, told his customer that his next departure to Seattle, Flight 305, was scheduled to leave at 2:35 pm but was currently running late.

"That's a 727, right?" the customer asked.

Lysne assured him that Flight 305 was in fact a Boeing 727, the relatively new aircraft introduced a few years earlier and widely favored in the airline industry before jetways were commonplace. 727s enjoyed their reputation because they possessed their own internal stairway system—an aft stairs that could be lowered down to the tarmac, thus eliminating the need for cumbersome "air stairs" to be rolled into place.

Lysne's passenger was the last to purchase a ticket for Flight 305 and he identified himself as "Dan Cooper," which Lysne reportedly wrote on the ticket.

Dan Cooper was wearing a dark suit, a white shirt and a narrow black tie. Over that he wore a lightweight black raincoat.

He also carried a briefcase, possibly made of cloth, and toted a brown, or green, paper bag with contents unknown. He was tall, about six-foot, and trim, around 175 pounds. He also had an olive or "swarthy" complexion. However, he spoke with no discernible accent.

The ticket agent said Cooper stood off by himself in the passenger waiting area, staring out the window until the boarding call was issued. Essentially, Cooper looked and acted like a businessman heading home for the Thanksgiving holiday.

Flight 305 had spent the day hop-scotching across the United States, starting in Washington, DC early on Wednesday morning. When it reached the NWO hub in Minneapolis it received a fresh flight crew—one destined to be hijacked—and continued westward, stopping at Great Falls and Missoula, Montana; Spokane, Washington; and then headed to Portland (PDX). The Seattle leg was scheduled to be its last jump of the day.

"I loved flying like that," Flight 305's First Officer Bill Rataczak told me in 2009. "All those take-offs and landings—it was a lot of great flying."

Rataczak also told me that his co-pilot, Captain William Scott, "Scotty," and he swapped duties at every airport. One pilot would fly into a city, and the other would handle the subsequent take-off. Since Rataczak flew into Portland, Scotty was slated for the run to Seattle. In the cockpit, Rataczak and Scott were joined by the flight engineer, Harold "Andy" Anderson. After the skyjacking, all three would continue to have distinguished careers as Northwest flight captains.

In the passenger cabin, Flight 305 had three flight attendants: Purser Alice Hancock in first class, and newbies Florence Schaffner, 23, and Tina Mucklow, 22, in the economy section.

There is some question on the number of passengers aboard Flight 305, but the general consensus among researchers concurs with the *Seattle Times*, which published thirty-six names in its account of the skyjacking. The passengers were offered "open seating," and Dan Cooper sat in the last row on the starboard side of the aircraft—the right-hand side of the plane as one looks ahead towards the cockpit.

At first, Cooper sat down in the aisle seat, 18-D, but during the hijacking he moved over one seat to the middle of the row, 18-E. Passenger William Mitchell, a 20 year-old college student returning home for the holidays, sat directly across the aisle from Cooper in seat 18-B, and as a result, Mitchell had one of the best views of the skyjacker. Along with the three flight attendants, Mr. Mitchell is considered a prime witness to the skyjacking.

As Flight 305 rolled down the runway a few minutes after 3 pm, Cooper turned toward flight attendant Florence Schaffner sitting behind him in a galley jump seat, and handed her a note tucked inside an envelope. Schaffner, a former beauty queen from Arkansas, put the paper unopened into her pocket. A few moments later Cooper gave her a prompt. "Miss, I think you better have a look at that note," he said. Schaffner retrieved the message and read it: *Miss, I have a bomb in my briefcase. I will use it if necessary. I want you to sit next to me. You are being hijacked."*

At this point Cooper was sitting in the middle of Row 18, and Schaffner promptly sat beside him in the aisle seat. Cooper opened his briefcase and showed her what he claimed was a bomb—four, or possibly eight, red cylinders that Florence believed to be dynamite, and a couple of large batteries with wires attached. Cooper explained that he was hijacking the plane and instructed Florence to write a note with his demands to take to the cockpit. He wanted four parachutes: "two back chutes" and "two front chutes," which were understood to be two main parachutes and two reserves, and $200,000 in non-specified "negotiable currency." Knowing that the flight to Seattle was less than forty minutes, Cooper demanded that they circle above Puget Sound until the money and chutes arrived at Sea-Tac airport. There, he promised to release the passengers. He also wanted a fuel truck parked nearby when they landed. "No funny stuff or I'll do the job," Cooper added.

Florence complied with the note-taking but became increasingly agitated. She told Tina what was happening, and Flo later admitted she thought she was going to die that night in a mid-air explosion. As Florence's fears escalated, Tina intervened. First, she informed the cockpit crew of the skyjacking via the plane's intercom, known as the "interphone," and then took Flo's seat next to the skyjacker.

Initially, Tina made a joke about the hijacking, which she assumed to be one of the airline industry's weekly unscheduled outings to Havana. "You know Northwest Orient has strict policies about traveling to Cuba. Can't bring home rum or cigars. Customs confiscate them in the airport." Cooper laughed.

But the seriousness of the situation returned. Rattled, Florence headed to the safety of the cockpit, and when she left Cooper donned the infamous wrap-around sunglasses that he wore for the remainder of the hijacking.

When Florence arrived in the cockpit with the ransom note, she "dropped it in Scotty's lap," according to Rataczak, and Captain Scott became so anxious that Rataczak had to assist him in completing the take-off.

But back in Row 18, Tina lit cigarettes for Cooper because he kept his hand inside the briefcase, which remained on his lap. Tina, a former smoker, lit a few for herself. She also tried to engage the hijacker in conversation, both to defuse tensions and to elicit information. Cooper rebuffed her.

After Tina had stabilized the situation with the skyjacker and the cockpit crew settled down, Alice Hancock moved the aft passengers up to the forward section of the aircraft to minimize the chance of their taking matters into their own hands and causing injuries. Hancock cited weight and landing concerns, and the passengers moved without incident, including Mitchell. As a result, no passenger sat closer to Cooper than Row 14.

Over the next two and a half hours, Tina sat next to the skyjacker in relative isolation as 305 circled Puget Sound. She continued to probe him with questions, including their famous repartee: "Do you have a grudge against Northwest?" she asked.

"I don't have a grudge against your airline, Miss. I just have a grudge," Cooper answered.

Tina and Cooper even laughed at a passenger's joke, according to Jack Almstad, who told me that he stood behind Tina and Cooper as he waited to use the rear lavatory. "If this keeps up much longer they can serve us our turkey dinners up here," Jack joked with the pair in Row 18, who chuckled at his witticism. However, this incident is not recorded in any of the crew debriefing reports filed by the FBI, and contradicts Hancock's claim that no passengers were able to approach Cooper.

Overall, Tina's actions are seen as heroic. "Tina saved our lives that night," Bill Rataczak told me. "If it wasn't for her I wouldn't be here talking to you right now. She's one-in-a-million. She did a tremendous job that night, sitting next to him for hours."

Rataczak also said that he considered Tina to be the "brains of the outfit," and after the skyjacking he bought her a bottle of

Channel No. 5 perfume on behalf of the entire crew. He attached the following note: *A gift to you. Remember that there were three guys sitting in front of you in the cockpit that survived that night because of what you did.*

As for Cooper, Tina and Florence both reported that the hijacker acted like a gentleman, with Tina stating that the hijacker "wasn't nervous... (and) he seemed rather nice. He was never cruel or nasty. He was thoughtful and calm all the time."

However, Special Agent Ralph Himmelsbach and author of *NORJAK—The Investigation of DB Cooper,* consistently describes Cooper as a "rotten, sleazy crook" who used "foul language." But, Himmelsbach has never offered any specific behaviors to support this characterization.

Despite the uncertainty, the passengers also remained calm throughout the skyjacking and never challenged Hancock's ruse of a mechanical problem.

In the cockpit, the flight crew realized that Scotty needed to concentrate solely on flying the airplane, so Rataczak and Anderson focused on the communications, which quickly became complex discussions between Tina—relaying instructions from Cooper—and Flight 305 to NWO flight operations in Minneapolis and the FBI at Sea-Tac, and FAA personnel in Portland and Seattle conferring with the aircraft and NWO.

"But we passed all decisions through Scotty," Rataczak told me.

Astutely, the skyjacker had few interactions with the cockpit crew, and none directly with the FBI. Tina used the interphone to talk with Rataczak and Anderson, and Florence remained in the cockpit and took notes of all communications.

During the hours they circled over Puget Sound, Cooper indicated the lights of Tacoma to Tina, leading many investigators to believe that he was familiar with the area. In addition, Cooper reportedly said that he did not want military parachutes, such as might be obtained from McChord Air Base. In doing so he revealed that he knew the Air Force facility was about thirty miles south of Sea-Tac.

At 5:39 pm, the FBI informed Flight 305 that the money and back parachutes had arrived at Sea-Tac and the front chutes were expected shortly. Hearing that, Cooper allowed 305 to begin its decent, and at 5:45 pm the plane landed at Sea-Tac, parking on an isolated section of runway.

On the tarmac, the boss of NWO ground operations at Sea-Tac, Al Lee, waited with the money and parachutes. Ironically, the aft stairs were not used and NWO brought in airstairs mounted on a pick-up truck. It docked at the forward door, where Tina got off before the passengers and retrieved the bank bag with $200,000 from Lee.

Jack Almstad says he clearly saw Tina come back on board with the bank bag and what looked like "bricks or bundles of money" bulging in the sack. Nevertheless, neither Almstad nor anyone else realized that they were witnessing a skyjacking. "No one suspected what was going on," Jack told me in 2012.

The exact sequence of events after Tina brought the money aboard is muddled, but transcripts of the crew debriefings suggest that Cooper allowed the passengers to disembark at this point. However, some authors claim that Tina also had to bring the parachutes aboard before Cooper released the passengers.

Nevertheless, Almstad says he and his fellow passengers left the plane without any interruption. "Northwest had a bus waiting for us when we got off the airplane," he said.

As they were leaving, Cooper hid in the lavatory. When all the passengers had left the plane, Cooper re-emerged and instructed

Tina to bring the parachutes on board, according to the debriefing transcripts. She needed to make three trips—first bringing one back chute, then the two smaller front reserves, and finishing with the second back parachute. After Tina brought all the items aboard, Cooper told her to close all the window shades to thwart any sniper activity.

During this time, the FBI screened the passengers in the terminal and in that process the skyjacker received a new name, "DB Cooper," the moniker by which he is known to history. There are several versions of how that happened, but here is the predominant scenario:

In those days airlines used passenger manifests that identified each individual by last name and first initial. Hence, the FBI realized their skyjacker was "Cooper, D." They immediately contacted the Portland Police Department and asked if they had any known criminals named "D. Cooper." A detective reportedly said that they had a small-time burglar named "DB Cooper," and the feds instructed the Portland police to pick up the suspect. An Associated Press reporter named Clyde Jabin was standing next to the detective and overheard the Portland half of the conversation. Jabin asked the cop for details and was told that the police were now looking for DB Cooper, which was true but misleading. In turn, Jabin told his AP editor and the information went over the news wires. Hence, Dan Cooper became "DB Cooper." Soon, even the FBI began calling the skyjacker DB Cooper.

Once the passengers were ushered to safety, a great disagreement arose in official circles on how to deal with Cooper. Author Geoffrey Gray, who had unprecedented access to FBI files and case agents, reveals in his *Skyjack—The Hunt for DB Cooper* that many in the FBI felt there should not be any accommodations given to the skyjacker.

This jibes with the perspective of the FBI in other hijackings. In the late 1960s and early 1970s, the United States experienced about one skyjacking a week—all political before Cooper. As a result, the FBI advocated a tough approach toward hijackers.

But the airlines preferred a more conciliatory—and cheaper— posture. Essentially, the airlines felt it made better business sense to fly a plane load of grumpy travelers to Cuba occasionally than to provoke an armed confrontation with a hijacker and risk millions in damages to the aircraft and injuries to the passengers.

Thus, the relationship between the Bureau and the airlines was uneven, and the FBI was widely seen as a bunch of "cowboys" who had to be controlled by the cooler heads in corporate board rooms. Along those lines, Rataczak confirmed to me that FBI officials were not cooperative with 305 while it was on the ground, and "played games" with the refueling.

The first attempt to refuel 305 was interrupted by the FBI, who told the cockpit that there was a "vapor-lock problem." However, this was a mechanical glitch that only occurred in the hot temperatures of summer, and the bluff was not believed by anyone. Further, Cooper knew that the plane should have been completely refueled in less than a half-hour, so when the process stretched out beyond that time he became antsy, which in turn made the crew nervous.

Rataczak had to get pushy with the feds and ultimately ordered them to proceed without delay, since lives were at stake. "I laid down the law; and yes, I raised my voice, and that's all I'm going to say about the matter," Rataczak told me.

His words carried sufficient weight, apparently, and a second fuel truck arrived. However, it developed some legitimate problems and a third was dispatched, only to discover it had too little fuel to complete the job.

Eventually, a fourth truck was required to complete the task, but by then Cooper had become distracted with the process of preparing his parachutes, and tensions aboard 305 dissipated.

As for his ransom money, Cooper had originally wanted the bills in a "knapsack" and not the bank bag, but none was provided. So Cooper tried to fashion a suitable container from a reserve parachute bag, but was unsuccessful. Instead, he cut several shroud lines from the chute itself and lashed the bank bag closed, along with weaving a kind of rope handle that he attached to himself.

In addition, Cooper donned a main parachute before take-off, supposedly putting it on "like it was an everyday occurrence," according to author Richard Tosaw from his 1982 interview with Tina.

Cooper allowed Alice and Flo to leave with the passengers, but he held Tina on board as a hostage, and to show him how to lower the aft stairs once they were airborne. After her colleagues departed, it is believed that Tina spent about forty-five minutes alone with Cooper. However, what they said or did has never been revealed. In total, Tina Mucklow spent nearly five hours in the company of DB Cooper.

For the getaway, Cooper instructed the cockpit crew via Tina to prepare to fly to "Mexico City or anywhere in Mexico." He also gave them a list of unusual demands on how to fly the plane: go no faster than 200 mph with the wing flaps set at fifteen degrees, have the wheels down and locked, ascend no higher than 10,000 feet and keep the cabin unpressurized. In addition, he wanted to take-off with the aft stairs down even though they might get torn-up dragging along the runway.

The crew was aghast, and detailed negotiations between the cockpit and Cooper ensued over these metrics, especially Cooper's insistence to depart with the aft stairs deployed. Paul Soderlind, NWO flight operations boss in Minneapolis, advised his pilots not to take-off with the aft stairs lowered, which triggered an argument with Cooper. The skyjacker assured them such a take-off would be safe. Apparently, Cooper knew that such departures were possible, perhaps from flight tests that had been conducted by the military in Vietnam.

But Scott was adamantly opposed, and eventually Cooper relented to the captain's demand. The aft stairs remained closed.

The pilots were also concerned about flying with the aft stairs lowered. However, according to Ralph Himmelsbach in his book *NORJAK,* Soderlind and NWO were assured by the CIA and Boeing officials that 727s could fly with the aft stairs deployed because the military was doing that during covert operations in Vietnam.

Once their fears were allayed, the pilots additionally told Cooper that they wouldn't be able to fly to Mexico without another refueling stop. They wanted to get more fuel in San Francisco or Los Angeles, but they also had an ulterior motive for these choices. "It was like war," Rataczak told me. "He wanted to get us and we wanted to get him. I wanted to fly down the coast, out over the ocean, and let him jump out there—let's see how long DB Cooper could hold his breath with twenty-two pounds of twenties tied to his waist!"

But a less confrontational approach was recommended by Soderlind, who was following the non-provocative tone established by NWO's boss, Donald Nyrop. Hence, a compromise was offered: refuel in Reno, Nevada. Cooper agreed.

Finally at 7:36 pm, Flight 305 took off from Sea-Tac on Cooper's getaway run. As they lifted off from runway 16L, Tina was in back with Cooper, while Scotty, Bill and Andy were in front soaring into the Big Unknown.

Fifteen-hundred miles away at a Northwest Orient repair facility in Minneapolis, airline officials turned on the intercom system so their employees could follow the drama unfolding at Sea-Tac. Listening closely was a jet mechanic named John Rataczak, the father of Bill, the guy flying the plane.

Chapter 2

Getaway

Climbing above Seattle, Bill Rataczak was at the controls and Captain Scott manned the communications. Behind them, Second Officer Andy Anderson monitored the weather as usual, but now he had to closely watch their fuel consumption due to Cooper's ungainly flight requirements. In aviation slang, Flight 305 was flying "dirty."

But Cooper's instructions to fly to Mexico at 10,000 feet were seen as brilliant because it forced 305 to fly over predictable terrain. Cooper knew where he was without having to reveal a specific flight plan to the authorities, and here's how that happened:

Leaving Sea-Tac for any southerly destination but flying no higher than 10,000 feet only allowed two options: over the ocean, or due south down an eight-mile wide air corridor known as Victor 23 (V-23). The ocean route was ruled out even though it was Rataczak's preferred choice, so 305 had to fly V-23, which parallels the Interstate 5 corridor. It is heavily used by small private planes that need to avoid the peaks of the Cascade Mountains lying to the east, as Mount Rainier has an elevation of 14,409 feet and dominates the urban Seattle skyline so dramatically that "The Mountain" is pictured on every Washington State license plate. From Rainier southward, the Cascades possess numerous peaks over 10,000 feet all the way to Mount Shasta at 14,179 feet in northern California.

Compounding this issue, Oregon's Coastal Range lies west of I-5 and also has some elevations that need to be avoided. Thus, south-bound traffic out of Sea-Tac is funneled into the narrow channel of V-23, which runs directly above metro Portland and south over the farmlands of Oregon's Willamette Valley. However, once 305 climbed out of Sea-Tac and entered Victor 23 the plane's exact location became surprisingly difficult to determine. "I really don't know where we were," Bill Rataczak told me when I asked him in 2009.

With this kind of uncertainty, 305's flight path is fiercely debated because it is nearly impossible to determine where Cooper landed if the plane's position when he jumped can not be pinpointed. The FBI has historically claimed that 305 followed V-23 all through Washington and Oregon. They say their maps draw upon FAA radar readings and calculations from the NWO's Paul Soderlind, who was closely monitoring the flight. Former Cooper case agent Larry Carr places 305 smack dab in the middle of V-23, and most researchers accept the FBI's position that the flight stayed in V-23 all the way to northern California, where it turned left at Red Bluff and headed to Reno.

But there are strong voices of dissent. Most prominent is Ralph Himmelsbach, who told me that he is convinced 305 flew much farther east of V-23, perhaps as far as 15-20 miles eastward and over the Washougal River watershed. "Why do you believe that, Ralph?" I asked during our one brief and unpaid conversation in 2011.

"Because that's what Rataczak told me," he answered. Besides Himmelsbach, Rataczak has told others a different story than what he told me. Some journalists claim Rataczak told them he was east of V-23, while other have reported that Rataczak said he could see the lights of Portland and suburban Vancouver, WA, which is within the V-23 flight path.

Researcher Jo Weber claims that the latter is exactly what Rataczak told her. This perspective was further supported in 2015 when crew debriefing reports from the FBI surfaced on the DB Cooper Forum, in which Flight Engineer Andy Anderson told officials they were "coming up on the suburbs of Portland," and were able to see the city's lights glowing through the clouds.

Nevertheless, here is the exchange I had with Mr. Rataczak: "Flight 305 didn't have the capacity to determine its exact location," he told me. "Only the air traffic controllers could determine our position." However, Rataczak told me that he had been given the freedom to move outside of any designated air corridors, and that the air space around 305 had been cleared of all other air traffic.

This has been confirmed by other pilots, such as Everett Johnson, who was flying a San Juan Airways Piper Aztec inbound to Seattle from Friday Harbor. Johnson told me that he and many other aircraft had to endure the skyjacking in large holding patterns throughout the Pacific Northwest. In fact, Johnson ran low on fuel while circling Puget Sound and had to make an emergency landing at Boeing's Paine Field in Everett, Washington. Subsequently, he spent hours waiting for the aerial traffic jam to dissipate.

But Rataczak offered me another version near the end of our 70-minute conversation: "The winds had blown us off Victor 23 to the east," he said. "How far? Nothing dramatic, a couple of miles probably... the FBI or the FAA may have our exact position and flight path." Rataczak also declared that Soderlind was an instrumental voice that night and was coordinating, if not overtly directing, Flight 305's movements in the air. "Paul Soderlind was a very experienced flight captain himself and he did the research on the wind and he also gave us the weather forecasts," Rataczak said. But later, Rataczak specifically stated, "We were east of Victor 23."

Another dissenting voice is Marianne Lincoln, now a Microsoft programmer and a former Bethel School Board member from Spanaway, Washington. In 1971, she was a 14-year old listening to the skyjacking on her father's VHF radio, mounted in his airplane parked at the family's home at Shady Acres Airport in Spanaway. Marianne remembers vividly the communications she heard from "Seattle Center," the FAA's command post. She says that 305 flew east of V-23 over the Washougal River and turned left at Gresham, Oregon. Then it headed up the Columbia Gorge. Her claim dove-tails with the mind-set Rataczak told me he possessed that night—*it was war; he wanted to get us and we wanted to get him.* Did Rataczak fly over the rugged lands of the Cascades and the Columbia River Gorge hoping to deposit a skyjacker in the most dangerous terrain possible?

Even more confounding, federal agents Russ Calame and Bernie Rhodes write in their book *DB Cooper—the Real McCoy* that Captain Scott told Ralph Himmelsbach at the latter's retirement party that 305 was flying over Woodland, Washington, which is 30 miles **west** of the Washougal. So, the issue of the flight path and Cooper's LZ is obviously problematic.

Nevertheless, before he jumped Cooper learned from Tina how the staircase operated. Geoffrey Gray says that Cooper opened the access door to the staircase before take-off, and Tina showed him how to push the stairs' control lever forward, a very simple maneuver in actuality. Shortly after this, they became airborne, and Tina grew anxious because she was afraid that she would be sucked out of the aircraft if Cooper deployed the stairs while they were still standing in its doorway. Cooper assured her that she was safe since the cabin was not pressurized—one of his requirements with the flight crew.

She also told him that she was concerned about the bomb, and Cooper reportedly told her that he planned to disarm it or take it with him. After that, he sent her to the cockpit. On her way, Tina turned around at First Class to close the curtain. Gray says that she saw Cooper lasso-ing the bank bag to his waist, while author Richard Tosaw in *DB Cooper—Dead or Alive?* says that Cooper waved goodbye. Regardless, Tina pivoted and entered the cockpit at approximately 7:45 pm, about ten minutes after take-off.

No one has ever seen DB Cooper again, but his movements were closely monitored. A couple minutes after Tina left Cooper, the skyjacker called the cockpit on the interphone and told Rataczak to slow the plane because he was having trouble getting the aft stairs deployed. Rataczak reportedly extended the flaps to 30 degrees, reducing the plane's speed from 225 mph to 170 mph.

At 8:04 pm, according to Tosaw, the crew felt movement in the plane and realized that the aft stairs were finally opened. They could also hear the engine roar more plainly. About 9 minutes later, at 8:13 pm, the crew felt a sharp spike in cabin air pressure. "There he goes," Rataczak shouted.

Rataczak made that assumption based upon the following aerodynamics: When Cooper released the aft stairs they did not drop fully into the air and only extended a few feet into the slipstream. But when Cooper descended the staircase he forced it fully open. Then, when he jumped off the stairway they sprang upwards much like a diving board does when a swimmer dives into the water. As the stairs re-bounded they pushed air into the cabin, which the crew perceived as a "pressure bump." The spike was also recorded on the plane's instruments.

The bumping motion also made the aircraft "curtsy," with the tail rising, apparently a couple of times. Rataczak had to counter these oscillations and "trim" the craft back into horizontal flight.

These oscillations and the pressure bump were later re-created by the FBI when they jettisoned a 200-pound weight off the aft stairs of a 727 at 10,000 feet and 200 mph. The crew, which included Andy Anderson, reported identical readings to the Cooper jump.

But where was 305 at 8:13 pm? "It remains an enigma," Rataczak told me. But he is very certain about the time: 8:13 pm.

"We were quite confident that the pressure bump indicated when Cooper jumped," Rataczak said. Rataczak also informed the air traffic controllers that Cooper had left. "I told them to mark it on their shrimp boats (radar screens)," he said.

As for the time of the jump, Rataczak's time of 8:13 pm is confirmed by Richard Tosaw, but Bernie Rhodes and Ralph Himmelsbach write 8:12 pm in their respective books. Others cite different times, and some at the DZ chat room on Norjak claim as early as 8:10 pm, while others as late as 8:15 pm based upon flight path calculations. One minute can make a lot of difference as Flight 305, even at its reduced speed, was traveling at three-miles-per-minute.

Nevertheless, once DB Cooper left Flight 305 the search began.

Chapter 3

Search for DB Cooper

The aerial search was immediate. Two F-106 jet interceptors attached to NORAD command took-off from McChord Air Base when Flight 305 left Sea-Tac. They followed Cooper down Victor 23, but were unable to fly safely at 305's speed, allegedly, and had to perform circular maneuvers to stay close to the aircraft.

In addition, an airborne T-33 training jet from the Idaho Air National Guard was diverted to tail Flight 305. However, none of these pilots saw Cooper exit, and if their radar screens recorded anything it was not made public.

At the same time, Ralph Himmelsbach and a second FBI agent raced from the FBI's command post at PDX and jumped into an Oregon Air National Guard helicopter. In the rough weather they couldn't gain enough headway to catch up with 305, which lumbered ahead of them through the skies of northern Oregon.

However, some of these official accounts are now questioned. A syndicated journalist from Tacoma, Adele Ferguson, wrote an account of DB Cooper's getaway that contradicted the official version. Ferguson said that Dan Dawson—who in 1971 was in charge of readying the F-106s at McChord, and later a Washington state legislator—told her that the national command at NORAD had ordered him to "back-off" from Flight 305.

In addition, Dawson also claimed that he was ordered by NORAD officials *not* to add chaff to a set of parachutes, which would have amplified their radar signals.

Along those lines, I asked Cooper case agent Larry Carr about the lack of tracking devices on the Cooper chutes. Carr told me that such electronic equipment had not been developed at that time. I find that spurious since similar technology was being used in the 1960s to monitor enemy troop movements along the Ho Chi Minh Trail, especially around the beleaguered Marine combat base of Khe Sanh. Further, they were used on the McCoy skyjacking five months later in April 1972, according to the FBI's Salt Lake City, Special Agent in Charge (SAC) Russ Calame.

Similarly, no reports of Cooper's exit have been released publicly from NORAD's super-secret SAGE radar system at McChord. As a result, sleuths at the DZ have speculated that DB Cooper may have gotten a free pass on his getaway because the Air Force didn't want the Russians to know how sophisticated their new detection equipment was. Or conversely, the military didn't want the Russians—*and* the American taxpayers—to know if SAGE was a boondoggle and unable to pick up a skydiver descending from 10,000 feet at 1,000 feet per minute only 75 miles away.

Nevertheless, by the time Flight 305 landed in Reno—shortly after 11 pm—it is generally believed that Soderlind had deduced from FAA radar and NWO monitoring systems that Cooper had jumped northwards of Battleground, WA. Accounting for wind drift to the northeast, Soderlind sketched a potential landing zone of about four-miles wide and six-miles long emanating southwest from the gritty logging towns of Ariel and Amboy Washington, about 25 miles north of Portland. This area was the aforementioned "LZ-A," and was a moderately populated region that featured rolling hills and farmlands. However, a myth quickly developed that LZ-A was rugged wilderness.

Outside of the FBI, Cooper is widely believed to have successfully deployed his parachute, landing on the ground at approximately 8:30 pm after descending through a thick cloud layer at 5,000 feet and scattered clouds at 2,000 feet.

The case for Cooper making a successful descent is supported by the fact that all the copycats who jumped after him made it, some without any prior parachuting experience. In fact, one successful copycat, Martin McNally, had to be shown how to put on his parachute.

Further, if Cooper knew the capabilities of the 727 he would probably know the optimum techniques for deploying his chute, which would be to open it while on the stairs and letting it squib into the winds rushing past the aircraft. This would alleviate the need for a problematic free-fall through the slipstream and would allow Cooper to carry an asymmetrical load of money. Most sky-divers agree that if Cooper was able to open his parachute he would have landed successfully.

But it would have been a rough ride. The temperature was 22 degrees Fahrenheit at his departure point of 10,000 feet, but it was raining through the lower air column. Astonishingly, few witnesses concur on how hard the precipitation was falling at ground level. Official reports indicate that the night of Wednesday, November 24, 1971 was just another drippy, dreary autumnal evening. But, local residents report that the weather was hellacious.

Meyer Louie, a college student driving home for the holiday, told the audience at the 2011 Symposium that the storm he experienced was so intense that he was afraid for his life as he drove along I-84 through the Columbia Gorge. He said he thought he might be blown off the road. "Ever since then, I use that storm as the judge for how bad a storm can be," he told us.

Another member of the symposium said she drove through Portland on I-5 that evening and characterized the wind and rain as "fierce." Dona Elliott, owner of the Ariel Tavern and hostess of the renown Cooper Days Festival, claims that the rain was falling so hard that she couldn't see the other side of the street at her home in nearby Amboy, Washington. Another Amboy resident, Margaret Culp, told me that the storm that night was "simply terrible," and Ralph Himmelsbach writes that "the weather was absolutely rotten."

Nor does everyone agree on how windy it was. Official reports put the wind as variable throughout the air column to 10,000 feet, with gusts up to 30–40 mph from the southwest, which is fairly typical for a November storm in the Pacific Northwest. Rataczak acknowledged that the weather was rough and that the flight got a "little bumpy." However, Ralph Himmelsbach writes in *NORJAK* that a Continental pilot named Tom Bohan, flying into Portland a few minutes behind 305, faced a cross-wind much higher—gusting up to 80 knots—and blowing from due south, which made his east-to-west landing at PDX dicey.

Regardless, it is believed that DB Cooper made it to the ground, either alive or dead, by 8:30 pm. But the subsequent ground search is filled with inconsistencies and rumors. Simply, it is unclear when it actually began or what was done initially to apprehend DB Cooper.

LZ-A had been tentatively established on the night of the sky-jacking, but no road-blocks or check-points in LZ-A were established, apparently. At present, there is no record of them nor any mention of who manned them, but Tosaw reports that the "main roads" between Woodland and Vancouver did have road blocks, even though that is outside the main landing zone. Further, it is generally thought that some form of ground search began on the morning of Thanksgiving Day, but there is no concrete evidence describing who conducted the search, when they started, or where they operated. In his book, Himmelsbach infers that some elements of law enforcement went looking for DB Cooper at day-light on Thanksgiving Day, but even if that is accurate then the skyjacker had at least an eleven-hour head start on his pursers. But, he probably had much more time, perhaps 36–40 hours.

Even though Himmelsbach suggests that some ground searching began on Thanksgiving morning, he writes definitively that the landing zone was not determined until the afternoon of Thanksgiving Day. He also states that the ground searches com-menced on Friday, November 26 at 7:30 am, which would have given DB Cooper at least a 36-hour head start. This comports somewhat with information I received from the officer leading the ground search in LZ-A, Clark County Under-sheriff Tom McDowell. However, McDowell told me that his team didn't actually deploy until the afternoon, which would have given the skyjacker a 40-hour lead.

Besides searching for Cooper, the FBI was busy looking for witnesses to the skyjacking. Himmelsbach states that immediately after the skyjacking and through the Thanksgiving Day period the FBI scrambled to interview cabbies, bus drivers and other wit-nesses at PDX, and to ascertain how DB Cooper got to the airport.

Since the FBI also maintained a command and communi-cation presence at the Woodland City Hall to support the local aerial and ground searches, they were stretched too thin to actually slog through the woods looking for Cooper. These factors led the Bureau to out-source the ground search to local County Sheriff's deputies and selected volunteers.

Specifically, the task for searching for Cooper in LZ-A fell to the aforementioned Clark County Sheriff's Department, while deputies from Cowlitz County searched north of the Lewis River and LZ-A, and deputies from Lewis and Wahkiakum Counties searched south and east.

McDowell told me he had two or three teams of sheriff deputies and volunteers, with each group numbering about five to ten individuals. As a result, a total of about 25 to 30 men went looking for a skyjacker in LZ-A. "The FBI were not part of any actual team on the ground," he told me in 2012, adding that the feds were on standby in case the locals found something.

McDowell and his teams focused their search along Cedar Creek Road, the main road west of Amboy and just south of Ariel. Their instructions from the head of the operation, FBI agent Tom Manning, were simple. "Look for either a parachute or a hole in the ground," McDowell recounted. The search teams found neither.

McDowell and his teams covered only a small area in LZ-A, perhaps a square mile or so, leaving about 20 square-miles untouched before the FBI shut down the local operations on the Monday after Thanksgiving. Why is unclear, but poor weather may have played a role.

Supporting this account, Himmelsbach writes in his book that the search in the Ariel-Amboy area was terminated after four days. Media coverage of the initial search further confirms it was light. Pictures in the *Seattle Post-Intelligencer* show Manning addressing a roomful of about 20 to 30 deputies and volunteers at the Bureau's command post in the Woodland City Hall on Friday, November 26.

But Richard Tosaw writes that the ground search was much more robust. In his *DB Cooper Dead or Alive?* he claims that the ground and air search began in earnest at daybreak on Thanksgiving Day, with searchers hiking on foot from Woodland to Lake Merwin, a distance of 13 miles. However, he offers no substantive details on who performed that task.

For his part, Ralph Himmelsbach writes that he climbed into his personal airplane on Thanksgiving morning and surveyed LZ-A for 2 ½ hours. The next day, Friday, Himmelsbach writes that the weather was too stormy to continue any reconnaissance.

Nevertheless, the FBI obtained six helicopters from local logging companies and two from the Oregon National Guard for their aerial surveillance, but this operation was severely limited due to inclement weather. Himmelsbach reported that Saturday had "partial clearing," which allowed for a resumption of the air search, but the rains came back and stayed throughout Sunday.

On Monday, November 29, five days after the skyjacking and the day they terminated the LZ-A search, the FBI sent a large flotilla of fixed-wing aircraft and helicopters to search Victor-23 in its entirety, from Seattle to Reno. However, nothing was found from the skyjacking.

Participating in the effort, Himmelsbach flew the left flank of V-23 through the entirety of Oregon, from the Washington border to California, while three helicopters and another fixed-winged craft covered the center and right flank of V-23. According to Himmelsbach's account in *NORJAK,* the FBI's primary goal was to spot a parachute snagged on a tree top, but found was none.

With this much uncertainty on who, how, and when the search for DB Cooper was conducted, especially in the Ariel-Amboy area, it begs for clarification from the FBI agent who had the greatest responsibility for the Cooper investigation, case agent Charlie Farrell. Sadly, his 300-page account of his actions in Norjak has never been made public, nor is his family willing to share it, apparently, despite numerous requests.

Officially, the FBI discontinued the search at the local level after seven days, and I have been unable to ascertain what, if any, searching was done in the twenty square-miles not examined by McDowell's team. Strangely, the FBI suspended their operation in LZ-A due to excessive snow, according to federal records presented by Geoffrey Gray at the 2011 Symposium. However, local residents and Sheriff McDowell say there was no snow in LZ-A over the Thanksgiving weekend, although they've confirmed that snow was present at the higher elevations to the east.

Oddly, the FBI continued looking in snow country after it suspended its official search in the rainy lowlands of LZ-A, according to a former FBI agent and audience member of the 2011 Cooper symposium, Gary Tallis.

Tallis said he flew as a spotter in a one of the FBI's commandeered helicopters for nearly two weeks after the hijacking—one week past the time the ground and aerial search in Amboy was ended. Tallis said he coursed over the snow-covered highlands of the Cascadian foothills in the general area of the Washougal River drainage, and his primary objective was to spot a parachute. None was found.

Further, Tallis, who is a former collegiate skydiver, also told me that he volunteered to re-enact the Cooper jump over Ariel but his offer was rebuffed by J. Edgar Hoover. "I felt really disappointed," Tallis said.

This suggests that the FBI believed that Cooper jumped east of Amboy and into the Washougal River drainage. Perhaps they concentrated their search efforts there while sending the local cops, looky-loo's, and the press on a wild-goose chase in LZ-A.

Nevertheless, a second ground operation was launched four months later to search the Ariel-Amboy area, beginning in March 1972 and stretching into April, and employing over two-hundred soldiers from Fort Lewis, Washington.

But Amboy resident Margaret Culp told me this second ground search appeared haphazard, as it began with a helicopter full of FBI agents landing in her pasture and asking for directions, apparently not knowing where they were. They also interrogated her son as a suspect because he had the temerity to photograph the agents tromping through the neighborhood.

Despite all this searching nothing has been found, and this is the quintessential fact of the DB Cooper case. "We didn't even find so much as a belt-buckle," one FBI agent allegedly muttered.

Nevertheless, some items from Flight 305 were retrieved eventually. A Boeing placard on how to deploy a 727's aft stairs was found in the woods east of Castle Rock, Washington several years after the skyjacking. It is believed to have been from Flight 305, as Boeing acknowledged that when they repaired the aft stairs on Cooper's plane it was missing its instructional laminate from a protective sleeve mounted on the doorway.

Other evidence was retrieved in Reno, including: multiple sets of fingerprints, a clip-on tie and pin, and eight cigarette butts in the ashtray of seat 18-E. Also recovered were hair samples from its headrest. Nearby was an unused 26-foot back chute packed inside its Pioneer harness, along with a deployed reserve chute spread across several seats, minus several strands of parachute cord.

Then in February 1980, an eight-year old boy found three bundles of Cooper's twenties at Tina Bar on the Columbia River, twenty-five miles southwest of Ariel.

But that's it. No body, no parachutes, no bomb, no briefcase, and no paper sack has ever been found. Not a single twenty scattered in the woods was ever found despite the thousands of seekers who combed the woods looking for a valuable souvenir.

Clearly, we've got a mystery.

Chapter 4

Sketches of DB Cooper

The first drawing of DB Cooper, known as "Composite A," was developed by the FBI immediately after the skyjacking and was created by one of their top-notch sketch artists, Roy Rose.

Composite A is commonly described as the "Bing Crosby" sketch, as it bears a resemblance to the famous crooner. It was drawn from the accounts of the flight attendants, and since Florence Schaffner was the only crew member to see DB Cooper before he donned his sunglasses, her input had strong influence.

Since Cooper wore his sunglasses for the remainder of the skyjacking, they were added to Composite A as well.

Composite A, with and without sunglasses. Courtesy of the FBI

However, many eye witnesses objected to Composite A, claiming it was not an accurate portrayal of DB Cooper.

"I didn't agree with that first sketch. It was missing the jugular thing," claimed Bill Mitchell, the passenger sitting nearest to the skyjacker and describing a loose fold of skin under the skyjacker's skin.

Mitchell's input carried significant weight in the development of Composite B, and Florence Schaffner's less so, reportedly because her agitated state was deemed to color her recollections.

Composite B has more detail, making DB Cooper appear older with a more mature look. "B" is now considered to be the most accurate description of DB Cooper.

Composite B with sunglasses added. Photo courtesy of the FBI.

In response, Florence developed her own sketch in the 1980s, at the behest of a documentary film crew.

Florence Schaffner's Composite "C," as presented on Sluggo's
DB Cooper website. Used with permission

In an attempt to reconcile the dispute, Norjak aficionado Sluggo commissioned a "composite of the composites" by artist Joshua Ryals. His version includes all of the previous renditions.

A, B and C, "super" composite. Picture courtesy of "Sluggo."
Used with permission.

Sluggo has also commissioned a Composite B "age-regressed" drawing that he posts on his website.

Age-regressed Composite B by Sluggo. Used with permission

In 2011, Geoffrey Gray commissioned another version of Composite B, this time incorporating the "marcelled" hair and russet suit jacket described by passenger Robert Gregory. Although Gray gives Gregory's characterizations great weight because of the passenger's career as a paint salesman—thus possessing a sharp eye for color and detail—Gregory reportedly told the Seattle Times that he only saw the skyjacker for a brief period of time while exiting.

Nevertheless, flight attendant Alice Hancock gives some credence to Gregory's description, as she reports DB Cooper's hair was "wavy."

However, Gregory's portrayal of the skyjacker is viewed skeptically by many researchers since most of his other characterizations are strongly at odds with other depictions, such as age, height, and clothing.

This gives further heft to the argument that the FBI is seeking to shift the publics' perception—away from being a cultural hero, "The Man who beat Da Man"—to one of mundane incompetence.

Geoffrey Gray's composite B, developed in 2011.
Used with permission.

Chapter 5

Profile of DB Cooper

Although DB Cooper's identity remains a mystery, there are some things we know about him as a skyjacker. We know for certain that his name was not DB Cooper, and it is widely assumed that his original moniker, "Dan Cooper," is also an alias.

Further, "Dan Cooper" was a male Caucasian in his mid-to-late 40s, or possibly even early 50s. In fact, the first official report to reach Northwest Orient flight operations pegged the skyjacker at 60. But later, a passenger reported Cooper was in his mid-30s, and Alice Hancock described Cooper as 38. Nonetheless, criminologists feel that even the younger end of this range it is still very old for such a rigorous and innovative crime. Confirming that perspective, most of the Cooper copycats were men in their twenties.

The detailed physical descriptions given by the passengers and flight attendants vary somewhat, but there is a general consistency in their accounts.

Cooper was wearing a dark brown or black suit, white shirt and thin clip-on black tie. Over this he sported a lightweight black raincoat. He wore loafers, possibly dark brown, or some kind of slip-on shoe that might have come to his ankles. He may have been wearing a set of thermal underwear beneath his business attire. In addition, Cooper's hair was dark brown or black, and short. It was parted on the left side.

As for the specific reports from the flight attendants, Tina Mucklow offered the following description to the FBI, as posted at the DZ and attributed to "Ckret," aka case agent Larry Carr:

> White male, mid-40's, 5-10" to 6', 180 to 190 lbs, medium to dark complexion, medium build, dark straight hair with narrow sideburns to mid-ear parted and combed back, dark plastic wrap-around sunglasses, dark top coat, dark brown suit possibly with a thin black stripe, brown socks, brown ankle length pebble grain shoes—not the tie type. He had a low voice with no accent; she did not see scars, marks or tattoos, the man did not have on any jewelry she could see.

Florence Schaffner, the flight attendant who made the first contact with the hijacker, reported the following:

> White male, mid-40's, 6', 170 to 175, average build, brown eyes, straight black hair medium length and parted on the left side, olive skin, black business suit, white shirt, thin black tie, black overcoat, black shoes, black brief-case, dark-framed sunglasses with brown lenses, no scars, marks or tattoos, he had a normal, calm voice and appeared to be of Latin descent.

Florence, who is the only flight attendant to talk with Cooper before he put on his sunglasses, characterized Cooper as having dark brown "piercing" eyes.

Alice Hancock's perspectives can now be added, as a copy of the FBI's crew debriefing was posted on the DB Cooper Forum in 2015. In these never-before-seen transcripts, Alice confirms the skyjacker had an olive complexion, was about 6'1", 170-175 pounds with a slim build. She also thought that the skyjacker's sunglasses were prescription glasses. Hancock placed Cooper between 38–45 years old, which is a bit younger than her colleagues' estimates.

Cooper may have had either a square jaw or a saggy chin. Passenger Bill Mitchell says that Cooper had a loose fold of skin under his chin, a "turkey gobble," but again Bill is alone in that observation. In addition, Mitchell claimed the hijacker's hair "looked awful" and might have been dyed, but he is the only one to make such a statement.

Fellow-passenger Robert Gregory described Cooper's hair as "marcelled," a wavy pattern that is in sharp contrast to what Tina and Flo have reported, but it is supported by Hancock's statement that Cooper's black hair was "wavy." Gregory also claimed Cooper's hair was "greasy, with a patent-leather sheen."

Cooper is generally cited at 6-foot or maybe 6'1", but some passengers thought he might have been 5'10". Mitchell is 6'2" and 225 pounds, and said he was "way bigger" than the sky-jacker. But, Gregory puts Cooper at 165 pounds and 5'9" in height. Nevertheless, most eye-witnesses say Cooper was trim and about 175 pounds. Of note, Tina, who is 5'8", stated that she needed "to look up to see Cooper."

Skin complexion seems to be a notable characteristic. Alice and Flo both described Cooper's skin as "olive," and Flo thought he might be "Latin." Others called Cooper "swarthy," and these observations lead some investigators to believe the hijacker might have been of Mediterranean descent. Gregory thought Cooper might have been a Mexican-American or of Native American ancestry.

Additionally, Gregory said that Cooper was wearing a reddish brown, "russet-colored" suit jacket with wide lapels. However, he is the only one to offer this description. Further, Gregory's claims are steeped in confusion because the FBI files say that he sat in "the same row as Cooper," but that is incorrect, and must be assumed to be a clerical error. Only Mitchell, Tina, Flo, and the skyjacker sat in Row 18.

More troubling though, Gregory's claims must be viewed skeptically since many of his claims are outliers—5'9", mid-30s, marcelled hair, and a russet jacket. Giving further doubt to Gregory's account, the *Seattle Times* claimed that Gregory only saw Cooper for a few moments when all the passengers stood up to disembark after the skyjacking.

Continuing, most observers agree that Cooper spoke with no discernible accent, and some investigators speculate he may have been raised in the Midwest during his formative years. Hancock added that the skyjacker was "soft-spoken."

Cooper was not observed to be wearing any jewelry or a watch, nor did he wear a hat. In addition, Cooper carried a briefcase and toted a brown paper bag, according to a DZ post by Larry Carr. The bag was also reported to be a burlap sack. The FBI crew debriefing notes also claim that the bag was green in color. Besides his dark sunglasses, Cooper also carried a knife, and Carol Abraczinskas of the Citizens Sleuths says that the FBI files declare it to be a "pocket knife." Not displayed during the early stages of the hijacking, it was later used by Cooper to cut the parachute cords used in securing the bank bag.

As mentioned previously, Cooper stood off by himself in the passenger waiting area, and Gray reports that the NWO gate agent Hal Williams claimed Cooper stood out from the rest of the passengers by wearing "all black," and appeared to be a "lone wolf."

Although he had no visible tattoos or distinguishing anatomical features that are known publicly, it is rumored that the FBI knows of a small scar on Cooper's hand that it has not revealed to the public. Additionally, his fingers were reportedly discolored from tobacco smoke, indicating that he was a heavy smoker.

Most reports say that Cooper drank a single Bourbon and water during the 2 ½ hour wait over Sea-Tac. However, Richard Tosaw writes that Cooper had two drinks. Mitchell claims that Cooper spilled his one drink.

Cooper was also vigilant about not leaving evidence, especially his fingerprints. He was so concerned that he pocketed the blue "Sky Chef" matches that he and Tina shared. Since Sky Chef was a popular airport restaurant chain and an airlines catering service, investigators later posited that DB Cooper ate in a Sky Chef facility before hijacking his airplane or aboard a flight catered by Sky Chef.

Himmelsbach describes Cooper's behavior as desperate and crude, but he offers no specific behaviors or language to support that declaration. In contrast, the flight attendants describe Cooper as mostly calm and thoughtful. "A gentleman," Tina recalled, and Hancock said the skyjacker was "good-natured during the flight."Oddly, Himmelsbach has acknowledged in his book that some passengers described the skyjacker as "relaxed."

But when Cooper received the money, he acted "childlike," according to Larry Carr at the DZ, and was "jumping up and down," which comes from Florence's account in the crew debriefing report.

Additionally, Cooper is widely reported to have become agitated when the refueling process stretched out past the normal time of 20–30 minutes—shouting and banging the seat in front of him, according to Tosaw and others. Tosaw also reported that Tina was so concerned when the refueling got delayed that she thought Cooper was going to blow up the plane.

During calmer moments, though, Cooper frequently used a few colloquial expressions. One was "funny stuff," and at the beginning of the refueling he had warned the crew not to attempt any "funny stuff or I'll do the job." Cooper also used the expression, "Let's get the show on the road."

Besides knowing the specifics of refueling a 727, Cooper possessed a deep knowledge of the plane and possibly parachuting. In fact, his level of knowledge was that of a classified military secret.

This latter detail—DB Cooper's knowledge of the plane and the jump requirements—may be the greatest clue in Norjak, and plumbing those depths has been key to the Norjak investigation.

Chapter 6

Interview with Passenger Bill Mitchell

As discussed earlier, the passenger who sat nearest DB Cooper was a twenty-year old college student named Bill Mitchell. He sat in 18-B, across the aisle from Cooper in 18-E, until he was moved up in the cabin by Purser Alice Hancock. It is believed that Mitchell spent about 20 minutes in close proximity to Cooper.

When Bill spoke with me in December 2014, it was one of the few times he has spoken to a journalist since the hijacking. Prior, he appeared briefly in a 2007 British documentary. Additionally, Mitchell has given a detailed account of his hijacking experience to the Washington State Historical Museum for their 2013 COOPER exhibit. Fortunately, the WSHM has provided public access to an audio tape of the interview.

Currently, Mitchell is the only person who sat near or next to DB Cooper who is talking directly to researchers and journalists, even if he's selective. Galen Cook interviewed Mitchell in person a few years ago, while flight attendants Florence Schaffner has refused to speak to any journalists since 2008, Alice Hancock hung up the phone on me when I finally found her in 2015, and Tina Mucklow hasn't spoken in public for nearly forty years for reasons that are unknown.

Bill has provided some important elements: one, the passengers entered the plane using the aft stairs. Hence, DB Cooper boarded and exited from the same stairway. Also, it was sunny when they boarded. In fact, Bill donned his sunglasses as he crossed the tarmac and wasn't surprised when DB Cooper put on his shades later.

However, Mitchell says that he doesn't remember much about Cooper. But, he clearly remembers being snubbed by the cute stewardesses who paid a great deal of attention to the "old guy" sitting across from him. In fact, the individual appeared "geeky" and his hair "looked awful." As stated previously, the old geek also had a distinctive layer of skin under his chin that Bill called a "turkey gobble."

Why aren't they paying any attention to me? Bill recounted to me and the WSHM team.

Further, Mitchell told the WSHM that he was "way bigger" than Cooper. Bill stands 6'2", and weighed 225 pounds, and this comports with the flight attendants' recollections of the skyjacker, who put Cooper at six-feet tall and about 170–180 pounds.

Mitchell has spoken extensively with the FBI, especially in the initial stages of the investigation, and was a major force in the development of the Composite B sketch.

Galen Cook offers this account of Mitchell's role in the Norjak investigation:

Composite B, according to FBI records, which I've reviewed in Seattle, shows a more complete and detailed facial profile of the hijacker. There is a reason why the FBI returned to Mitchell for follow-up interviews. They didn't do this with the stews. Composite B is considered the most accurate version by the FBI and other experts. I can also tell you this: Mitchell looked at a few pics when we were together and both Duane Weber and KC (Kenny Christiansen) are not on Mitchell's list. Mitchell is very studious and has an eye for detail. Mitchell was not under threat during the hijacking, thus his perceptions and recollections carry greater weight than those who knew the hijacking was taking place and were under direct threat.

Additionally, those who speak with Mitchell protect his privacy fiercely, and neither Galen nor the staff at the Washington State Historical Museum would share Bill's contact information, nor pass on any requests from me for an interview.

Nevertheless, I knew that Bill lived in the Puget Sound area so I tried to contact him independently. But, after calling dozens of Bill Mitchells I gave up. However, in September 2104 a fellow Cooper sleuth and friend, Vicki Wilson, made contact with Bill in an effort to find out if her father, Mel Wilson, was DB Cooper.

Vicki's father has been missing since September 1971, and her request apparently softened Bill's resolve. In late summer, he spoke with Vicki and reviewed photos and videos of her father. Here is Vicki's email account of Bill's reckoning:

He found that my father's facial features were more consistent to what he remembers. He had hesitations about the size of my father in the video from 1970—the lake shot—and thought Mel was too big. But according to the Unsolved Mysteries episode, my father was 6' and 180 lbs at the time of his disappearance on September 15, 1971.

Excited by this breakthrough with Mitchell, I emailed Vicki and asked if she would intercede on my behalf with Bill. A year earlier, Vicki and I had spent a solid day looking for Bill during the 2013 Cooper Symposium—she seeking answers about her father—and I just wanted to talk to the guy who sat next to DB Cooper. Vicki agreed, and kindly passed on my contact information. "Be nice to him," Vicki entreated me when she sent me an email confirming that she had told Bill about me.

To maintain his privacy, Vicki knew Bill would prefer to initiate the contact. She didn't give me his contact information and I had to wait and receive his phone call.

In December 2014, Bill called me. Here is my account of our phone call:

"Hi. This is Bill Mitchell, DB Cooper's best friend," he announced on my message machine. "I thought you might like to talk about something that happened forty-three years ago."

He left his phone number, and I dialed. He laughed when I called and said that I wanted to talk about his "best friend."

"Forty-three years was a LONG time ago," he chortled.

After the good-natured joshing, I told Bill that I was equally interested in hearing about his experiences in the Norjak saga, past and present. We rambled across a range of topics, starting with what he remembered from 1971.

"I didn't agree to the first sketch," he said "When Vicki showed me a picture of her father the only thing I could tell her was that DB Cooper had that 'jugular' thing, as did her father."

"You mean the 'turkey gobble' fold of skin under his chin?"

"Yeah. I remembered that; not sure it was any help to her. I also remember being upset that Tina was paying SO much attention to that older guy."

I laughed and commiserated with Bill. "Yeah, Bill, I have a crush on Tina, too."

"No kidding?" Bill laughed again. "Have you ever met her? I'd like to meet her someday. I think it would be interesting to talk with her, to hear what she went through that day."

Bill and I talked a bit about Tina and my investigatory encounters with the Mucklow clan. Then he launched into a description of his many emotions and feelings about the guy in 18-E.

"DB Cooper was romanticized. All my friends and me, we, um, looked at him as 'beating the man'—y'know. But he had six sticks of dynamite and was sitting next to me!... I wasn't, like angry, but more like puzzled. But you have to remember—when people called him a hero he also had a bomb and was threatening to blow me up.

"When I went home that night and was just sitting around watching the TV, my dad said, 'The way they're building this guy up—there's going to be a million copycats.' And there was, not a million, but a lot."

I asked Bill about the FBI and his experiences participating in their investigation.

"You could tell that the veteran FBI agents had the holiday weekend off because when I got off the plane, all the agents I talked to were young guys."

I asked Bill if he remembered the names of any agents.

"Nah, not really. It was forty-three years, ago, remember!"

Bill continued, and told me he went back to college after the Thanksgiving weekend. At school, he saw FBI agents two or three times per week for a year and a half, reviewing at least ten pictures per visit. Surprisingly, Bill was a little anxious about their presence.

"You have to remember, in Eugene, even then it was hippie-dippie-ville, and I was, um, a sophomore and not in a fraternity, yet, but in the dorm, and there was um, a lot of drugs around. I told the FBI that I didn't do any drugs, but I was concerned that some of my friends, or guys in the dorms, might get into trouble with the agents coming around so much. So, I asked the FBI about that and they said, 'We don't worry too much about that.'"

As Bill reflected he mentioned that most of the agents he dealt with in Norjak were based in Eugene. He vaguely remembered Ralph Himmelsbach, the agent from Portland who went on to fame as the FBI's public-face for the DB Cooper story, but Bill acknowledged that he didn't have any direct dealings with him. When I mentioned the actual Norjak case agent, Charlie Farrell, or his Seattle colleagues Special Agents John Detlor and J. Earl Milnes, Bill had no recollection of them whatsoever.

"But all of the agents I met were impressive," he reassured me.

Bill discussed the events at Sea-Tac in detail, especially his dealings with the FBI, who recommended that Bill discuss the case with caution and prudence.

"You're one of the prime witnesses they reminded me," Bill recounted. "The FBI said, 'Look, we don't know who this guy is or where he is, but he threatened to blow you up along with the plane so use good judgment in deciding who to talk with.' They recommended that I not talk to news reporters, so I didn't."

Bill said that a lot of media has called him through the years but he has refused them all. Besides protecting himself and his privacy, Bill was further discouraged from talking to the media by the widespread inaccuracies they were reporting.

"It was a long time before I read a newspaper article that I felt was true to what I knew. I was amazed that so many stories got the facts wrong—that was one of the reasons I wasn't too eager to talk to journalists."

Bill figured that Tina Mucklow also went through the same kind of treatment. "I'd love to talk with Tina and see what she's had to deal with."

When Bill landed at Sea-Tac he was tired and eager to connect with his father, and head home for a good meal. "It was supposed to be a thirty-seven minute flight, but it took three and a half hours."

Bill remembered some of the details of that night with great clarity: "It was dark and rainy when we landed—and way out on the tarmac. You could hardly see the terminal... I had been moved up to First Class by the flight attendant who looked like she was in charge, and she also looked stressed. I moved, but I really didn't want to. I was happy to just stay in back and sleep. I moved up, but I forgot my coat, and instead of going back to get it, the flight attendant went and got it for me."

Further, Bill says he remembers the money bag coming aboard, and also the parachutes. "But I still didn't think that we were being hijacked."

Later, as he descended the stairs to the tarmac he heard someone call out, and an FBI agent answered, "Yes, you've been hijacked."

"That was the first I knew of it," Bill said. "We started walking towards the terminal, which was a long ways away. Then a bus came and we got on. Then the FBI started calling names from a list and they called my name first, 'Bill Mitchell.' I said, 'Here,' and then they called 'Dan Cooper' and there was nothing. No one answered. So, we realized that was the skyjacker.

"Then, it hit me—the FBI had three and a half hours to investigate *me*! I wondered if they had been investigating me since they had called my name first. I was thinking... I had paid for my ticket in cash, I was a 20-year old college student from Eugene... did they think I was the hijacker?"

After a pause, I asked Bill about some of the notables of Cooper World. "Do you remember Galen Cook? I think he's interviewed you several times."

"The guy from, um, Alaska?"

"Yes."

"Vaguely. I do remember that a book that was on sale at the exhibit in Tacoma. I didn't recognize it when I saw it. My name was in it, but I don't remember talking to anyone about it."

"*Skyjack? The Hunt for DB Cooper,* by Geoffrey Gray?"

"Maybe."

"You didn't talk with Geoffrey Gray?"

"I might have, but I don't remember. But, somehow my name got in that book. But I do remember Jo Weber. She called me several years ago. She's a wacko. She sent me all these pictures of Duane (Weber, her husband, who purportedly confessed to being DB Cooper.) Now, remember that Duane's ears are HUGE, and I would have made fun of them, so what I told Jo was: 'I know for a fact that I would have remembered those huge ears.'"

Bill also enjoyed recounting his getaway from Sea-Tac.

"All the passengers were sitting in the VIP lounge at Northwest and the FBI was asking us what we remembered about the guy in the back of the plane. I was just sitting there and being quiet. When they got to me I said, 'Well, I was sitting next to the guy,' and then they all got in my face!"

At the same time, Bill's father was waiting for him in the parking lot at Sea-Tac.

"I had called him from Portland just before I got on the plane and told him it was just a thirty-seven minute flight, so I'd see him soon. But it took three and a half hours!"

Bill said his dad waited in his car at first, and then heard about the hijacking on the radio. Hearing the news, he went inside the terminal to the Northwest counter, where the waiting families were gathering and becoming visibly agitated. "They brought all the families into a room and told them, 'Yes, it was a hijacking.'"

Bill's mom was home cooking "her baby boy's favorite dinner," and was watching the TV. She saw the news coverage, especially the fire boats circling in Elliott Bay, waiting to retrieve wreckage in case the plane exploded over the harbor.

"She was going nuts," Bill said.

Earlier, Bill's dad went back into the public waiting area and was standing next to a fellow wearing NWO mechanics clothes. "When the individual's walkie-talkie crackled, he reached inside his coat and my dad could see he had a machine gun slung over his shoulder. It was kind of crazy," Bill said, "But my dad is an ex-Marine, so he wasn't too fazed by anything."

As the "guy who sat next to Cooper," the FBI kept him longer than any other passenger. As a result, a scrum of 200 reporters waited for him to exit. "My dad was waiting for me just outside of them, so I told the FBI I had to leave that way. They recommended that I take a ham sandwich, take a bite as I leave the room and keep chewing as I walked past the reporters. When they pushed me out the door the light bulbs flashed, and everybody started shouting. It was just like in the movies. But a state trooper barged ahead and cleared a path for me. I kept walking right through them, and after we got past the first line of reporters it lightened up. I just kept walking over to my dad, and we continued out of the terminal and went home."

Mom had a turkey dinner waiting for Bill, and life returned to near-normalcy. "I went back to college after the weekend—Sunday or Monday—and I told my circle of friends. But really, everyone in Eugene knew about it. But I didn't talk about it publicly, and I turned down all the media requests."

Bill did write an essay about his experiences, though, but in a foreign language! "I had an assignment in Italian class, to write a story in Italian, so I wrote about the hijacking. When my teacher read it she pulled me aside and said, 'Is this for real?'"

After the Richard McCoy hijacking in April 1972, Bill got a surprise call from two *Newsweek* reporters. They had obtained a photograph on McCoy, and located Bill through a family friend. They showed the photo to Bill, who told them the likeness didn't match his recall of Cooper. However, the next day two FBI agents also showed up with a picture of McCoy and were really miffed to learn that two *Newsweek* reporters had preceded them. "So, who tipped-off *Newsweek*?" Bill mused.

I asked Bill if he ever tries to figure out DB Cooper's identity or fate. "Well, sure. I mean, I worked for Boeing for thirty-five years, so we talked about it a lot. But most of the FBI agents I've talked with told me they figure Cooper died in the jump. But everything was so well planned...."

Several days after I posted the above story on the *Mountain News*, Bill called me again, but this time he said he didn't want any further contact with me or anyone else in the Cooper firmament. He said that Jo Weber had contacted him the day before and had caused some kind of ruckus.

So, it appears that Bill Mitchell has chosen to keep quiet in the face of angry encounters with people who insist on being part of the DB Cooper story.

Chapter 7

Investigation Intensifies

When DB Cooper hijacked his airplane it was considered a bold and innovative crime. Many in the FBI considered DB Cooper a master criminal, and Walter Cronkite used that exact term in his broadcasts.

Some FBI agents openly shared their respect and hoped Cooper made it, although their names were omitted from newspaper accounts. Others thought the November jump was too tough, including many agents in the Seattle office, and felt the skyjacker most likely died in his escape.

On the cultural spectrum, DB Cooper was revered by many for "beating the system," and that distinction still holds as evidenced by the many movies and songs—even a rap tune—praising his accomplishment. Gatherings continue to be held in his honor, such as the annual DB Cooper Days Festival in Ariel, Washington.

However, most skydivers believe that Cooper made it, and the day after the skyjacking many parachutists muttered, "Why didn't I think of that!" Similarly, the FBI assumed Cooper must have been a skilled skydiver because they viewed the jump as highly problematic, and as a result they investigated the parachuting community heavily, especially professional skydivers.

Recently, it has also come to light that the FBI also interrogated many airborne commandos from the Special Forces, particularly the super-covert unit known as the Material

Assistance Command-Vietnam-Special Operations Group (MAC-V-SOG).

Initially, Cooper's broad set of skills were appreciated, such as his superior knowledge of the 727. The pilot, Bill Rataczak, characterized Cooper as a learned adversary.

"When he told me to set the (wing) flaps at 15, I knew he knew something about airplanes," Rataczak told me in 2009, adding, "The 727 was the only Boeing product at that time that had a 'predent' (predetermined) setting of 15 degrees." More importantly, Cooper knew that the 727 could be flown with the aft stairs lowered into the slipstream, which was a highly classified secret in 1971 and known only to a handful of select Boeing officials and the US military.

His knowledge of jumping from a 727 was sublime. Cooper instructed the pilots to fly the plane below 10,000 feet so he would have enough oxygen to breathe, and to keep the cabin unpressurized so that he could safely open the sealed hatchway to the aft staircase. But surprisingly, Cooper did not seem to know *how* to lower the aft stairs, and this suggests that wherever Cooper had learned the details of jumping from a 727 he had never opened the aft stairs by himself. However, Cooper was familiar with avionic terminology and properly identified the stairway used by airlines to load passengers as an "airstairs," and the intercom system as an "interphone."

Cooper's choice of destinations—"Mexico City or anywhere in Mexico"—is considered to be astute as it put him in Victor 23 and over predictable terrain.

Further, his management of the onboard situation was masterful. His choice of seat 18-E was viewed as ideal for monitoring events inside the plane during the hijacking. Plus, there were no windows for Row 18 on his 727-100 airplane, which lessened the risk of a sniper attack. Additionally, he had the passengers in the rear of the aircraft moved forward without incident and used the flight attendants as couriers to keep the cockpit crew at a distance, minimizing his exposure to eye witnesses. Additionally, Cooper wisely kept his original hijacking note. Further, Cooper insisted that the fuel trucks be positioned to the port side of the plane, which gave him optimum visibility of events outside the plane.

Despite persistent rumors, neither Captain Scott nor any of the cockpit crew came aft to meet with Cooper. The skyjacker also insisted that meals be brought aboard for the crew even though they never ate them. But according to Bill Rataczak, the German Shepherds used in Reno to search for the bomb ate the food before doing any sniffing.

Additionally, Cooper reportedly brought several tablets of Benzedrine to keep the crew alert, but they apparently never used them.

Cooper displayed military-like abilities as well. Specifically, the bomb was a tactical upgrade from weapons used by other hijackers because Cooper was able to foil any attempt by the FBI to simultaneously rush him from multiple directions. In fact, Himmelsbach characterized Cooper's use of a bomb as "a game changer" when I spoke with him in 2011.

In addition, Himmelsbach also described the hijacking as well-planned and executed. Along those lines, the SOG troopers I have interviewed characterized the Cooper skyjacking as having the earmarks of special ops planning and execution.

Himmelsbach also possessed some admiration for the skyjacker, writing in his *NORJAK:* "As much as I hate(d) Cooper, I know this about him. He was no wimp. The guy had guts—that I had to concede."

Initially, Cooper's getaway by parachute was considered daring but not impossible, a perspective supported by the fact that the five DB Cooperesque skyjackers who jumped, the so-called "copycats," successfully made it to the ground.

In fact, many in the FBI considered one of the imitators, Richard McCoy, was actually Cooper doing a second hijacking. Russ Calame, the FBI agent who captured Richard McCoy, is still convinced that McCoy was Cooper. In fact, Calame told me in 2008 that many in the FBI held the same opinion, including the Norjak case agent in Seattle, Charlie Farrell. However, the current thinking in Seattle is that McCoy was not Cooper.

Intriguingly, the FBI's assessment of Cooper's abilities shifted during the 1970s, eventually calling Cooper inexperienced and ill-equipped for a successful hijacking. Over time most agents felt that Cooper died during his getaway, and that belief is now written in stone within the FBI. Why the FBI switched their thinking is not fully known, but it may be partially due to the Bureau having no definitive physical evidence prior to the money find in 1980.

They also had little compelling soft evidence, such as a credible family member coming forward saying they had a missing husband or brother who looked like DB Cooper and had suddenly vanished over the Thanksgiving Day weekend.

Nonetheless, many suspects were investigated by the FBI. However, most of them were linked to romantic quarrels and considered bogus. At last count, the Bureau has investigated over 1,100 suspects in the DB Cooper case.

These dynamics may have fueled an organizational pressure to "do something," leading to a campaign to discredit DB Cooper and dampening his cultural appeal as "The Man who beat Da Man."

As a result, the historical arc of the Norjak investigation cuts a broad swath across the decades, and the variance may reflect the political pressures upon the FBI as much as it does any probing analysis. Simply, the FBI's present perspective that Cooper knew just enough to get himself killed, may say more about the Bureau's concern with its public image than its abilities as a crime-fighting organization.

With so little physical evidence the key is how to evaluate DB Cooper himself—his knowledge, behavior, and decision making. Central to the reversal in FBI thinking was Cooper's selection of parachutes from among the four delivered.

DB Cooper's Parachutes

Was DB Cooper an expert skydiver or was he a "whuffo?" The latter is what the skydiving community calls an inexperienced *wannabe,* and this is the current FBI perspective. Or was DB Cooper a deft and daring parachutist, as most skydivers currently maintain despite the FBI's disbelief?

Here is the known evidence: DB Cooper received "two back chutes and two front chutes" as part of his deal with the FBI. He also demanded "D" rings to attach the front chutes to the harnesses of the back chutes, but he did not receive any.

The "back chutes" refer to the main parachutes worn on one's back, and the two front chutes are smaller reserve parachutes worn over the abdomen or torso. As a result, a fully-rigged skydiving outfit would be a main parachute worn on the back, with a reserve parachute lying atop a skydiver's belly or chest and secured by metal "D" clips.

Back Chutes

The first parachutes to arrive at Sea-Tac airport were the two "back" chutes, and they are the most hotly disputed elements of

Norjak. Key are the issues of ownership, the types of parachutes presented to Cooper and their capabilities, and how the chutes were transported to the airport.

More troubling, FBI documentation on this matter is misleading or incorrect, and adds to the muddle. This kerfuffle reveals that the Bureau had poor record keeping in the early days of Norjak, coupled with inadequate oversight. No one caught the errors in the paperwork, suggesting that there wasn't an adequate system of review in place at the Seattle FO.

Adding to the confusion is skydiving terminology. A main parachute has two components to the "rig"—first is the actual parachute, known as a canopy—and secondly the "container," which is the harness and bag, into which the canopy is placed. As a result, a military parachute rig, like a Navy pilot's emergency chute—the acclaimed NB-8—may have a civilian chute inside the military container.

Every aspect of the back chutes are in conflict. One narrative posits that **Norman G. Hayden**, a Kent, Washington businessman and acrobatic pilot is the owner and provider of the back chutes, and delivered them to Sea-Tac via a taxi. His view is supported by the official FBI documents.

The second and highly contentious perspective was presented by **Earl J. Cossey,** who said he was the owner of the back chutes, and trumpeted his claims through many *ad hoc* pronouncements and was buttressed by FBI agents despite their own records. Inexplicably, Cossey says he sent his parachutes first to Boeing Field by taxi, where they switched to a private car for delivery to Sea-Tac.

The issue of ownership is not insignificant as the two men say they provided different kinds of parachutes.

Hayden says his chutes were two identical, civilian-type Pioneer chutes, with 26-foot diameter canopies, suitable for a pilot of an acrobatic airplane.

Cossey, now deceased, but in 1971 a Woodinville, Washington skydiving champion and certified parachute rigger, claimed he sent two different parachutes—one a military parachute and the other a luxurious civilian, "sport" model. However, his recall of exactly what types of these chutes has varied over time.

Cossey told me in 2009 that he had provided a military NB-6, which is akin to the Navy's NB-8, but smaller. Yet, Cossey, who preferred being called Coss, said he stuffed the container with a 28-foot canopy even though the NB-6 would normally take a 26-foot canopy. Cossey later reversed his statement in 2011 and said it was a larger NB-8 container with its customary 28-foot canopy. Nonetheless, he did tell the FBI about the NB-6 because additional federal parachute documents indicate that as fact.

Coss also sent along a civilian sport parachute, and when pressed for details he claimed it was a 26-foot Pioneer although initially he told me it was a "Paradise." He had also told other investigators that the second back chute was a "Paracommander," a popular skydiving chute at the time that had great steering capacities.

As for the transportation dispute, the FBI apparently never questioned Coss why he initially sent the chutes to the wrong airport—Boeing Field in Seattle rather than Sea-Tac. But when I posed that question to Coss in 2011, he shouted, "Fuck you," and hung up.

Also, the driver of the private car that supposedly took Cossey's errant chutes to Sea-Tac has never been identified.

Nevertheless, both Cossey and Hayden agree that a 26-foot Pioneer **container** was a part of the package they provided to DB

Cooper. However, what kind of **canopy** was inside is still unresolved. But, there was one back chute found at Reno—a sport Pioneer with a 26-foot civilian Steinthal canopy—which Hayden says is his parachute. So, Cooper may have jumped using the NB-6 or NB-8 as per Cossey's scenario, or the second of the two 26-foot civilian Pioneers as provided by Hayden.

Front Chutes

The two reserve "front" parachutes are also burdened with controversy. What is indisputable though, is that they were the last items to arrive at Sea-Tac, and when they did Cooper allowed his plane to land. These reserves came from the Issaquah Sky Sports skydiving facility, located about 25 miles east of Seattle, and were brought to Sea-Tac by troopers from the Washington State Patrol (WSP).

Strangely, one of the reserves was a "dummy" chute used for indoor training exercises, and its panels were sewn shut, making it inoperable. This chute had a white "X" sewn onto it, and the "how and why" it was given to the WSP is unknown. Further, this reserve was not found on the plane in Reno, so presumably it went out the door with Cooper, but we don't know if it was used as a reserve, a storage sack, or simply discarded.

As for the second reserve chute, the "good one," Cooper opened it long before he jumped and cut the shroud lines to use as rope. Tina Mucklow was on her way to the cockpit when she saw Cooper use the cords to cinch his money bag and secure it around his waist, and that's the last eye-witness account we have of Cooper's actions.

Since the main chutes came without "D" rings, the front chutes were nearly impossible to use. Conceivably, Cooper could have tied a reserve chute to the rear harness with rope somehow, but many skydivers scorn that idea because parachute cord is too stiff and thick to tie into a reliable knot.

Cooper's choice of words, asking for "front" chutes instead of the proper skydiving term, "reserves," and similarly calling his mains, "back" chutes, is offered by some as proof that Cooper was a whuffo. Others say he was just a smart hijacker who knew to use common parlance so that his demands wouldn't get screwed up in the transfer of messages from flight attendants-to-cockpit-to-FBI-to-the skydiving supply house.

Parachute Controversy Deepens

Until the release of Geoffrey Gray's *Skyjack—The Hunt for DB Cooper* in August, 2011, the "Common Understanding," long cited by FBI officials, authors, and armchair sleuths, had been that Cossey owned the two main chutes and that DB Cooper had used one of Cossey's military chutes, either an NB-6 or NB-8—as Cossey has claimed both—to make his getaway.

But Gray writes in his book that FBI documents state the two back parachutes were owned by Hayden, and that Coss only inspected and packed the parachutes for Mr. Hayden. This was the first time most DB Cooper researchers had ever heard of Norman Hayden, and the first time anyone had challenged Earl Cossey's version of events.

To support his announcement, Gray cited a never-before-publicly-seen FBI document that clearly states Hayden was the owner of the back chutes. However, it says, cryptically, that one back chute was a *military* 26-foot conical canopy packed inside a *civilian* Pioneer bag and harness, and the other was a full 28-foot military-type rig, such as a NB-8. Further, the FBI document also says their information comes directly from Mr. Hayden. However,

Hayden refutes both claims, and says he neither talked to the FBI nor did he provide any type of military parachute.

Here are the actual files, from pages 226–227 of a larger Cooper case file:

> Civilian luxury type, tan soft cotton material outside, 26 foot white canopy inside. The parachute inside is a military parachute. The parachute has a foam pad cushion and a fray mark down the rib on the back from rubbing on metal.
>
> A military backpack parachute, standard olive drab green on outside, a 28-foot white canopy on inside. He (Norman Hayden) stated that this parachute also has a foam pad cushion.
>
> He (Hayden) stated that both parachutes bore lead seals which had not been broken and it is possible that his seals bear a confidential number, such as a rigger's number. He (Hayden) stated that both of his parachutes were assembled for him by Mr. Earl Cossey, who works at Seattle Sky Sports in Issaquah, Washington.

Author's Note: I've come to this file via a curious route—I stole them. But I pinched them from the person who lifted them from the FBI, as the files were apparently first taken by Geoffrey Gray, who had access to the FBI files and evidence room, and was unsupervised in any direct manner. Thus, Geoffrey had the opportunity to copy these files and hide them in cyberspace in a kind of private file of his own. One of the sleuths in the DropZone chat room, "Snowmman," discovered Gray's secret cache and gave me—and the DZ—the access code, which is how I was able to obtain the files for use here.

At quick glance, this seems to be only a minor glitch in federal record-keeping, and the gravest consequence is seeing how badly the FBI got the facts wrong. But the documentary mess brings into question the actions by the FBI—can Cossey be trusted and if not, why did the FBI draw Cossey so deeply into their Norjak investigation?

Initially, the FBI brought Cossey into the Norjak investigation at the beginning and sought his advice on what kinds of abilities DB Cooper had as a skydiver. Coss told the FBI that a skydiver did not have to be an expert to "do the Cooper jump," only needing a handful of practice jumps to prepare for a night-time November jump into an unknown Pacific Northwest landscape. As a result, Coss was able to dissuade the FBI from monitoring professional skydiving gatherings or individual skydivers. This information comes from author Geoffrey Gray, who posted the following on his Cooper website:

> During a time when many in the Bureau were convinced that Cooper never survived the jump, Cossey met with agents and told them the jump wasn't as perilous as they thought. Cossey's opinion was that Cooper could have survived the jump, even with minimal parachuting experience.

Cossey is mentioned in FBI documents stating that view. Further, in the early days of Norjak, Cossey told at least one family member, Richard Bowyer, that Cooper had made it. Coss also expressed the same view with many professional skydivers, such as the renowned skydiving champion Ralph Hatley. But over time Cossey changed his tune. Then, the FBI changed theirs. Was the flip-flop based on solid analysis or did other factors influence this change? Historically, here is what we know:

In the middling stages of the investigation Cossey began telling the media that DB Cooper most likely panicked and died in the jump. Cossey further proclaimed that Cooper had chosen an inferior parachute, the NB-8, and had ignored a better chute—the civilian model—presumably the 26-foot Pioneer, all of which proved Cooper was a whuffo.

To what degree he fostered this argument inside the FBI is not known publicly, but it appears that Earl Cossey eventually became the *de facto* technical expert for the FBI on matters of the parachutes. Regardless, Coss always spoke authoritatively, as if he had the full backing of the FBI.

In 2009, Coss gave me the details supporting his flip-flop on Cooper's abilities. Key to his argument was that Coss had made modifications to the NB-8 that had made it more difficult to operate and likely caused Cooper to "no-pull." Coss characterized the ***chosen parachute***—the NB-8—as a "VW Bug," and described the ***not-chosen*** civilian Pioneer chute as a "Cadillac."

Specifically, Coss told me that he had changed the placement of the ripcord, making it harder for a whuffo to find in the tough conditions of a November night jump. He also installed a pouch to hide the ripcord so that it would not be snagged while getting on board a jump plane, and as a result the user would need to "double-pull" on the ripcord—"out and up"—to get the chute to deploy properly. Again, much tougher for a whuffo to use.

Further, the NB-8 had a "sleeveless" design, which Coss said made for harder openings, and it didn't have padded leggings such as the Pioneer, making the NB-8 a rough ride and a bad choice for a nighttime getaway.

In contrast, Coss praised the sport chute because it was a luxury model and had padded leggings, improved deployment designs, and an easy-to-find ripcord. Plus, it possessed steering capacity, which Cossey claimed would be important when DB Cooper landed into an unknown forest.

Because of the NB-8 modifications and the lack of a steering capacity, Cossey concluded that the NB-8 was an inferior parachute to the civilian rig. Hence, Cossey claimed that Cooper was an inexperienced whuffo for not knowing to pick the better parachute.

The FBI fully embraced Cossey's assessment and that view is now written solidly in federal stone.

But the NB-8 is a Navy pilot's emergency parachute (**N**avy **B**ackpack—2**8**-foot canopy), so this begs the question of why a rigger would modify a pilot's rig to make it harder to open when a pilot is struggling for his/her life. This is critical since military pilots do not wear emergency reserves on the front side of their body. "Front" chutes are unwieldy to wear while flying an airplane, and as a result pilots rely solely on their main chute if they have to bail out.

Coss indicated to me that he made these modifications to satisfy his own personal requirements for a recreational parachute, and wasn't offering the chute to military pilots as a bail-out rig. But why go to all that trouble? It seems spurious.

Coss also voiced harsh opinions about DB Cooper during our 2009 interview in sharp contrast to his initial public comments. "He didn't make it," Cossey told me emphatically. "I don't believe he pulled the ripcord. He augered into the ground somewhere."

However, Geoffrey Gray penned a revisionist account of Cossey for the May 3, 2013 issue of *Esquire* Magazine, and recast Coss from a "he-didn't-make-it" guy back to being a true believer of Cooper's moxie. In a piece titled, "The Man Who Believed in DB Cooper," Gray presented a remarkably different view of Earl Cossey than the one Coss presented to me:

> As an expert skydiver in the area, Cossey was summoned to see Bureau agents in the days after Cooper disappeared. At the time, according to the Bureau's original Cooper case files, many of the lead agents hunting for the hijacker were convinced that Cooper was a master skydiver if he indeed pulled off the jump. Agents were so gung-ho on this theory they went through over 14,000 registration cards for skydivers in the Pacific Northwest. The Bureau even sent undercover agents to a skydiving contest across the border to Canada to look for suspects.
>
> 'The feds were wrong though,' Cossey said. 'Cooper didn't need to be a pro skydiver to pull off the jump.' According to documents that outline his Bureau interviews, Cossey told agents that with only six or seven jumps with an instructor the hijacker could have landed safely in the forests of the Pacific Northwest.

Before this revisionism in 2013, though, the FBI's Larry Carr had fully embraced Cossey's flip-flop in 2009, stating often that he thought the skyjacker was inexperienced and unsuccessful. Carr seemingly used Cossey's script and consistently described a fumbling, bumbling, tumbling skydiver who died in the jump. Further,

Carr, and most of the FBI, claimed that Cooper's decision to cut up his only good reserve chute was the action of an inexperienced jumper who could not recognize a bogus parachute with an "X" sewn onto the container.

Nevertheless, Cossey's flip-flop analysis seems quite thin and casts his beliefs in a cynical light. Plus, he most likely lied about owning the parachutes. In sum, the FBI is placed in a critical light for accepting Earl Cossey's beliefs and allowing him to participate in their investigation of DB Cooper.

So, we are left wondering: did Earl Cossey scam the FBI?

Cossey Sticks to His Guns

Coss was adamant about his ownership of the parachutes during every interview I had with him. When I pressed for an exact accounting of what happened on the afternoon of November 24, 1971, Coss told me NWO's chief of *ground* operations at Sea-Tac, Al Lee, contacted him at home and asked for two back and two front chutes.

Cossey says he told Lee that he had only back chutes, and he placed two of them in a taxi that he directed inexplicably to Boeing Field in Renton, WA before the parachutes worked their way to Sea-Tac via the unspecified private car and unidentified driver.

This scenario is repeated by author Richard Tosaw and the renowned Cooper researcher known as Sluggo, and they specify that Lee made the calls looking for the parachutes. The "Common Understanding" unfolds from there.

To the end Coss stuck to his guns. When I asked him about the ownership dispute he replied emphatically, "Well, Northwest Orient paid me for the chutes. That should tell you something!"

Relationship Between Cossey and the FBI

The connection between Coss and the FBI goes much further than just simply a shared understanding on the parachutes, or offering his advice as a consultant in the early days. Cossey was touted by the Bureau as their spokesperson for parachuting issues.

The depth of this relationship was clearly demonstrated in 2009 during the discovery of the so-called "Amboy chute," when many thought a parachute found half-buried in Amboy might be Cooper's getaway canopy. In April 2009, I called the public information officer for Norjak at that time, Robbie Burroughs, and asked her if the Amboy chute was Cooper's. She replied, "That's the kind of question you should ask Earl Cossey."

Taking her suggestion, I made my first ever phone call to Coss. He told me that the parachute found in Amboy, Washington was not from Flight 305.

"It was too large—34-feet in diameter—and it was made from silk, not nylon." Coss added that it had been a cargo chute and was of WWII vintage.

Subsequent research by members of the DB Cooper Forum have confirmed Coss' assessment.

But Coss added to the confusion by telling a reporter from the *Oregonian* in early April 2009 that the Amboy chute was DB Cooper's rig. The scoop made the wire service for a few hours and jolted Cooper World. However, Cossey later recanted his statement and claimed his deception was "Just an April Fool's joke."

More disturbing though, Coss also told me that when he delivered his Amboy chute findings to the FBI, the Bureau had asked him to "keep the information quiet for a few days." Cossey told me that he thought the FBI wanted to "milk" some positive media attention from the discovery. Coss also characterized the FBI as being "stupid" in its Cooper investigation, a dismissive attitude that he often expressed.

But the allure of Norjak may have been quite strong for Coss. Besides being the FBI's parachute expert, Coss was widely sought for expert advice in the Cooper case by media, film crews and documentarians, such as the National Geographic documentary on DB Cooper filmed at Thun Field in 2009.

Yet, the questions about Coss are plentiful. Was he truthful when he said he owned the chutes? Did DB Cooper really use an NB-8? Why did Cossey send the chutes to the wrong airport? Why did he reverse his perspective on the survivability of the jump?

Why was he so convinced that Cooper chose an inferior parachute? Why was he so deceptive about many details of the case? Did he trim the truth in the pursuit of fame?

Cossey is Rebuked by Skydivers

Cossey's assessment of Cooper's skills and parachute choices—and by association the FBI's analysis as well—is *strongly* challenged by other skydivers. Voicing the most notable dissent is Mark Metzler, who gave a searing analysis of Cossey's views at the 40th Anniversary DB Cooper Symposium in Portland.

Metzler, aka "377" at the DZ, avoided the ownership question entirely and focused solely on Cossey's assessment of a NB-8. Metzler, a skydiver since 1968, declared that DB Cooper likely picked the best chute when he chose the NB-8 because it normally contained a 28-foot C-9 canopy, a military chute designed for high-speed jet ejections. "The C-9 is the pit bull of parachutes," Metzler said.

"Cooper made the right choice by selecting the NB-8," he added, explaining that Cooper's 727 was estimated to be flying at slightly over 200 mph when he jumped, and the "not chosen" civilian parachute was designed to open at speeds no higher than 150 mph. Metzler, an engineer, said a mere 50 mph of extra speed would nearly double the stress on the civilian canopy, which could have failed if it were deployed at 200 mph.

Metzler has made his own "DB Cooper jump" from a DC 9 passenger jet through the rear airstair door in 2006, and also presented an alternative to a high-speed opening or prolonged free-fall. At the Symposium, he showed a film clip taken over Thailand during the Vietnam War that pictured military jumpers parachuting from a 727 slowly deploying their canopies while exiting out the rear airstair. The canopies were opened via static lines and filled with air, taking the shape of a squid body. As a result, this on-the-stairs-opening of a parachute is called " squidding."

This technique, had it been known to Cooper, could have been duplicated by facing forward on the stairs and pulling the ripcord, thus allowing the inflating canopy to pull him off the stairs with no free-fall and no risk of uncontrolled tumbling. It would also refute the many claims that hold Cooper would have been paralyzed by the freezing temperatures, or tumbled by the fierce slip stream.

However, if Cooper decided to go into a regular skydiving free-fall, he would have slowed down eventually to a speed closer to his terminal velocity of approximately 115 mph, which refutes many of the concerns that the 200 mph of Flight 305 was too fast an exit speed to survive.

Also, Metzler said that some reports claim that Tina Mucklow described Cooper as putting on the parachute rig with ease, indicating that the skyjacker had significant experience. As proof, Metzler had an audience member attempt to put on a NB-8 to demonstrate how difficult it is for the uninitiated to don. The subject took many minutes trying to figure out the chest and leg strap configuration.

Additionally, there are some accounts that say Cooper pulled the packing card from the NB-8 to see the data on the type of canopy inside. Metzler challenged another audience member to try to find the packing card on his NB-8, but the subject could not locate it after many minutes of searching, as it is very well concealed in a pocket behind a fabric flap.

Metzler, an aviation buff, also put great weight on the fact that DB Cooper knew the 727 could be jumped, something few people knew including skydivers. "In 1971, I had a 727 flight manual detailing all the 727 systems. Even with that information I didn't even know a 727 could be jumped," exclaimed Metzler, "nor did the pilots, the flight engineer or anyone at Northwest Airlines operations center."

Metzler also touted Cooper's skills, as he knew the aforementioned metrics necessary to safely exit from a 727—cabin unpressurized, gear down, wing flaps at 15°, and speeds not over 180 knots (about 205 mph) and at a height not to exceed 10,000 feet.

As for not selecting a steerable, civilian chute Metzler feels that Cooper again made the correct choice. "Steerability (which requires forward canopy velocity) could actually be an disadvantage," declared Metzler, adding that in his opinion the safest way to enter an unknown area in the dark might be via the straight down descent of a C-9 canopy. Metzler said that the forward speeds of steerable chutes in 1971 could reach 10-20 mph depending on weight and canopy configuration.

"Why take a chance on flying into something, or adding 15 mph to the speed of an unintentional downwind landing?" he asked.

Norman Hayden's Uneven Relationship with the FBI

Although the FBI's files indicate that Norm Hayden owned the back chutes and cite him as a source of their parachute findings, the majority of the information in the Bureau's documents conflicts with Hayden's recollections. In particular, Norman says the two chutes he provided were identical—both Pioneers with 26-foot civilian canopies, with at least one identified specifically as a Steinthal. However, the FBI documents declare the chutes were different, as per Cossey's general view.

More confounding though, the FBI documents say that both canopies were military parachutes, which conflicts with both Cossey and Hayden. Seeking to clarify these issues, I traveled to Kent in 2011 to visit Norman and inspect his Pioneer. Upon the advice of many in the skydiving world, I invited Bruce Thun to accompany me. Bruce is the manager of Thun Field in Puyallup and has been around airplanes, pilots, and skydivers all of his life. In addition, he is intrigued by Norjak, confessing to me that he puts himself to sleep at nights by thinking about DB Cooper.

Bruce and I met with Hayden at his shop and inspected his "not used" civilian parachute, now returned to his possession after a court battle with the FBI. However, in 2013, Hayden sold it to the Washington State Historical Museum and it was a featured part of their COOPER exhibit. Norman also told me that several years after the skyjacking NWO had paid him for the "rental" of two chutes.

Mr. Hayden was very gracious when we arrived, and straightaway he showed us the Pioneer parachute that went aboard Flight 305.

"Here it is."

The parachute was small and very thin—not much larger than what a lot of kids use to carry their books home from school. In fact, I didn't think it was a parachute when I first saw it. I assumed it was a harness system and pouch that would receive some kind of parachute in another bag to be fully operational.

"No, that's the parachute," Norman said without a chuckle.

I picked it up. It was very heavy. *This is only twenty pounds? It feels heavier.*

Putting it down I tried to take notes and listen to Norman, but the notion that this parachute was once carried aboard Flight 305 by Tina Mucklow and inspected by DB Cooper was too huge for me to digest. *Wow...*

Continuing, Norman described his participation in the events of November 24, 1971. The day was busy, and what Norman told us mostly jibed with the FBI's records. Specifically, Norman said he was contacted by George Harrison, the flight operations manager of Northwest Orient Airlines at Sea-Tac, who asked for the two back chutes. Norman had them at his manufacturing shop in Kent and placed them in a cab, sending the chutes off to Sea-Tac. A later memo from Harrison to his boss at NWO further confirmed that Norman's two chutes were delivered to the Northwest Orient Air Freight Office.

My understanding of this whole scenario was solidified by Barry Halstad, a former sales manager at Pacific Aviation, and an individual listed in the FBI files as instrumental in the procurement of the back chutes. Halstad is also friends with Norman, and a colleague.

Barry told me that he worked at Pacific Aviation at the time of the skyjacking, and since his company sold airplanes and aviation gear, George Harrison knew to call them to purchase chutes for the skyjacker.

However, when Harrison called Pacific Aviation he learned from Barry that they had only "seat packs" and not the "back pack parachutes" demanded by Cooper. Hence, Halstad recommended that Harrison contact one of his customers, Hayden, who had two back parachutes and was located nearby in Kent.

Following that discussion Norman received a flurry of phone calls. The first came from Harrison asking for the chutes, but Norman thought it was a prank call and hung up. Harrison tried again, and Barry also rang. Eventually, Norman sorted out the clamor. Then, the three individuals strategized how to get Norman's two parachutes to NWO.

Norman says he was too busy at work for him to leave and deliver the parachutes himself, so he placed the parachutes in a taxi and gave the cabbie the address. He also handed the driver a receipt book so that Harrison could sign a document acknowledging that NWO was "leasing" Norman's two parachutes. Norman says the cabbie returned with the signed receipt, but Norman can't find it presently.

The FBI documents are completely muddled on this point and state the parachutes went first to "Boeing Flight Services in Seattle," but that facility does not exist, apparently. "I used to work for Boeing and I never heard of that place," Barry told me, revealing how incorrect the FBI records are.

In addition, Norman says he never spoke directly to the FBI during the parachute delivery or subsequent investigation, yet, the Bureau's parachute document claims that their detailed parachute files are based on interviews with Norman. However, the language in the FBI's document sounds like it came from Cossey, and Norman was dismayed over the FBI's inaccuracies when I read him the Bureau's parachute documents.

Besides the mix-up in the files, the overall relationship between the FBI and Norman was strained. Norman says the return of the parachute was highly contentious, and he had to sue in court to get it back from the FBI.

"It took years, and it was a court in Washington, DC, too," Norman told us.

Norman's difficulties with the FBI didn't conclude in the court room, and the actual transfer in Seattle was tense. "The FBI guy who gave it back to me was downright rude," says Norman. "I asked him if he could write out a little note, you know, giving me some-thing official, proving that it was, you know, part of the skyjacking. Well, he just said, 'I'm not giving you nothing,' and turned away. So, I just called out, 'Well, if you ever need any more help from me in the future, I'm not gonna give you nothing,' either!'"

Ironically, Norman has never used the parachute, either before the skyjacking or since. "Why should I leave a perfectly good airplane in flight," he told me, cracking a smile.

As for the parachute ownership debate, Norman is non-plussed. The most emotion he displayed was when he told me, "Earl Cossey is sometimes full of beans."

Coss is hot, though. When I told Cossey that Norman insists he is the owner of the chutes and his claim is backed up by FBI documents, Coss screamed: "Norman Hayden is full of shit." I was surprised by Coss' vehemence since both he and Hayden told me that they had never met the other even though Coss packed his parachutes in May 1971.

After I printed this exchange on the *Mountain News,* Norman informed me that he wanted no further contact, saying that he didn't wish to be caught up in any mud-slinging with Cossey. Norman has been true to his word, but has spoken occasionally with other researchers and has participated in the Washington State Historical Museum's 2013 exhibit on Cooper.

Halstead was less dramatic when I asked him about this dispute. In fact, he was astonished to learn that there was any controversy about Norman's ownership, and he had never heard of Earl Cossey or his claims. Along those lines, Barry openly wonders if NWO received *four* back pack parachutes that day—two from Norman that were identical civilian rigs, and two from Earl Cossey that were a mix of military and civilian.

So, was Earl Cossey telling the truth? I don't think so because he deceived me too many times to receive the benefit of the doubt, and I wonder, along with many others, if Cossey's deceptions may have contributed to his murder in 2013.

But there is one thing about Earl Cossey that everyone agrees upon. Coss, a certified rigger who worked at Issaquah Sky Sports, folded and packed all the chutes that went aboard Flight 305, even the reserves. The picture below shows Norman Hayden's rigging card from his Steinthal/Pioneer rig, signed by "EJ Cossey" on May 21, 1971.

Chapter 8

Murder of FBI Consultant Earl Cossey

Cooper World was rocked when Earl Cossey was found dead in his Woodinville home on April 26, 2013. Coss' daughter discovered her father's body lying on the garage floor, and authorities determined that Coss had been murdered three days prior. He was 74.

The King County Sheriff's Office (KCSO) said that Cossey was killed by a blow to the head, but PIO Sgt. Cindi West declined to describe where on the skull he had been struck or by what type of instrument. "We're not releasing that kind of information at this time," she said. The cops remain mum to this day.

However, the looming question in the Cooper investigation is whether Coss was killed because of his involvement in Norjak. Specifically, was his murder linked to the fact that his credibility had crumbled in the past few years from the issues discussed in the previous chapter? Was Cossey deemed a "loose end" by a Norjak insider who controls the investigation and wanted to keep a possible cover-up intact? I posed that question directly to Sgt. West.

"I have had many calls asking if this case is related to the DB Cooper case," she told me, "But, we have **NO** information that leads us to believe that this case has any relation to the Cooper case.'"

Many speculate that Cossey's death was for a mundane reason like interrupting a burglary or an angry ex. Supporting that notion, Coss' driver's license and credit cards were mailed back to him postmortem by a Good Samaritan, who presumably found his wallet a few days after the murder. But that person has never come forward despite entreaties from the family and police.

However, there was a dark side to Earl Cossey that posits something more sinister. I interviewed several of Coss' friends and was surprised to learn that he was a big-time gambler, specializing in poker and sports betting. One of his friends, Steve Baird, told me that Coss was known to "look for action" daily, and generally carried large sums of cash—at least $500 and often thousands, $25,000 in one estimate. Cossey's gambling buddies in Seattle called the KCSO and gave detectives the names and places they thought might lead to whoever murdered Coss.

However, the friends never saw the police investigate any of the establishments or individuals they cited, nor did the detectives ever call them back for more information. As a result, these friends felt the cops had dropped the ball on Coss, and told me they suspected a cover-up.

Coss' case got bumped up to the Major Case squad soon afterwards, but the KCSO has not released any additional information on the case.

Nevertheless, more troubled dealings were revealed when I spoke with a colleague of Cossey's, Ralph Hatley, in 2014. Hatley operates a skydiving operation in Eagle Creek, Oregon, and is widely respected in the skydiving community. Hatley and Coss were skydiving competitors for many years, and Ralph told me he considered Coss a good friend. Hatley said that Coss did more than gamble or earn kudos as a beloved math teacher in the Leota

Middle School of Woodinville, and Coss made most of his money in property development, especially with a series of house rentals. "Coss embezzled those houses from his mother. That's how he got his start," Hatley told me.

With these allegations in mind, Cossey's death requires us to take a much closer look at his difficulties in truth-telling and his relationship with the FBI. We now know that Cossey was wildly deceptive throughout his sojourn in Norjak, as discussed in the previous chapter.

To recap and amplify: In 2011, I asked Coss for a clarification on the story that he had stuffed a 28-foot canopy into an NB-*6* container rather than the larger NB-*8* sack. He told me the stuffing story was "pretty much accurate."

The FBI clearly believed his NB-6 story, because Gray revealed in 2011 that FBI documents state explicitly that Cossey had supplied an NB-6. Additionally, Larry Carr believed Cossey, and spoke publicly about Coss shoving a 28-foot canopy into the NB-6.

But in a follow-up interview Cossey told me that he had no idea how the NB-6 story got started. Plus, Coss told me that he *never* discussed the technical aspects of the Cooper jump or the parachutes with the FBI. That statement is blatantly false. Cossey was an FBI consultant and his skydiving expertise is recorded in the written FBI records. Further, Special Agent Larry Carr described his many technical conversations with Cossey on the DZ. Carr even discussed the NB-6 stuffing scenario directly with Cossey:

> ... I asked Cossey why he packed a 28-foot canopy in the NB-6 and he just shrugged. Kind of like, 'it was my chute; I did it because I can. (Larry Carr, DZ post, 6.12.08).

Carr also believed Cossey's view on the NB-6, and Coss' ownership claim.

> The NB-6 and the Pioneer were Cossey's chutes, he had them at his house... (Carr, DZ, 6.12.08).

Carr also confirmed that Cossey had told the FBI in writing that one chute was an NB-6.

> In Cossey's statement to the FBI on 11/26/1971, 4th paragraph: "... he described the missing back pack parachute as having a sage green nylon container, model NB-6 with sage green nylon harness, which harness has no "D" rings to mount a chest pack." (Larry Carr, DZ, 12.17.07).

Yet, in a second 2011 interview Cossey emphatically told me that he had provided an NB-8. Sadly, Carr was in error about the true parachute picture, and Cossey never clarified events for the case agent. In fact, Carr clearly respected Cossey despite his *mishigas*.

> I liked that guy. I could have talked to him all day, but he grew tired of me in about an hour. (Larry Carr, DZ, 6.12.08)

Therefore, how much legal responsibility must Cossey shoulder for confusing Larry Carr? Did Cossey impede the investigation by muddying the Norjak waters, or was he just a wannabe that wanted to sip the champagne bubbles of Norjak fame? Regardless, Carr was seriously mixed-up about the parachutes.

Carr's confusion included the transport issue as well. On the DZ, Carr reverted to the official FBI documents at first, but finishes by supporting Cossey's perspective.

> The chutes were secured through NWA's Seattle flight operations. The flight ops manager called an individual from Pacific Aviation who in turn called an individual he knew who had two back packs...

> ...This person put the two back packs in a cab and the cab driver delivered them to Boeing Field and then onto Sea-Tac by private car." (Larry Carr, DZ, 12.17.07)

Carr revealed his persistent confusion in other posts:

> Yes, we have the serial numbers and interviewed the rigger. One chute was returned to its owner, two were never found and one is in evidence. (Larry Carr, DZ, 1.1.08).

As noted, Hayden received his one, unused parachute back from the FBI. Only Cossey claims he didn't get any of his parachutes returned, according to Geoffrey Gray. This affair casts strong suspicion not only on the relationship between the FBI and Cossey, but also the FBI and Gray. Did Geoffrey have to make a deal with the FBI to get official access? Did Geoffrey have to promise not to reveal the dirty little secrets of Norjak, such as why the feds reversed their view of DB Cooper? Or worse, is Geoffrey now part of a spin job, sanitizing Cossey's reputation?

I've asked Geoffrey, but have not received a substantive answer. Regardless, Cossey's reputation is now scrubbed clean. As of 2014, no one in the media describes Earl Cossey as the owner of DB Cooper's parachutes, and Coss is only identified as the rigger. Clearly, Coss' role in Norjak has been altered.

But, if Cossey's persona problem was fixed, why would someone murder him? Just to cleanse some lingering blemish on the FBI's public image? Or is something more pernicious in play? Here is one hypothesis:

Suppose Coss knew someone who had an interest in controlling the Norjak narrative because they wanted to protect a bigger secret.

Suppose this "puppet master" had encouraged Coss in the early days to develop a storyline that would provide reasonable assumptions that DB Cooper was inept and probably dead, thereby allowing the Bureau to toss cold water on the publics' belief that Cooper was heroic and "beat da man." With that insight, did Coss have knowledge of how the FBI actually conducted its investigation? Did Coss know why the FBI was so concerned about changing the DB Cooper story?

Was Coss considered a liability once his credibility became compromised and the Cossey–FBI partnership was spiraling downward? Suppose that the puppet master didn't trust Coss to keep his secrets any longer.

Would that be a reason to kill him?

Chapter 9

Analysis of the Flight Path, Weather, and Clothing

The flip side of the parachute examination is: where did Cooper land, even if he died upon impact? The key to answering that question is knowing where was Flight 305 when Cooper exited the plane, and for that we need precise information on the flight path and the time of the jump. Surprisingly these issues are not fully resolved, which begs another question *why not?* Is it due simply to the turgidity of bureaucracy? Or is there a cover-up?

Tom Kaye, the leader of a quasi-official investigation group known as the Citizen Sleuth team, attempted to clarify these issues at the 2011 Symposium. Using never-before-released FBI documents, including radar maps that were an amalgam of radar transcripts from McChord Air Base in Tacoma and the FAA's Seattle Center, Kaye said that he had examined 100 percent coverage of the landing zones. However, Kaye did not display any of the original data.

Additionally, Kaye accepted the claim that elk hunter Carroll Hicks found Flight 305's instructional placard for deploying the airstairs near Silver Lake, Washington, and thus Kaye placed 305 smack dab in the middle of V-23. Kaye also acknowledged that the placard most likely drifted about 2 ½ miles eastward in the wind, but said it was still within the central corridor of V-23.

Graphically, the flight pathway that Kaye presented appears to be a zig-zag, generally heading southward, and why 305 didn't fly a straight line is unknown. Nonetheless, Kaye said that after Silver Lake, 305 then passed over nearby Toledo, Pigeon Springs, Ariel, Highland and Battleground, Washington, finally crossing the Columbia in the western Portland metro area. Kaye accepted the general assumption that Cooper jumped somewhere near Battleground and drifted northeast to Ariel, but he challenged the conventional wisdom on the type of landscape within LZ-A.

For years most people assumed that Cooper landed in a dense and dangerous forest, but Kaye reviewed topographical maps of the area and found there were very few sections that would be considered heavily forested or "wilderness" at the time of the skyjacking.

"There were no 'death woods' in 1971," he declared, characterizing the landing area as a mix of trees, hills and farm fields, and filled with light from homes and developed areas. In fact, Kaye described LZ-A as decent spot to land because it was a benign agricultural area. Kaye added that there would be a lot of ambient light from the houses, stores, and street lights in the area, all of which would have bounced off of the clouds as well.

He also challenged the FBI's assertion that there was too much snow on the ground to continue an effective search. "There was no snow," he stated simply, refuting Geoffrey Gray's pronouncement made earlier in the Symposium when he had shown FBI documents from Seattle to Bureau headquarters in Washington, DC claiming the LZ had too much snow and the ground search needed to be postponed until spring.

Additionally, Kaye delivered details on the cloud cover, saying two cloud layers existed—one of "broken clouds" at 3,000 feet, and a second "overcast" condition of at least 85 percent cloud cover at 5,000 feet. Hence, Kaye said that Cooper could not see the ground from an elevation of 10,000 feet, nor could anyone on the ground see Cooper bail.

As for flying east of Victor 23 over the Washougal, as espoused by Himmelsbach and Rataczak, Kaye said that he had not found any credible evidence to support this assertion. Simply, Kaye rejected the hypothesis that the money floated down to Tina Bar from the Washougal Basin.

"There was no natural means to move the money to Tina Bar," he said, stunning the Portland audience.

He also suggested that the money was delivered to the beach by human hands, speculating that Cooper had landed successfully and hitchhiked a ride to Portland Airport. Kaye theorized that Cooper rewarded his benefactor with three bundles of ransom money, which the driver buried at Tina Bar out of a pique of guilt and fear.

However, few audience members believed Kaye then, or now, and the issue of how the money got to Tina Bar remains wide open.

Flight Simulation

Adding more fuel to the fires of flight path controversy, Cooper aficionados at the Internet's DB Cooper Forum have established a flight simulation for 305 through the disputed areas between the "Malay Intersection" near Castle Rock, WA, and Portland, Oregon. According to the flight path maps provided by the FBI to Kaye and featured on their DB Cooper website, the flight times between checkpoints do not jibe. Flight 305 would have had to double its speed and then greatly reduce it to match the time-marks the FBI has indicated on the maps.

Is this simply a transcription error? Or is it a tell-tale sign of something else at work, such as obscuring where 305 actually was flying at the times presented? At the very least, it indicates the flight data from the FBI is not accurate. In addition, these accelerations occurred as 305 allegedly performed sharp turns to the left and right.

The FBI has not explained these discrepancies.

Conditions of the Jump

Another contentious issue is the clothing DB Cooper wore. Was he critically under-dressed for a nighttime skydive in a November rain storm?

"You bet!" most folks say, such as researcher Jerry Thomas, since DB Cooper was wearing only loafers, a thin business suit and a lightweight overcoat. Yet many skydivers say that such concerns are overstated. Alan MacArthur, former president of the Boeing Employees Skydiving Club, says that he has jumped successfully in all kinds of weather including snow, and his gear has often been minimal. In fact, he even confessed to jumping in sandals during a youthful escapade. Other skydivers have posted on the DZ saying that they have parachuted naked, which certainly presents extreme levels of wind chill exposure.

Further, a founding member of the Boeing skydivers, Sheridan Peterson, reportedly jumped in the 1960s wearing a thin, black business suit—just like DB Cooper did years later—which helped place Peterson near the top of the FBI's suspect list.

Currently, many investigators wonder if Cooper may have brought extra gear with him concealed in the briefcase or in his brown paper bag. Perhaps he had a roll of duct tape or ace bandages to bind his ankles, and gloves and goggles for wind chill protection?

MacArthur told me that such gear would be adequate for the terrain Cooper would face.

Regardless, Cooper's descent through the 10,000 feet would take less than ten minutes, so his exposure was modest. Further, jumping in a rain storm in the Pacific Northwest is not uncommon, and according to Metzler the best place to be when it's raining is under the "umbrella" of a parachute.

Nevertheless, jumping into intermittent nighttime rains with temperatures below freezing and being unable to see the ground or the horizon are offered by the FBI as proof that Cooper was inexperienced and foolhardy. But during the Vietnam War, HALO (High Altitude, Low Opening) commandos parachuted from 14,000 feet in sub-freezing temperatures—conditions that exist year-round in the tropics—and they landed in unknown jungles with people waiting for them with guns.

Further, the weather conditions during the jump have been greatly exaggerated by the FBI and several authors. The temperature at 10,000 feet is now generally understood to have been about 22 degrees Fahrenheit, but many authors report the air temp to be -7 degrees, which it was, but they often fail to mention this number is Celsius, not Fahrenheit. Additionally, the air-temp at ground level was in the mid-40s.

Further, the windchill factor is routinely miscalculated. According to many skydivers, the actual wind on the stairs is virtually nil due to the perturbations of the slipstream around the stairs. In fact, one skydiver on the DZ said that when he jumped from a 727, a Styrofoam coffee cup placed at the top of the stairs didn't even move since there was no wind whatsoever at the upper portion of the stairway.

Along those lines, many skydivers have stated that there is very little turbulence immediately upon jumping. After a few moments however, a skydiver does hit the slipstream and it gets rough. Skyjacker Robb Heady said that once he hit the slipstream he tumbled for about fifteen seconds. But his plane was also traveling at a speed almost double to that of DB Cooper, so the air turbulence would have been much more severe.

Where is His Gear?

If Cooper did land safely—or crashed—where is all of his stuff? Did he lash everything together in one huge bundle so he could find it on the ground, or did he track it with some unknown electronic device? Or, if it was a privatized commando operation, did Cooper have a ground crew monitoring both his location and his gear?

The Citizen Sleuths (CS), a band of private investigators organized by Larry Carr in 2009, have revealed that Cooper cut a lot of cord from a reserve chute, so he could have secured a bundle. Tina Mucklow confirmed that some of this rope was used to close his bank bag and form a kind of handle and/or cinch. However, the CS reveal inconsistencies in the official FBI documents regarding the rope, and official records indicate that two or three lines were cut from the reserve chute depending on which file one reads. However, five separate cords are missing from the chute in the evidence room. This discrepancy is difficult to resolve at this point, but the five lengths of rope would total nearly 80 feet.

Even if the lower number of shroud lines is used, Cooper still had 30–45 feet of rope. That's enough line to secure the bag, affix it to his body, and have a few feet left over for the bundle. Perhaps Cooper landed, buried the bundle, and it has never been found.

Another scenario exists and is held currently by the FBI—Cooper not only died in the jump, but he took all his gear with him by splashing into a lake and drowning, or "cratering" into a remote hillside and entombing himself and his bundle. Variations of this theme are profuse, with numerous speculations on what body of water or remote mountain peak Cooper impacted, and they dominate FBI thinking to this day.

Could the bundle have been disposed by setting it on fire, though? Maybe Cooper's bomb was not made of dynamite but was actually a set of road flares that the skyjacker could use to burn the leftover equipment? As bizarre a notion as this may be, there is circumstantial evidence to suggest that something like this may have happened.

The "Fiery Object"

In 2011, Galen Cook announced that he had received some intriguing documents from the estate of Richard Tosaw, which cast light on the possibility that Cooper incinerated his left-overs.

Galen had been a friend and fellow-researcher with Tosaw, spending time with him at Tina Bar in 2005 and 2008. After Tosaw's death in 2009, some of his associates gave Galen selected copies of their mentor's field notes. One mentioned a "fiery object" seen over Vancouver, Washington on the night of the skyjacking. The notes reveal that a woman from Vancouver had contacted Tosaw in the mid-1980s when Tosaw was on Portland TV discussing his Cooper book. The woman, known as "Janet," sent a note to Tosaw describing what she had seen in the skies over Vancouver and she later met with him. However, Tosaw had never told anyone about the woman or her claims.

Tosaw recorded that Janet lived in the eastern suburbs of Vancouver near Mill Plain Road. She and her husband had seen

TV coverage of the skyjacking at 6 pm, so they were familiar with the events on-going in the skies above them. Shortly after 8 pm, they left their house and saw a low-flying plane to the west, heading south. They immediately saw a bright glow directly underneath the plane. It was so brilliant it illuminated the belly of the aircraft.

Then the glow burst into a flame and they saw a fiery object arcing away to the west. Whatever it was stayed lit for about five or six seconds, eight tops, she told Tosaw, and then faded. "That must be DB Cooper's plane," the wife shouted at the time.

The next day the couple wrote the FBI and described what they had seen. Several days later, Janet says she was visited by two men. One fellow stayed in the car and the other, who was wearing a suit and dark coat, approached the house. He identified himself as an FBI agent but he never showed his badge or any other identification. He asked for the couple who had written the letter, and the wife confirmed that she had contacted the FBI. Janet reported that the "FBI" guy became intimidating, and told her to never tell anyone about what she saw, shocking her with a crude outburst: "Keep your fucking mouth shut." She did, and never told anyone until Richard Tosaw was on his book tour ten years later. However, Tosaw's reasons for never revealing her observations are unknown.

Galen says that after he received Tosaw's notes he was able to contact the wife and husband, who are now divorced but still living in the Vancouver area. Galen says the story they told him comports exactly to what he read in Tosaw's account. In addition, Galen says that he has received two more reports of folks witnessing a burning object over Vancouver, and he has interviewed the other parties.

All three witnesses were in different neighborhoods of Vancouver, and Galen says that their placement of the glowing object triangulates to the same spot, a position just to the west of the I-5 bridge as it crosses into Portland. Additionally, they all said the fiery object arced westward towards Tina Bar. Was Cooper burning incriminating evidence? The FBI has never commented on this finding.

Despite the reports of extensive cloud cover, which presumably would have hidden the plane and any burning object descending from it, there is supporting information that something was observable from the ground. "I heard it fly over my house that night," Dona Elliott told me and several others at the 2012 Cooper Days shin-dig in Ariel. "It was loud! It's wasn't flying at 10,000 feet. It must have been more like 3,000 or 4,000 feet,"

Official transcripts add more mystery to this matter because Flight 305 wasn't always at 10,000 feet. Radio transmission between Flight 305 and the FAA's Seattle Center—as provided on the FBI's website and Sluggo's research site—indicate the pilots were flying faster and *higher* than has been generally reported, climbing to nearly 11,000 feet in an attempt to deprive Cooper of oxygen.

DB Cooper's Behavior

One of the best pieces of evidence for DB Cooper's skills as a skydiver may be his demeanor—he never broke a sweat. Despite sitting in an airplane for six hours with people that he had threatened to kill, it seemed like another day at the office for DB Cooper. He calmly smoked cigarettes, buffered inquiries from Tina Mucklow, and orchestrated a unique major crime—seemingly with aplomb.

What kind of man does that? A whuffo?

More Questions

A nagging question hangs over the investigation—how did Cooper get to the Portland Airport in the first place? Despite extensive questioning of bus drivers and cabbies, airport and ground personnel, plus the staff of local motels and restaurants, the feds still have no idea how DB Cooper got to PDX. Such was the era before surveillance cameras became ubiquitous.

Regardless, let's explore the discovery of the only definitive physical evidence ever found in the DB Cooper case—the $5,800.

Chapter 10

Money Find

On a Sunday afternoon in early February 1980, an eight-year-old boy named Brian Ingram uncovered three bundles of DB Cooper's money during a family picnic at a Columbia River beach known as Tina Bar. Brian discussed his famous discovery with me at the 2011 DB Cooper Symposium in Portland, and gave me a straightforward description of his remarkable find.

"Yup, I found the bundles near the surface under a few inches of sand, and they were stacked atop one another, with each bundle slightly askew from the next," Brian told me.

He also said they were worn around the edges and appeared weathered, as if they had been buried in the sand for awhile. Each bundle was wrapped with a rubber band, which Brian said were intact when he found them, but they soon crumbled.

After discovering the bills, Brian said that he and his family—his parents Dwayne and Patricia, his aunt Crystal Ingram and her five-year old daughter, Denise—scoured the rest of the beach looking for more bills. "Of course, we went looking," he told me. "We wanted to find more money!" But they found nothing else, Brian said.

The next phase of the story I learned from "Georger," a frequent poster at the DropZone website and an associate of the Citizen Sleuths. Georger says that the Ingrams brought the money back to their apartment and planned to take the money to a bank to be redeemed. But the bills were stuck together and any attempt to pull them apart broke the wad into chunks. Brian's mother tried soaking the bills in the kitchen sink but they wouldn't separate. She added dish soap and even Clorox.

Discussing their find at work the next day, one of Dwayne's fellow employees suggested to Dwayne, who was from Oklahoma and unaware of DB Cooper, the money may be from the hijacking and he should contact law enforcement. Dwayne called the Sheriff's office and they put him in touch with the FBI in Portland, who checked some of the serial numbers Ingram provided and realized immediately that is was part of Cooper's ransom.

After meeting with the family, Himmelsbach assembled a retrieval team and headed out to the beach, known as Tina Bar, as in *sand bar*. By late Tuesday, February 12, 1980, dozens of FBI agents, newspaper reporters and camera crews had descended upon Tina Bar.

The beach is owned by the Fazio family, and is part of a large and varied ranch operation that includes a cattle business and a sand and gravel company. In those days, the Fazios let people use the beach at Tina Bar and a jar was placed at the beach gate for a 25-cent donation. It was a popular spot for fisherman.

Al Fazio told me he was not at home when the FBI arrived. In fact, he first encountered the feds as he was returning from a cattle auction and was stopped by agents on Lower River Road, about five miles northwest of Vancouver, Washington. He was not allowed to proceed onto his property even though he showed proper identification. But eventually he gained access.

Once on the property he headed to the beach and joined his brother, Richard Fazio. Al says that they were soon hired by the FBI to bring their backhoes onto the strand and participate in the dig.

In 1980, Tina Bar looked much different than it does today. Then, the beach sloped gently from the edge of the pasture lands down to the water's edge. Nowadays, the beach is much steeper because the dredged channel muck is deposited inland for environmental considerations, rather than thrown back directly on the beach. Without the replenishment, the shoreline erodes quickly. Currently, the slope at Tina Bar has a 2–3 foot cliff at the upper edge of the riverbank and then drops sharply to the water's edge. As a result, the actual locale where the money was buried is now an imaginary spot a couple of feet in the air.

The change in the placement of the dredge spoils occurred in 1974. FBI indicate that the Portland State University hydrologist who inspected Tina Bar, Leonard Palmer, declared the money came from soil layers above the last on-shore dredge deposits in 1974, proving that the money arrived at Tina Bar after that date. The "Palmer Report" also suggests that the money was never deposited at Tina Bar by any dredging operation.

However, since the bills were compressed and did not separate easily, it is possible they had been buried in the sand for a lengthy period of time, perhaps at a great depth and only discovered once the shoreline eroded enough to reveal the money. But how they might have arrived at that depth is unknown.

But other evidence challenges a long-term burial at Tina Bar. Brian claims that the rubber bands that enclosed each of the three bundles were intact when he found the money, and Tom Kaye of the Citizen Sleuths has declared that the manufacturer of the rubber bands said that they would only stay pliable for a few months in the wild. Nevertheless, Kaye says they could have lasted longer if they were buried in wet sand.

Further, Galen Cook has employed a team of local soil and hydrology scientists to evaluate the Tina Bar environment and review all of Dr. Palmer's findings. Galen says that extreme river flooding may have deposited the money at Tina Bar, and says Palmer's Report indicates that the money arrived at Tina Bar only 9–12 months before discovery, which would be about mid-1979. This time frame corresponds to a period of flooding following the severe drought of 1978 when water levels on the Columbia were at their fourth-lowest level ever recorded.

In addition, Galen says one of the bundles did not have a rubber band around it and was missing several bills. Galen feels that this bundle may have been the source of the money shards reportedly found strewn about the beach and sighted by many others, including the FBI and the Fazios, even though Brian says that he and his family didn't see a single piece of extra money. Like most things in the DB Cooper case, there is plenty of controversy about most aspects of the money find.

Despite Brian's claim that he found nothing else on the beach, Himmelsbach writes in his book that he and his team found fragments of bills on the beach and buried in the sand as deep as three feet in some instances. Similarly, Himmelsbach's PIO, Dorwin Schreuder, told me in 2010 that they had found "thousands of shards" throughout the sand column and they placed them in plastic baggies.

Specifically, Dorwin says they found the shards "evenly placed throughout the top 3–4 feet of sand for a radius of 20 feet" from the spot where Brian had found the three bundles, and that they found them through lots of shovel work before Al Fazio and his brother arrived with their backhoes. In particular, Dorwin said that they dug at least four holes to that depth and found shards each time. "No matter how deep we dug we found money, homogeneously mixed to a great depth," he told me.

Dorwin told me that some of the bill fragments were sizable—about two or three inches across, and had enough of a serial number on them to confirm that they were part of Cooper's ransom. However, most were small, about the size of a quarter.

He also said they worked diligently and methodically. Pictures in newspapers confirm that the beach was sectioned into six grid zones, with dozens of FBI agents and volunteers digging with shovels. They even established a screening pit. "We went at it like archaeologists," Schreuder said, and claimed that once they went past the 20-foot radius the money field diminished, and that was when they brought in the backhoes. The FBI continued recovery efforts at Tina Bar for a week after the Ingram's initial discovery.

Supporting the Bureau's claims, another FBI agent at Tina Bar, Special Agent Mike McPheter, told me that he was on "shovel detail," and was digging with other agents on the "high-tide line," where they found money fragments. McPheter told me that he retrieved about a dozen pieces, either on the surface or buried about a foot or two down into the sand. "Down about a shovel blade's length," he told me.

However, when I called McPheters in 2015 to confirm where a high-tide line was on the Columbia River in February 1980, McPheters declined to answer, and hung up.

Nevertheless, the Fazios told me that they do observe tides at Tina Bar, as the ocean will occasionally push water up the 60 miles to the beach. However, I did not see any kind of tide line at T-Bar when I visited in 2009, nor have I ever seen any pictures of one. In fact, the river's downstream current is very strong at Tina Bar, perhaps 5–8 knots.

More disturbing is the fact that few shards or bags of fragments are in the evidence collection in Seattle, according to the

Citizen Sleuths. In addition, there is no documentation in Seattle pertaining to where the shards were found. In short, the Seattle FO has no record of what was found by the Portland agents under Himmelsbach's command at Tina Bar.

I have asked Ralph Himmelsbach repeatedly to clarify this issue, sending him letters and emailing his trusted associate, Jerry Thomas. As of this writing, I haven't heard anything definitive other than Jerry's comment, "Ralph told me that everything was sent up to Seattle."

If so, where is it? There are snippets of comments on Internet chat rooms that say the shards went to FBI headquarters in Washington, DC for analysis. But, if so, are they still there?

Worse, I haven't received any information on this subject from the Cooper case agent at the time of the money find, Ron Nichols. As Cooper case agent, Nichols was stationed in Seattle, and if he made any attempt to monitor the money retrieval or document it, he's not talking.

Worst, though, are the rumors that Himmelsbach retained the shards and kept Nichols in the dark, forcing the FBI in Seattle to learn of the money find by reading the Seattle newspapers.

Complicating the matter, Schreuder also told me that they found more than just money. "We found about a-half-to-a-third of Cooper's briefcase," Schreuder said.

However, he also claimed that the money and briefcase came on shore as part of the channel dredging—that everything got scooped off the bottom of the Colombia and thrown on the river bank. Schreuder is alone in his briefcase claim, however.

Dorwin admits that his memory may be faulty, as he says he recalls the Army Corps of Engineers (ACE) had their dredge, the "Bedell," at Tina Bar during their recovery operations, but ACE records show the Bedell was in California when the money retrieval was ongoing at Tina Bar in early 1980. Yet, the dredging scenario is compelling because the money find seems like the equivalent of a shotgun splatter of money hitting the beach during a dredging operation.

But the uncertainty is compounded by Al Fazio, who adamantly claims that the FBI didn't find a single shard buried anywhere. "They didn't find anything buried. That's just a lot of government crap," Al told me in 2009. "I should know, I was there, right on top of a backhoe, doing the digging."

Schreuder says that the Fazios and their backhoes were brought in when the feds discovered that the money find had petered out, but the Fazios claim they had never seen any money on their beach before the Ingram find. However, Al and Richard do say that they saw money shards along the tide line during the dig. Al is convinced the money washed in via a recent tide and he posits that the bundles were covered with a bit of sand brought in by natural wave action.

Continuing, he says many of the shards he saw were discolored or black, which confounds the claims of the Citizens Sleuths who say the blackening occurred *after* the FBI applied a silver nitrate compound to test for fingerprints.

Nevertheless, Al is convinced the shards were actually part of the top bundle of Brian's three, and says the actions of the tides, river currents, and floating driftwood tore up a few of the surface bills and deposited them along the "tideline."

Casting more doubts upon Dorwin Schreuder and his findings, researcher "Georger" shocked the Cooper World in 2015 when he reported on the DB Cooper Forum that Schreuder had told him the FBI had found a 60-yard plume trail of fragments emanating southwards and upstream from the primary money find area. How a plume field could develop upstream is baffling, as is Dorwin's selective storytelling since he never mentioned this development in our conversations.

In addition, Galen Cook contributes more uncertainty with recent findings. In 2012, he spoke with fishermen along the Columbia and met two men who claimed to have seen money shards at Tina Bar just prior to Brian's discovery in February 1980. They said they were aged 12 and 14, and fishing for steelhead trout in January 1980. They claim they found a dozen pieces of twenties buried in a hole in the sand a few feet away from the spot where Brian discovered the three bundles. Intriguingly, the fishermen say the pieces were the corners of torn-off twenties, with the numeral "20" clearly showing as if someone had deliberately cut them off the bills. In addition, the fishermen told Galen that a week later they found a few more shards about 100 yards downstream. They also told Galen that they didn't attach any significance to their find so they didn't tell anyone.

But it does raise the question of what the FBI did in the days and weeks after the money find in 1980. Did they talk to fishermen along the shoreline? Did they explore other sections of the river front? If not, why not? If they did, what are their findings? Where are their findings?

The fishermen's claims tie into another discovery near Tina Bar. When Galen released the news about the teenagers finding fragments, he was reminded of Richard Tosaw's 1988 discovery of a "pilot chute" snagged on a wooden river groin in twenty-feet of water, about a mile upstream from Tina Bar.

A pilot chute is a small rectangular parachute about 2–3 feet across and designed to help pull the main canopy from a parachute bag, such as pulling a Steinthal canopy from a Pioneer container.

Combined with the fiery object and the testimony of the teen-aged fishermen, Galen now wonders if DB Cooper concealed a pilot chute in his briefcase and waited until the Columbia River to ditch his bundle of gear. As he passed over the water he ignited the bundle with the sticks of dynamite—which were actually road flares—and attached the pilot chute so that the bundle would slowly float down to the surface and give him a long look at his landing zone. As a result, Galen now wonders if Cooper landed in Oregon on the southern shore of the Columbia River. "This is why the case is unsolved after forty-two years," he wrote me in 2012. "Everything is out of whack and ripe for a really good conspiracy storyline."

Supporting the notion of a new LZ are numerous reports that Larry Carr told many sleuths shortly before he left the case he was convinced Cooper jumped far south of the FBI's original landing zone in Ariel. Galen said to me that Carr had told him that Cooper jumped much closer to Portland—in Orchards, Washington—and landed far to the south of Ariel. However, I have not found any definitive statement from Carr that moves the LZ south from Ariel.

The money find and its associated investigations have one additional twist—the role that Richard Tosaw played in the lives of many of those connected with the case.

The FBI confiscated the money from the Ingrams immediately after the money find in 1980, claiming they needed it for evidence. In response, the Ingram's hired Tosaw to get it returned to them. Tosaw, who had already established himself as legal expert for inheritance recovery cases, needed years to convince a court to grant the Ingrams some of the money. Because of their compressed, torn and compromised state, the total could only be estimated to be about $5,800, or approximately 290 twenty-dollar bills. The settlement in June 1986 gave the Ingrams half, and a similar share went to NWO's insurance company, Global Indemnity. The FBI was awarded fourteen bills for evidentiary purposes.

In the course of helping the Ingrams, Tosaw became immersed in the Cooper saga and wrote the first major book on DB Cooper. He was also the last journalist to interview Tina Mucklow. Further, Tosaw became fixated on the notion that Cooper crash-landed in the Columbia River near Tina Bar, and perished. But he couldn't prove it conclusively. Nevertheless, he spent summers camped on the shores of the Columbia looking for Cooper, and hired many locals to help him. At one point, he even rented a spot on the Fazio's property. Eventually, Galen joined him for two summertime stints at T-Bar, and their collaboration continued in a robust fashion until the venerable investigator died of cancer in 2009.

The last investigatory oddity is the fact that the FBI and their hydrologist Leonard Palmer, plus many others including members of the DB Cooper Forum, call the beach "Tena Bar." Why is unusual, since the sign at the beach clearly states "TINA BAR." But suspicions run deep that the FBI is trying to obfuscate the association between the location of the money find and Norjak's primary witness, Tina Mucklow, who lived only a few miles upstream in Gresham, Oregon when the money was found in 1980.

However in early 2015, Smokin'99 from the DZ, challenged that assumption. Smokin' discovered historical documents from the 1920s that indicate the property was owned by a "Tell Tena" prior to the Fazio family, and as a result she posits that Tena Bar is the correct spelling, with the present sign in error.

Chapter 11

Tina Mucklow, the Primary Witness

Tina Mucklow is the most enigmatic figure in the DB Cooper saga. Even though she is the prime witness to the skyjacking, she hid from public view for thirty years until a bevy of journalists and private investigators discovered her whereabouts in 2010.

When I and other researchers, particularly Galen Cook, found Tina, we also discovered that she had undergone a personality change. Once a competent and compassionate flight attendant, Tina is now a social isolate quick to anger. Galen and I felt that if we could understand why, or how, Tina changed we might know more about Norjak.

The general feeling expressed by the public, certainly at DB Cooper forums on the Internet, is that Tina has suffered PTSD from the hijacking. Supporting this notion is a FBI report found by Geoffrey Gray that describes her as verbally unresponsive to Al Lee at the bottom of the airstairs during the money exchange, and Lee deduced that Tina was in emotional trouble.

However, the video clips of Tina after the skyjacking show her to be a confident and articulate woman. In media interviews she discusses the skyjacking calmly and with composure, clearly showing her concern for her passengers. Further, Tina seemed comfortable in front of the cameras.

Compared with video archives of Florence Schaffner, the contrast is striking. YouTube clips reveal that Florence was still anxious years after the hijacking, steadfastly proclaiming she was afraid she was going to die that night in a mid-air explosion. If one had to project who would suffer long term impacts from the sky-jacking, Florence would be the choice, not Tina. Yet, Tina is the flight attendant seemingly most affected.

Additionally, many followers of the case, especially members of Tina's circle of family and friends, vociferously claim that Tina's behavioral changes are a response to the media hordes hounding her for a juicy skyjacking story, compounded by residual trauma from the hijacking.

However, both Galen and I feel that something else has occurred. Perhaps another event or a series of circumstances cascaded into a psychological tidal wave that pushed Ms. Mucklow into a troubled state of mind. This scenario may be connected to the money find or not, as Tina disappeared shortly after the $5,800 was found on her namesake beach, which was only a few miles away from where she was living at the time. Most troubling, though, are reports from authors Richard Tosaw and Russ Calame that indicate Tina was having significant cognitive impairments and memory loss when they spoke with her in the 1980s.

So what happened? Aboard 305 Tina clearly demonstrated that she was the right person in the right place at the right time. She handled Cooper with aplomb. In fact, she was singularly skilled in dealing with a man who threatened to kill her and her passengers. Bill Rataczak clearly recognized these capabilities and has called Tina, "The brains of the outfit." Could a woman as capable as Tina truly get derailed by pesky journalists?

One of my concerns is that Tina may have been subjected to official pressures after the skyjacking, perhaps to maintain company secrets or to refrain from answering troubling questions concerning the FBI's stalled investigation. I am worried that something sinister may have befallen Tina, such as a Manchurian candidate-like scenario, as attributed to governmental MKULTRA mind-control programs. However, I have no solid evidence indicating what those circumstances might have been.

Regardless, something has happened to Tina Mucklow, and it seems to have something to do with Norjak. Hence, it challenges the mantra uttered by many that the DB Cooper skyjacking was a victimless crime and that no one was injured.

Galen shares my concerns, and by 2009 we had formed an informal partnership to explore these issues. Our quest had two components: First we had to find Tina, and then we had to determine why she had changed.

Researching Tina, we learned she is very religious and reportedly carried a bible on her flights. To wit: In pictures taken at Reno she appears to be clutching a bible in her arms.

Further, Galen said that Florence told him that she and Tina roomed together on layovers and that Tina was a real "bible-belter," constantly proselytizing. In addition, we knew that after the skyjacking Tina had been a cloistered nun at a convent in Oregon, and that Richard Tosaw had interviewed her there in the early 1980s.

So, the logical first step was to contact the nuns. My initial phone call to the Carmel of Maria Regina Monastery in Eugene, Oregon was met with a civil, but terse response. The woman I spoke with referred me to Sister Elizabeth Mary Saint Onge, who confirmed she was the "Mother Superior" and had been at the convent when Tina was a member.

Sister Elizabeth Mary was initially resistant to speaking with me. "I really don't want to get involved," she told me. But when I said I was calling because I was concerned about Tina's current well-being, Sister Elizabeth Mary relented. She confirmed that Tina had arrived at the convent in the spring of 1980 or possibly in 1979, and she stayed there until about 1991. Sister Elizabeth Mary said she was a little hazy on the exact dates, and declined to say where Tina went when she left the convent. Sister Elizabeth Mary also refused to discuss Tina's mental state or any other specifics of Tina's life at the convent. When I pushed, she cut me off. However, she was more forthcoming with Galen, and she allegedly said that "Tina never really fit in here" or words to that effect.

Seeking more information, I traveled to the convent in January 2011. The monastery is an ecclesiastical retreat nestled in the woods overlooking Eugene, and it reminded me of a stylish mix of mountaineering cabin and sorority house. As members of the Discalced Carmelite tradition, the nuns live a monastic life and have no regular interaction with the outside world. Not surprisingly, the living quarters and grounds are surrounded by a tall wooden fence. However, the chapel is open to the public, and small rooms are nearby where families can visit in private with their cloistered relatives.

When I arrived, I was nervous about encountering Mother Saint Onge in person, as I considered her to be *One Tough Cookie*. I walked up a steep hill towards the convent and rang a buzzer outside the chapel entrance. I spoke with an older-sounding woman who said she would meet me in the tiny gift shop adjacent to the speaker box. Within a few moments the door opened, and I was invited inside by a diminutive woman about 70-years old. She was dressed in typical nun garb—a blue and white habit and a light blue dress with white trim. Despite the habit's rim her face was unobstructed. "I'm Sister Teresa," she said warmly, extending her hand in greeting.

We shook hands and I gave her my business card. She asked about the nature of my visit, and I told her I was investigating the DB Cooper story and was concerned about Tina. "We don't want to get involved with that," she told me.

"Why not?" I replied.

"We've been stung too many times by the newspapers," Sister Teresa said.

"Really? Which papers? I've never heard or read anything uncomplimentary about the convent. What did they say?"

"I don't want to discuss any of that," Sister Teresa countered.

In response, I launched into a soliloquy about Tina and her retreat from mainstream life. I told Sister Teresa I was concerned about Tina's health, and added that I thought she had important information to share about Cooper. Silently, Sister Teresa thrust back my business card and began to move away. Passing beside me I could see a grimace on her face, as if she had a smoldering rage inside.

"Why are you so angry at me?" I asked her.

"I'm not angry," Sister Teresa replied.

"Well, you look angry," I countered.

"Well, you're just seeing the face that God has given me."

"But why are you angry at *me*?" I continued.

"I'm *not* angry," she stated again, but with more emphasis.

"But you *look* angry," I said, with my own elevated enunciation.

"That's *just* the face God has giving me," Sister Teresa insisted.

"Look, Sister Teresa," I replied, "There is very little I know about the Bible, but one line I do know—and the one that I truly believe in is—'The truth shall make us free.' I would add that the truth can make us whole, and in doing so will make us healthy, too. There are a lot of people in pain because of the DB Cooper case, in my judgment. A lot of people are afraid to talk. They're anxious and appear intimidated. I'm not looking to 'get' anyone or make their lives more difficult. I'm just seeking the truth. I just want to know what's going on."

After a pause, I continued. "I came here looking for justice," I said. "In fact, I came here seeking a partner in my effort to find justice."

"I'm looking for justice, too," Sister Teresa said, "and I'm going to return to it."

"That sounds evasive, Sister," I said.

"I'm going to return to my prayers," Sister Teresa declared.

I nodded but continued, "I was hoping the monastery would partner with me in my search for justice."

"We're not looking for partners."

I paused, and tried a new tack.

"Is Mother Saint Onge available?" I asked.

"Mother Saint Onge is on a personal retreat for ten days," she replied.

Sister Teresa began walking away again and I knew we were done. "Thanks for your time and for listening to what I had to say," I told her. She smiled wanly, and after shaking hands she left. I opened the gift shop door and departed.

I was getting used to this kind of rebuff from anyone in the Mucklow clan. The month prior I had I traveled to Tina's ancestral home in Philadelphia to see what I could learn from her relatives and friends. Newspaper accounts of the skyjacking have given researchers plenty of background on Tina and her roots in Pennsylvania.

Tina and her older sister Jane had attended a Lutheran boarding school called The Lankenau School for Girls, located in Germantown, PA, a working-class neighborhood of Philadelphia.

In addition, there is a woman named Arlene Mucklow listed in the phone book near Tina's family home town.

I called on Arlene, who described herself as a cousin "or something like that." When I approached Arlene's house it was just getting dark on a late December afternoon. The Christmas lights were on in the neighborhood and a gate blocked Arlene's pathway from the street. I debated about opening it, then took a breath and passed through. As I neared the house, however, all the interior lights went off, along with her outdoor Christmas decorations. It was as if a power outage was triggered by my presence. But I was only a couple steps away from the door, so I continued. I knocked, and a Voice from inside called out, "Who is it?"

"Hi. My name is Bruce Smith and I'm a newspaper reporter doing a story on DB Cooper. I'm looking for information on Tina Mucklow and I was wondering if you were related."

"She's not here," said the Voice.

"Is she okay? I hear she may not be well. She's been in hiding for thirty years," I replied.

"Oh, yeah, she's fine."

"That's great to hear... Well, thanks for your time."

I stepped back and prepared to go. As I turned, I saw a wooden plaque on the siding next to the door. It read: "No one gets to see the wizard. Not no one, not no way."

I smiled. I knew I was in the right place. As I passed back through the gate, though, the Voice spoke again—through another door.

"Wait!"

The door opened, and a woman about fifty approached me.

"Do you have a business card?" she called.

"Yeah, sure," I replied.

The woman was surrounded by a pack of yapping dogs that leapt at me from their side of the fence, but I arched my arm high over the railings and Arlene took my card. "I'd love to talk with you," I said. "Could I call you?

"Okay. Give me a piece of paper and I'll write down my cell phone number."

I passed her my notebook and she gave me the number. Within a few minutes, I had located a pizza joint and called her. We talked cordially for about twenty minutes. I also learned that she was very misleading, too. Arlene said that Tina had gone "on lots of vacations," but was unable to tell me where. Later, I realized that Arlene had lied to me when she told me that Tina no longer lived in Oregon. Nevertheless, Arlene reassured me repeatedly that Tina was in great shape and fully recovered from the skyjacking, even though she doesn't want to talk about it. I didn't accept Arlene's Pollyanna bromides and pushed back, saying that others, such as FBI agent Russ Calame, are reporting that Tina is not in the best of shape—that she is withdrawn and very different. Arlene acknowledged the truth of my words and said, "I guess she was traumatized that night."

After going in circles with Arlene for another five minutes, I changed my approach and starting talking about myself. I went into detail about how I had returned to New York for a few months to take care of my elderly mother. Arlene responded, saying that Tina had come Back East for a period of time to take care of her father. "She's one of the good people," Arlene said. "Not too many people would do that."

But Arlene stayed protective of Tina, and wouldn't give me any more details about her, so I decided to throw in the towel. I thanked Arlene for her time and hung up, then ordered a pizza and beer and wrote in my notebook about a very busy day.

Earlier, I had roamed the campus of the former Lankenau School for Girls (LSG), now part of Philadelphia College. I was thrilled to walk the campus knowing that Tina Mucklow had trod the same paths, and I felt closer to knowing the truth of Tina. I was stunned into some kind of quiet wonder in the administration building when I learned it had been the dormitory for both the nuns and women at LSG. *Nuns?* I pondered. I didn't know that the Lutherans had nuns, or that Lutheran girls would carry bibles when they worked as flight attendants.

Baptists maybe, but Lutherans? So many quirks to this story.

But, perhaps my most important encounter in Philly was meeting Dr. Susan Eisenhower-Turner. Several months earlier, Galen and I had spotted an Internet posting on a blog linked to a Minneapolis newspaper that was touting Bill Rataczak's retirement from Northwest Airlines. In the commentary section that followed, a woman named Susan Eisenhower-Turner asked if anyone had information on the whereabouts of her old friend and former classmate at the Lankenau School of Girls, Tina Mucklow.

I immediately responded to Eisenhower-Turner via the blog, but heard nothing. A Google search showed that a woman by the same name was a psychiatrist in the greater Philadelphia area. I hoped that Dr. E-T, as Galen and I began to call her, would partner with us in a joint therapeutic/journalistic effort to learn what had happened to Tina.

I sent a lengthy snail mail letter to Dr E-T describing my concerns and inviting her to join with me in a Good Samaritan partnership. Again, I received no reply. But the good doctor had responded to a similar outreach from Galen. He said that Dr. E-T had told him Tina should be left alone because she is suffering from a "permanent trauma."

Hearing that, I called Dr. E-T again. After leaving a couple of voice messages, I received one in return. Here is Dr. E-T's response:

Hi Mr. Smith,

This is Dr. Eisenhower-Turner returning your call. You had called me in regards to Tina Mucklow.

I have no information, and my feeling, as I explained to Galen, is that if Tina wishes to be interviewed she'll contact you in all likelihood, and if she doesn't, then perhaps we all need to respect her privacy.

Thanks so much, bye-bye.

But I wanted to learn more about the "permanent trauma" that Dr. E-T had revealed, even if we shared it off-the-record. In addition, I thought I could help Tina under the auspices that the "truth shall set us free." In fact, I felt it would be irresponsible not to act. The key issue for me was *how* to intervene, and I felt the best approach was to act gently, contacting as many friends and family as I could, and hoping someone could buffer my movement through Tina's emotional hot spots.

Hence, I went to Dr. E-T's office in the psychiatric unit of a suburban general hospital. However, there was no receptionist to inform her that I would like a word, so I knocked directly on her office door. She opened it, and was clearly in the midst of a session. Dr. E-T stepped into the doorway, and I explained who I was and why I was there. I asked if there might be an appropriate time for us to speak together, even if not for publication. She looked miffed and simply said, "No." She stepped back inside and closed the door. Dr. E-T has declined all further invitations from me to discuss Tina's well-being.

Upon my return home to Washington, I continued my search for Tina. From my sources on the DZ, I received information that Tina's sister, Jane, and her husband Lee Dormuth, were living near me in Olympia. In early 2011, I traveled to their home.

Lee Dormuth answered when I rang the doorbell. Besides being Tina Mucklow's brother-in-law, he is also a former FBI agent. But he was not very welcoming, so I took the initiative. I explained who I was and my concern with Tina. I was surprised by his response: "I don't want any part of it," he said.

But, after hearing more of my worries about her social isolation and suffering from possible "permanent trauma," Dormuth said that Tina was "fine," even though his contact with her in recent years had been minimal. He also declined to explain why his sister-in-law was not talking about the skyjacking. However, he inadvertently revealed that he did have some contact with Tina.

First, he intimated that he was aware of the Cooper-related mail Tina received.

Secondly, Dormuth told me that his wife had been "camped out" on the phone with Jo Weber the night before, allegedly to discuss my impending visit. Oddly, he described Jo as being "married to him."

"Do you mean DB Cooper?" I asked.

He nodded in the affirmative.

Overall, Dormuth's wary demeanor and cagey responses began to make Galen and I suspect that he was part of some kind of informal witness protection program for Tina—that family, friends, and perhaps even the nuns—were working hard to protect her by keeping guys like me at arm's length. But why?

At the same time, I was involved in a flurry of conversations with Galen and many others seeking Tina's whereabouts. Jo Weber told me that Tina was living in northern Oregon, and I began scouring the Internet looking for her. Finally after combing public records in 2010, I found Tina living in central Oregon. Since I don't know what is happening to her and have little way to gauge her frailties, I have joined with most researchers to keep her contact information confidential. However, Geoffrey Gray's book mentions Tina's current hometown, so I was concerned that the world was about to descend on her when *Skyjack* was released. In early August 2011, I knocked on her front door.

She lives in a cute and immaculately landscaped home. It's magical in an odd way—a glistening emerald in the midst of a run-down neighborhood. Through the screen door I thought I heard Enya on the stereo, and an opened bottle of white wine sat on a counter. When Tina answered my knock, she appeared to be a content woman in her sixties. However, her demeanor changed dramatically when I identified myself as a journalist. I pleaded to talk with her—even off the record. She closed the front door straightaway, saying, "You need to leave now." Her voice sliced the air with an icy rage.

Through the closed door I called out: "Arlene says we have a lot in common. I take care of my mother in New York the same way you took care of your father."

The door stayed closed.

I retreated to my vehicle parked at the curb. Frankly, I was angry that Tina and her family kept slamming doors in my face. In fact, as I wrote some notes and stewed, Tina came back to her front door and slammed it twice more, finally locking the deadbolt with emphasis. Nevertheless, I was the first reporter since

Richard Tosaw in 1982 to speak directly to Tina, even if she only said five words.

I empathize with Tina's plight, but I am frustrated with her. She is clearly a wounded woman who is super-quick to anger, yet I believe she has an obligation to talk about the skyjacking, a duty to seek justice. I want her to share my belief that honesty and trust are honored in society—that the FBI's bungling is not tolerated—and whatever the truth of DB Cooper we summon the strength to pursue it.

Despite the scathing remarks I receive on the DZ and elsewhere about my pursuit of Tina, I believe that I am a fair-minded journalist. I wasn't a creep sticking a microphone in her face or taking pictures of her from behind the bushes. How could I be any more gentle and respectful in my approach?

Really, Tina, what is your problem?

Since neither Tina nor any of her family talk substantively about her well-being, Galen and I began backtracking through her life to see if we could discern what has transformed a confident flight attendant into such a bitter person. The following timeline has been comprised through bits and pieces of information gathered from newspaper clippings and interviews with people who have known Tina.

It appears that Tina continued working as a flight attendant at Northwest Orient for about a year or so after the skyjacking. She then met and married a colleague at NWO, a flight dispatcher who worked out of Northwest's Chicago facilities. In about 1974, the couple left NWO and moved to California. However, they divorced less than two years later. Afterward, we believe Tina moved in with her sister Jane and brother-in-law in San Diego, where he was an active field agent in the local FBI office.

The timeline gets a little hazy after that, but Galen ascertained that by 1979, Tina had some kind of association with the Lutheran Health and Home facility in Gresham, Oregon. Galen and I assumed Tina had worked there, and probably lived nearby. Intriguingly, Gresham is only a few miles from PDX where she was hijacked eight years earlier. Also, Gresham is part of Ralph Himmelsbach's bailiwick, but he claims that he never spoke with Tina even though she was his primary witness in his biggest case.

Also, Gresham is just upriver from Tina Bar, and what possible connection may exist between Tina Mucklow and the money find is unknown. It could possibly be just a fantastic coincidence. Therefore, I sought more information and traveled to Gresham in 2013. I discovered that the Lutheran Health and Home Center was an assisted-living type of facility, once managed by the religious group that ran Tina's school in Philadelphia. However, at present it is administered by the Good Samaritan Society. When I asked the folks at the center for confirmation that Tina had worked there in the 1970s, I was shocked when they told me Tina had never been employed there, but rather had been a patient. Of course, the Society did not say *why* she was a resident, and I didn't ask.

Earlier, Galen had told me of a compelling rumor from flight attendants that Tina had a "nervous breakdown" some time in 1979 or before. I have not been able to confirm this possibility, but if true, I wonder if Tina recovered in Gresham.

In addition, we know from the nuns that Jane and Lee brought Tina to the convent sometime in the spring of 1980. We have not been able to learn if the convent was a continuation of her recovery. Perhaps the nuns run a pastoral psychiatric facility, or they might operate some kind of witness protection program. Or maybe the convent was just a place for Tina to pray for awhile.

Nevertheless, she spent twelve years there regardless of whether she "fit in" or not.

Further, her state of mind is characterized as being uneven while she was there. Galen says that Richard Tosaw had told him that Tina's memory was fuzzy when he interviewed her in the early 1980s, and that she answered most of his questions with some version of "I don't remember." Nevertheless, Tosaw quotes her extensively in his book, detailing many specifics of the skyjacking. But much of that may be additions he utilized via "poetic license."

Similarly, Bill Rataczak told me in 2009 that he worked extensively with Richard Tosaw on the latter's book, and said that Tosaw had told him that Tina had lost the ability to remember the events of November 24th. "It was like Tina took a white board and wiped it clean," Bill recalled.

Oddly, Tina's ex-husband seems to have been in the same state of mind. Rataczak told me that he tried to make contact with Tina years after the skyjacking, and when he couldn't find her he successfully sought her ex through NWO channels. But in some kind of *folie a deux*, Tina's ex-husband did not know who Bill was when he introduced himself, and the ex could not remember the name of Tina's sister or her brother-in-law, nor did he have their contact information or Tina's.

Adding to the possibility that Tina suffered some kind of neurological or psychological trauma is FBI agent Russ Calame's account of his phone interview with her while she was in the convent. In his book with Bernie Rhodes, *DB Cooper—The Real McCoy,* Calame states that at the beginning Tina's voice was "crystal clear" and her grammar "immaculate." But then something happened and her affect changed. Calame says that Tina giggled a couple of times about the spelling of her address. "Is Green Hill, one word or two?" Tina said. "I write so infrequently anymore I can't seem to remember," Calame reported.

More troubling, Calame also claims that Tina was unable to remember much about the skyjacking. Additionally, she was unable to remember the clip-on tie at all. These memory lapses thoroughly dismayed Calame. He became convinced that Tina Mucklow would not be able to give credible testimony at trial if the skyjacker was ever apprehended. In fact, Calame states specifically that Tina's testimony "wouldn't be necessary."

Along those lines, I asked Lee Dormuth if Tina was fragile. "Yeah," he replied.

I continued. "Would she have another nervous breakdown if I talked with her?"

"Well, I don't know," he replied. "I really couldn't say. We really have very little contact with her. I try to be very isolated from her."

But Tina certainly has friends rallying to her defense, protecting her from the fearsome media stampede. In 2012, a woman named Leslie contacted Galen and identified herself as a friend of Tina from flight attendant school. Galen passed the phone number on to me and I called Leslie, too, leaving a message. She called me back a short time later. "I knew Tina as a wonderful, sweet person," Leslie told me. "That's all I want to say."

Leslie was a strange mix. On one hand she was courageous enough to call me, but after delivering her declaration of support she wanted to go. She clearly did not relish chatting with a newspaper reporter about an old friend. But I was able to get Leslie to answer one question before she hung up: *why is Tina such an angry recluse?*

"Maybe because people are constantly going after her for interviews," she replied. "All I want to say is that people should respect her privacy, and I'm not going to say anything more." She didn't.

Even fellow Cooper sleuths won't talk. Jerry Thomas emailed me in 2011 to tell me that Tina was fine. In turn I asked how he knew. He phoned to say that he had promised not to divulge how he knew—he just wanted me to know that Tina was okay. "Ya know, Jerry, evasive comments like that make you part of the mystery," I chided.

"Well, then I guess I'm going to have to be part of the mystery." He is.

But Jerry is joined by Geoffrey Gray, who also emailed me at the same time to assure me that Tina was "okay."

I asked him how he knew that, but he didn't reply.

Chapter 12

Larry Carr, Norjak's Most Innovative Case Agent

Larry Carr became the Cooper case agent in 2007 and served until 2009. His tenure was historic because he revitalized the case and fed a resurgence that continues to this day. Adding to this ground swell were deathbed confessions, technological advances, and the declassification of top-secret operations in Vietnam by Special Forces, but Carr was unique because he recognized the growing technical opportunities emerging from the forensic sciences, such as the Internet and the power of DNA testing. Carr catapulted the Cooper investigation to new heights by marshaling the efforts of armchair sleuths, journalists, and the general public. In short, Carr reinvigorated the Cooper investigation with his dedication to a unique vision for the FBI—working with the public in an active partnership.

Arguably, his most vital contribution was joining the DropZone Internet chat room and sharing information on the DB Cooper case that had not been available previously: www.dropzone.com. The site is known colloquially as the "DZ," and with Carr's enthusiastic participation it emerged as the primary place to exchange Cooper info. Carr's posts as "Ckret" gave the DZ an unprecedented air of authority, which attracted the cream of Cooper sleuths from Cyber World.

Larry launched this new relationship with a superb gesture: he shared information about the presence of the clip-on tie—knowledge that was not available prior. Plus, he shared substantive insights into the Norjak investigation at the DZ, and displayed the actual physical evidence of the case via his video interviews with Seattle media, such as posted at the FBI's website: *https://vault. fbi.gov/D-B-Cooper.*

One highlight from Larry's early posts on the DZ was clarifying the source of the ransom money. Initially, official reports claimed that the $200,000 came from a variety of banks in Seattle, but Carr posted on the DZ that the money had already been gathered and photocopied long before the hijacking. Coupled with statements from other officials, it is now believed that the FBI had anticipated this kind of extortion and had stockpiled ransom money throughout the United States.

Carr also provided detailed information regarding the parachutes delivered to Cooper, and confirmed that Cooper was provided a Steinthal 26-foot canopy, model 60-9707, apparently packed inside a Pioneer container. This supports Norman Hayden's claim to ownership, and suggests that Earl Cossey is mistaken or lying because Coss never mentioned a Steinthal. Further, Carr also said that Cooper received written parachute instructions with the chutes, which Cossey never acknowledged issuing.

Carr was also very helpful on other issues. In the DZ, Larry described how extensive the Bureau's investigation actually was, declaring the starboard seats of Row 18 were taken out of the airplane and sent to DC for further analysis. He also shared intriguing tidbits, such as the fact that Tina was interviewed by the FBI both in Reno *and* Philadelphia, the latter being the place where she lived before moving to Minneapolis to fly with Northwest Orient Airlines.

In addition, Carr provided specific details pertaining to the jump, such as wind speeds and directions throughout the air column of Cooper's drop zone: 20 knots at 7,000 feet coming from the direction of 225 degrees, and 15 knots at ground level from 235 degrees. He also shared important information about Cooper, revealing that the skyjacker thought the aft stairs were deployed via a mechanism in the cockpit, an apparent military arrangement, which suggests that he was not familiar with their civilian usage.

However, Carr vacillated on some of his perspectives on the case, especially the issue of Cooper jumping into the Washougal watershed. Initially, the case agent supported the Washougal Wash-down theory, positing that the $5,800 found at Tina Bar arrived there by first dropping into the Washougal River basin, then working its way downstream to the Columbia and eventually burying itself at the beach—and taking eight years to accomplish this feat.

But he also defended the Victor 23 flight path and the Ariel–Amboy LZ as well. But, if the money landed somewhere in LZ-A, it would have entered the Lewis River Basin, and eventually would have joined the Columbia river six miles downstream from Tina's Bar, clearly an impediment for natural means to deliver the money to T-Bar. Adding to this conundrum, Carr stated often that he did not think DB Cooper survived the jump.

As a result, he struggled to tie the many conflicting bits and pieces of information into a coherent whole to support his explanation of how Cooper not only died, but how his body could still be missing. Perhaps Carr's most famous speculation of Cooper's demise was presented in the National Geographic documentary titled, "The Skyjacker Who Got Away," which aired in the summer of 2009.

In the film, Larry and Tom Kaye posited that 305 was in V-23 and Cooper tied all of this gear together and to himself. Tragically for Cooper, instead of landing in the woods of LZ-A, he crashed into the Lewis River. Since it was November and the water was icy cold, Cooper soon became hypothermic and drowned, ensnared in his bundle. Carr and Kaye then speculate that Cooper's remains floated down to the Columbia, where his body, bags and chute became hooked on a propeller shaft of a freighter going up river. Eventually, the whole kit-and-caboodle separated at T-Bar, and the $5,800 washed up. As it is with so many aspects of this case, though, Carr was unable to offer any specific evidence to support this wild hypothesis.

But, he did acknowledge that the skyjacker had some parachuting prowess. Carr accepted the notion that Cooper had a familiarity with parachutes and 727s, and had enough skills to at least think he could make the jump successfully. Carr speculated that the skyjacker might have developed his limited knowledge in a unique setting—aboard American cargo planes during the Vietnam War. Carr suggested that Cooper might have been a cargo kicker on air drops, such as were performed by Air America over Laos, Cambodia, Thailand and Vietnam. As a kicker, Cooper would have pushed cargo loads out the rear doors of a jetliner, possibly a 727, while wearing an emergency parachute, most likely an NB-8 or something similar. As a result, Carr felt it was reasonable to assume that Cooper picked the NB-8 because it was akin to something he knew from Vietnam.

Perhaps one of the strangest pieces of Larry Carr's legacy, and an item certainly from the *Out of Left Field* department, Carr embraced a wholly unique idea for the source of DB Cooper's moniker—the *Dan Cooper* comic books. These were French-language action comics popular in the 50s and 60s in France, Belgium, and

Quebec, and they describe the exploits of a Royal Canadian Air Force commando named "Dan Cooper," who skydives into action to make the world safe for democracy. Carr reminds us that the skyjacker identified himself to the ticket manager in Portland as "Dan Cooper," not DB Cooper. As a result, Carr touted an intriguing connection between DB Cooper and the Dan Cooper comics, one with international overtones. Since the comics are written in French and unknown in the United States, Carr speculated that they might have been discovered by an American airman stationed in the French-speaking parts of Belgium, such as at NATO headquarters in Brussels. Thus, Carr posits that his cargo-kicker spoke French, quite possibly had been stationed in Brussels, and at least got his *nom de guerre* from the comics or even derived the inspiration for the skyjacking.

So, did DB Cooper have any knowledge of the comic book action hero? Was his *signatore* a talisman? An inside joke? No one really knows. But, in true open-sourced fashion, Carr received this savory piece of evidence from civilian sources—the indomitable "Snowmman," who first discovered the Dan Cooper Comics in 2009 and posted his finding on the DZ.

Overshadowing all of these contributions, though, was Carr's block-busting revelation in 2008 that the FBI had lost DB Cooper's eight cigarette butts—their most valuable source of DNA. Further, he told us that the butts had never made it to Seattle but had been stored in the Las Vegas FO. This speaks volumes about how fractured the Norjak investigation has been, and the missing butts focus a harsh light on the evidence retrieval in Reno.

Digging more deeply, the chief of the FBI's Las Vegas Field Office, Special Agent in Charge (SAC) Red Campbell commanded both the evidence retrieval and crew debriefing in Reno. Since not only have the cigarette butts gone missing, but the fingerprinting

142 Bruce A. Smith

was smudged and the glossy in-flight magazines that Cooper read, which would have been an excellent source of fingerprints, were not collected, Campbell is viewed poorly by critics of the FBI. In addition, Cooper's clip-on tie didn't get to Seattle for four days after the skyjacking, which heightens the chain of custody concern, and suspicions fall heavily on Campbell for these failures.

In Campbell's defense, it must be acknowledged that an acceptable police practice in those days was to keep a *tell*, a piece of evidence from the crime scene, such as a tie, and held secretly by a detective. "What did you leave on the airplane?" would have been an ideal question to separate the wannabees from the actual skyjacker.

Nevertheless, Carr told me that because of the loss of the cigarette butts the current DNA profile of Cooper comes from epithelial cells taken from the hook of the clip-on tie, even though the chain of custody was not maintained by Campbell. Since fluid-based DNA sources are best and bodily tissue, such as from skin cells, are not as reliable, Carr readily acknowledged that his DNA sample was a weak source.

In addition, Carr posted on the DZ that sixty sets of fingerprints were recovered from Flight 305, but Calame writes in his book that only eleven sets of fingerprints were retrieved. Not surprisingly, Carr intimated to me that this evidence is flawed and inconclusive.

However, after his ignoble presentation of the Propeller Theory on the National Geographic documentary—and endless ribbing on the DZ—Larry Carr was relieved of his duties as Cooper case agent by early 2010. He was transferred reportedly to FBI headquarters in DC.

When he left Seattle, Larry also stopped posting on the DZ, although I believe he still follows the case. I have sent him a "personal message" on the DZ, a wonderful little feature of the website that provides secured communications between individuals. Although Larry did respond to my "PM," he wouldn't engage in a conversation. Further, a "SA Carr" posted on the *Mountain News-WA*, but again did not respond to my follow-up emails.

However, one of Carr's most lasting contributions to the DB Cooper case may be his Internet-based network of citizen sleuths. The leader of the Citizens Sleuths is Tom Kaye, who was Larry's side-kick on the Propeller Theory, but Kaye has publicly distanced himself from that infamous hypothesis. Nevertheless, Carr appointed Tom Kaye as leader of an elite group of DZ members, which has become known as the "Citizen Sleuths," a group of scientists interested in the case and willing to conduct private investigations.

Their contributions are extensive and will be examined next.

Chapter 13

The Citizen Sleuths

The Citizen Sleuths are perhaps the most visible expression of Larry Carr's efforts to enlist the public in the Norjak investigation. Carr hoped a team of citizen volunteers could be a parallel investigatory arm, providing the Bureau with plenty of free and innovative sleuthing.

The group has been known by a few names since its inception: the "Citizen Sleuth Team," and the "Cooper Research Group," but now it calls itself simply, "Citizen Sleuths." (CS). Although Carr left the case in 2010, the CS are still working and gave major presentations at the 2011 DB Cooper Symposium in Portland.

Tom Kaye is the CS leader and a self-taught scientist with many interests and skills. Despite his lack of a college degree, Tom is an accomplished paleontologist, with many publishing credits. He has worked as a contract researcher on dinosaur digs for the University of Washington's Burke Museum, and is also an inventor, and reportedly made millions developing paintball guns.

Kaye was recommended to Larry Carr by a fellow scientist named **Georger**, a university professor who wishes to maintain some privacy. Hence, I am withholding his complete name and simply using his DZ moniker. Georger was heavily involved in the initial formation of the Citizen Sleuths, but is not an active participant currently.

Carol Abraczinskas is known affectionately as "Abracadabra," and is both a professor and science illustrator at the University of Chicago. She is also a leading investigator into the connection between DB Cooper and the *Dan Cooper* comics. After Larry left the case, Carol seems to have picked up the mantle of discovery regarding the comics and she delivered an overview of the subject at the 2011 Symposium.

Alan Stone is a metallurgist and a key scientist working on the CS team, especially in the electron spectroscopy experiments that were conducted on the tie and money. Alan works at a private metallurgical research firm in Illinois.

The CS further expanded in 2009 just before Carr left the case, and included four associate members for a field trip to the Columbia River Basin, where they conducted experiments at Tina Bar and explored the Washougal watershed. This latter group included **Jerry Thomas**, and the fellow who found the money three decades before when he was a kid, **Brian Ingram**. In addition, the CS were accompanied by an in-house FBI journalist from Washington, DC, who would like to remain anonymous.

Also, **Geoffrey Gray** is mentioned by the *Oregonian* newspaper as participating in the group's activities. Additionally, Gray discusses his experiences with the CS in his *Skyjack*, especially his encounter with one of Jerry's wayward kids in the hills above the Washougal River. However, Geoffrey is not listed as a member on the CS website, nor does he claim any affiliation.

Kaye is more than just a leader of a group of volunteers, and is someone dedicated to a new and bold Norjak investigation. Kaye funded a large part of the Citizen Sleuths activities at the Columbia, according to Jerry Thomas, paying the motel and transportation expenses for Abraczinskas, Thomas, Ingram, and Stone.

Findings of the CS

The CS spent two major periods of time perusing the FBI files and evidence—first in 2009 under Larry Carr's tutelage—and then in August 2011 under the administration of Curtis Eng. Echoing the fact that little physical evidence has been found in Norjak, the CS reports that the Bureau's evidentiary collection is "sparse." Nevertheless, the CS focused on two items—the money and the tie.

Regarding the money, they asked some refreshing questions. In particular, the CS posed whether the microscopic analysis could tell the story of where the bills had been prior to discovery, particularly if diatoms and other biological or chemical residues were embedded in the bills. The answer to those questions has been inconclusive, but certainly the CS raised the big red flag of why some of the bills in the FBI's collections are so discolored. In fact, a few bills are virtually black in color. Why?

In addition, the bills have curiously large amounts of silver strands impregnated in the fibers. The two clues—the blackening and the silver residues—seem to be connected. The CS say the discoloration is due to the silver nitrate compounds used by the Bureau to test the bills for fingerprints. But, one would think that would be obvious to a seasoned FBI agent and a blackened bill wouldn't need any separate analysis, which begs a second question—why did the FBI encourage the CS to bother with the blackened bills? That question remains unanswered.

Also unexplained are the silver pieces found in the fibers of the bills. Georger told me that the CS had found these unusual amounts of silver, but this finding has not been confirmed nor clarified by Kaye.

Further, the CS put a few twenties under microscopes to look at the biological residues from aquatic creatures, such as diatoms, and to examine the curious little holes puncturing the bills. Kaye told me that the diatoms could function like a biochemical fingerprint, leaving unique signatures that could reflect the bodies of water the bills passed through on the way to Tina Bar. It was a very ambitious and thoughtful endeavor. However, it didn't seem to reveal much information.

"We didn't see any diatoms on the money," Kaye wrote me in September 2009. Further, Georger told me in 2013 that Kaye's findings indicated the money was buried deeply into the sand and didn't have any contact with the surface waters, which is where diatoms live.

However, Pat Forman has told me that Tom Kaye had told her the money had mineral residues on it, and had intimated that the bills had spent some time in a damp environment south of the Columbia River in northern Oregon. Pat felt this validated her belief that Barb had stashed the money for several years in an agricultural cistern in Woodburn, Oregon, about 50 miles south of the Columbia, and close enough to the surface for diatoms to thrive.

However, I have not found any corroboration on this claim. My relationship with Tom Kaye is spotty, and the CS "goes black" with frequency. So, the question of what Kaye told Pat Forman and what mineral markers have been detected, if any, has not been answered.

Nevertheless, Kaye confirmed in his presentation at the Portland Symposium that he thought the money did **not** float to Tina Bar. One reason he gave was that the bills seemed to have been stacked for a long period of time:

The money we examined was sort of adhered to the other bills in the stack and when they were separated, in some places a stack of bill chunks came with a single bill. You could see that the bills were all lined up one below the other when they were buried.

In contrast, Kaye said that his floatability survey conducted on the Columbia in 2009 indicated that bundles of money "fan out" when immersed in the water.

The CS also made ancillary inquiries, such as questioning the manufacturer of the rubber bands wrapped around the three bundles of twenties found by Brian Ingram. Tom Kaye says that the original manufacturers of the rubber bands claimed the bands would only last in the wild for three or four months. Yet, according to Brian the bands were intact when he picked the bundles out of the sand and only crumbled after handling.

"So this is in conflict with the idea that the bills were rolling down the river for seven years," Kaye told a reporter from KGW-TV during the 2011 Symposium in Portland.

Further, the CS website reveals some troubling information about the FBI's treatment of the money shards found at Tina Bar:

> ...the money... fragments recovered from Tina Bar were examined. Contrary to popular reports, there were only a few fragments in plastic boxes and ***no indication that there was a quantity of fragments found or any information on exactly where they were recovered***. (Emphasis added)

So where are the money shards that were recovered by Himmelsbach and his crew? The feds aren't saying.

Continuing, the clip-on tie was examined twice by the CS. First, in 2009, they took many "sticky tape" and "stub samples" for examination by scanning electron microscopy.

Initially, they were looking for pollen spores and chemical residues, and during the second visit in 2011, the tie was "thoroughly sampled using a variety of techniques including ultra-violet (UV) laser florescence and forensic vacuum for high density particle collection."

On the first assay the CS found significant amounts of pollen on the tie, specifically spores of Club Moss, which is commonly found in herbal remedies and homeopathic medicines. Conversely, no pollen residues from other plants were found, which was a disappointment since the CS had hoped to get geographical markers from this line of investigation.

More telling was the discovery of titanium fragments on the tie, suggesting that the tie—and most likely DB Cooper—had been exposed to metal filings sometime shortly before the skyjacking. In 1971, titanium was considered a "strategic" metal and used primarily in military aircraft and some civilian aircraft, especially in the mock-ups of the SST—the Super-Sonic Transport being developed by Boeing at their Renton, Washington facility. However, close analysis has revealed that the titanium shards were actually pure titanium, and that is even rarer than the alloy version.

At the 2011 Symposium, Alan Stone said that in 1971 there were six sites that could be considered as a place Cooper might have visited: four are in the United States, and one each in the UK and Japan. In addition, Russian processes some raw titanium sand. Intriguingly, one candidate is a titanium foundry in Albany, Oregon known as the Oregon Metallurgical Corporation, or Oremet. Did Cooper work there? No one seems to know.

Similarly, DB Cooper researcher Bob Sailshaw has reported on the DZ that pieces of titanium alloy and pure titanium were available in scrap tote-boxes in the alleyways of the 9-101 building at the Development Center in Seattle, next to the shop where innovative aspects of the SST were developed, such as heat-resistant paints. Sail, a Boeing engineer for over 30 years, wrote to me and said:

> A person looking through a tote-box could have easily picked up small machining and dust particles on their tie as it hung down into the tote-box while scrounging for free items. That lab had experimented with flame-sprayed metal, even pure titanium, on leading edge parts for high temperature protection. Sheridan Peterson (a prime suspect) worked in the 'Manuals and Handbooks Group' that had office space in the same building on the 2nd floor and right above the research lab in the late 1960's.

In addition, the CS found other bits of metal—in particular two microscopic shards of aluminum in a spiral form, as if from a drill bit. The CS also found traces of stainless steel and magnesium, plus exotic metals like bismuth. As a result, the CS feel strongly that Cooper may have worked at, or visited, a highly specialized metal fabrication plant before his skyjacking. Despite the assortment of metal shards, the CS focused primarily on the titanium.

> Of all the particles examined on the tie, the titanium particles were the most distinctive, the CS reports at www. citizensleuths.com/pollen.html.

Kaye seems to have vacillated about where Cooper might have picked up the titanium, and initially I thought he had suggested the SST manufacturing program at Boeing. But later, when I asked him to clarify this issue he told me explicitly that it was not Boeing.

The only connection of pure titanium to SST manufacturing at Boeing was the fact that when Boeing scrapped the SST project it collapsed the titanium industry.

But Sailshaw, a retired Boeing engineer, strongly refutes Kaye's perspective:

Boeing was working with all forms of titanium in the experimental shop, including pure titanium to flamespray on leading edge components. Pure titanium does not have the strength of alloyed titanium, but has better high-temperature characteristics. I think Boeing was possibly the only place the tie could have got the pure titanium machining particles. Kaye's 'not Boeing' is just a bad conclusion.

One element that can be clarified is Geoffrey Gray's contention that the titanium found on the tie was a raw form of titanium called "titanium sponge." Kaye has widely refuted that claim, saying Geoffrey jumped-the-gun as the CS were in the early stages of examining their discovery, ultimately realizing that the initial findings may have been in error due to contamination coming from match-head residues of chlorine and sulfur mixed into the sample from the tie.

One important finding of the CS is what they didn't see—they never examined the Amboy chute, the buried parachute unearthed in 2009 from Cooper's LZ-A. This is confounding, as I have not spoken substantively with anyone who knows definitely where it was found or even where it is stored presently.

Other problems were created by the presence of the CS themselves. The CS were apparently left unsupervised in the evidence room in Seattle, although Alan Stone said at the Portland Symposium in 2011 that Larry Carr was present with them in 2009. However, none of the pictures taken of the CS include Carr, which is odd considering that Larry loved media attention. As a result, the evidence may be considered legally compromised.

More disturbing is the disassembling of the tie reported in Geoffrey Gray's book, *Skyjack*. In this account, the CS decided to pull the tie-knot apart and look at its fibers more closely under an electron microscope. Were they authorized to man-handle the evidence in such a fashion?

Equally problematic is the question of how the members of the CS were selected. What qualified the members to be chosen? What happened to the notion of "equal access" for all citizens?

Fortunately, the knowledge gained by the CS couldn't be controlled by the Bureau. The CS functions separately and has independent access to media. Frankly, the CS has been more forthcoming than anyone in the FBI, and I learned volumes about the money find by talking to CS members in Portland. Tom Kaye and Abracadabra are quite chatty in person, and I was astonished to learn that they could not find any evidence of the money shards found at Tina Bar in 1980.

Lastly, did the FBI really fail to conduct a bio-chemical microscopic investigation of the tie and money in their own investigation? Certainly the FBI had electron microscopes and spectrographic instrumentation in 1980, so, it's hard to fathom why the feds didn't conduct some kind of analysis akin to the CS. But if they did, where are their findings? This raises the question of whether the Citizen Sleuths are truly that, or are they actors in a political show? In response, Georger, offers this rebuttal:

> (N)obody that I know of has ever contended that the FBI did not conduct its own finger printing and some analysis of some bills, but that was clear back in 1980 when methods were different than they are today.
>
> The difference in technology and methods in 1980 vs. today was more than enough reason alone to justify a more modern analysis, by somebody.
>
> The prior analysis done by the FBI in 1980 was commensurate with technology of that era, and their needs then. The new analysis extends the work previously done using newer technology to try and address issues Larry Carr and others posed in 2008.
>
> I don't see any conflict. The new work dovetails with the previous work the FBI did by extending the data base collected in 1980."

Georger also sheds a sharper light on the relationship between the FBI and the Citizen Sleuths. **"You have to remember, we (the CS) went to work for the FBI, not the public."** (Emphasis added)

In effect, this makes the Citizen Sleuths more beholden to the FBI and their organizational agendas than any public interest.

Thus, the Citizen Sleuths are more accurately described as "FBI auxiliaries." Along that line, Georger fiercely defends the ability of the Citizen Sleuths to protect the chain of custody in the evidentiary collection.

"The Citizen Sleuths are trained professionals," Georger told me. "They know how to preserve evidence and operated in a very careful manner. Plus, they were under the direct supervision of the case agent."

Georger also offered his observation that the Citizens Sleuths may be doing a better job at preserving the chain of custody than the Bureau has done for the forty years; specifically, the Bureau has kept the tie and other evidence in a clunky cardboard box, and the money fragments in loose paper file folders.

There are more troubling questions, though. Georger impeded my questioning by asserting he couldn't discuss a particular issue or person due to confidentialities that seemed obscure to me. One example was the Amboy chute.

"I could find it, but I'm not at liberty to say," Georger replied. Suppressing this information, while important to him, clearly demonstrated a less-than-free exchange, and is suspect. But, at least Georger was addressing the subject, and I was grateful because Tom Kaye and Carol Abraczinskas weren't.

Continuing, Georger did offer one treasured tidbit—an advanced analysis of the money find. Georger told me that the money found at Tina Bar had three main characteristics: first, it was in a compacted state when found initially, no diatoms were found on the bills, and the rubber bands were relatively intact. Georger acknowledged that this suggests that the bills were buried in the sand for a lengthy period of time before discovery.

Expanding, Georger said that the lack of diatoms indicated that the bills were not near the surface:

The test packets (of bills) that were placed near the surface at Tina Bar were found to be full of diatoms, and since no diatoms were found on the ransom bills that suggests that the bills were not near the surface.

Added to this finding, the compaction suggests that the bills were subjected to a significant degree of pressure. In addition, the height of the shoreline at Tina Bar had lowered since the time of the skyjacking, suggesting that it took years for the bills to come close enough to the surface to be discovered. Hence, the bills were probably buried at depth for a long time, perhaps since the night of the skyjacking.

Chapter 14

Open-Source Sleuthing

The DZ, the *Mountain News,* and the DB Cooper Forum

O pen-source sleuthing—where information is freely shared on the Internet—is a transformative development in investigative journalism. The emergence of Cooper chat rooms and websites have allowed reporters to bypass the usual constrictions imposed by law enforcement.

But, more than information is exchanged. Contacts are made and friendships formed, which in turn build impromptu sleuthing teams. Galen is my most significant partner, but I also joined forces with many of the folks I have meet on the Internet, such as Snowmman at the DropZone. But since it's open-sourced anyone can show up, including people you wouldn't want to rub elbows with under more ordinary circumstances.

One of the sites that most famously illustrates that dynamic is the **DropZone**, or more simply "the DZ." Until it's closure in 2014, it was one of the best online sites for sharing information about DB Cooper (www.dropzone.com), but it was often akin to a biker bar in cyber space—certainly a harsh but compelling place.

Although closed, the DZ remains open as an archive of critical information on Norjak dating back to its inception in 2007. Its pages reveal a classic example of open-sourced sleuthing at work—the good, bad and ugly of it all. Some days were filled with gems of information; others were bland exchanges of Cooper World gossip.

But the worst days were gruesome, and during those sordid moments the DZ was not for the timid or thin-skinned. Not only were treasured beliefs fiercely defended, but character assassinations were rampant. One low point was reached when Jo Weber repeatedly calling for my arrest as the killer of Earl Cossey simply because I had been part of the media coverage of his death. Irrational, real, and loud.

Yet, for those who could tolerate the cruelty—or side-step it—the DZ was, and is, a place to educate oneself about Norjak. Researchers, armchair detectives, and even the aforementioned FBI agent, Larry Carr, posted at the DZ.

The bad behaviors displayed at the DZ clearly indicate that the case has affected people psychologically—a dynamic I call the *Cooper Vortex*. It's a pull of emotions so strong they unleash a self-righteousness indignation that makes smart people do foolish things.

With all the name-calling and trash talking at the DZ, it required the services of a moderator, a fellow named "Quade." He admonished the worst perpetrators of uncivil conduct. Some took the hint and quieted themselves. Others didn't and were banned.

Yet, the DZ was also as warm as the TV neighborhood tavern in "Friends." Some nights I luxuriated on the DZ, reading a charming post about a bizarre Cooper encounter, or tangentially wafting about women. Those moments made the DZ feel down-right cozy, and I've cherished some of the friendships I formed at the DZ. Others, I endured.

Hundreds of people around the world read the DZ daily, and about a dozen individuals posted frequently. Many more simply came and went after delivering a pet theory or asking a burning question. Since its beginnings, over 40,000 commentaries accumulated on 2,000 pages of text. Since the DZ was so personality-driven, I think it may be useful to describe some of the characters.

Clearly, the most noted contributor to the DZ was FBI Special Agent **Larry Carr**, using the moniker **"Ckret"**. In fact, I collected more details on Cooper from Carr's postings at the DZ than I did from talking to Larry directly.

Besides Carr, **Jo Weber** was arguably the most dynamic figure on the DZ. She was certainly the most prolific poster, championing the Cooper-ship of her deceased husband, Duane Weber. Jo claimed her husband confessed to being the skyjacker in 1995, and she posted thousands of words every day. Jo had something to say on just about every aspect and every person in Norjak. Some visitors to the DZ dismissed Jo as a crank, but she has a deep knowledge of the case, and possesses a keen appreciation of issues affecting the Cooper investigation.

She is one of the few Cooper researchers to be knowledgeable of the MKULTRA program—the notorious CIA-run mind control project that ran concurrently with the Norjak investigation and has some potential links to the investigation, which we will explore shortly. Jo also has an advanced knowledge of JMWAVE, the largest CIA base in the United States, and a place where she says her husband served for a time before his alleged Cooper escapade.

One of those who slogged through Jo's DZ rants was the previously cited **Georger**, a smart guy who often got cranky himself. Besides being a professor at a Midwestern university, Georger has unusual ties to Norjak that are both familial and professional. Occasionally, Georger made reference to his FBI connections on the DZ, which seemed to be substantive if not fully revealed in their exact nature. **Galen Cook** has a wonderful description of Georger:

> He likes to cast himself as a 'backdoor observer' of the case, but he knows far more than he leads others to believe. G's knowledge of the case is vast. Yet, he remains a silent player in the investigation and prefers, it seem(ed), to engage others in the boisterous 'DropZone' sitc, where he is as nasty as he is allowed to be.

Perhaps the King of Attitude was **Snowmman**, certainly one of the smartest guys at the DZ and the undisputed expert on all things cyber. Snow summed-up his knowledge this way: "You have to remember, Bruce, I read the entire Internet every night." Some days it seems as if Snowmman has.

Snowmman has been invaluable to me in uncovering contact information for many individuals associated with the case. Without Snow, my research on Sheridan Peterson, Ted Braden, and Special Agent Dorwin Schreuder would be non-existent. However, because of his unrepentant surliness Snowmman was banned for life from the DZ in 2011.

On the other end of the spectrum, the regal voice of sanity at the DZ was an attorney from the Bay Area named **Mark Metzler**, who sported the moniker, **"377"**, the signage for his favorite Boeing aircraft. 377 is an avid skydiver and a dogged Norjak researcher, and his findings on the use of a 727 as a jump platform have been singular.

377 is also a buddy of Snowmman, and together they formed a solid team of Cooper sleuths. I was blessed that at least one of them was a gentleman.

Jerry Thomas (JT) was one of those DZ contributors who came and went, which wasn't a problem for those of us who appreciate proper spelling. In his defense, JT said he hadn't figured out how to use his spell checker. Regardless, Jerry is a long-time student of the case and a beloved sidekick to Ralph Himmelsbach. He was also one of the leading antagonists in the war of words with Jo Weber. Besides Himmelsbach, JT also enjoys an elevated relationship with others in the FBI and has access to case agent Curtis Eng. Currently, JT serves on the Citizen Sleuths, and is featured in Geoffrey Gray's book, *Skyjack—The Hunt for DB Cooper.*

Since 2010, one of the voices heard most often at the DZ was author **Robert Blevins**. Robert champions Kenny Christiansen as Cooper, which is the sole focus of his book, *Into the Blast—The True Story of DB Cooper*. Through his pronouncements on the DZ, Robert also found a way to infuriate just about everyone at the forum and in the larger Norjak investigation. Nevertheless, he has attended several Cooper Day festivals in Ariel and reported his findings on the DZ, including a video account of the Cooper phenomena.

Smokin99 was another of the DZ's solid researchers, and she has helped me locate several principals via back-door channels, such as Lee Dormuth. Similarly, **EVicki** also provided vital assistance, especially in helping me connect with Special Agent Nick O'Hara and passenger Bill Mitchell. In addition, Vicki has touched me with her heartfelt efforts to learn the truth of her father, Mel Wilson, a Cooper suspect and convicted felon who disappeared from her life in the autumn of 1971.

Another woman posting on the DZ was **Amazon**. She is an exceptionally accomplished skydiver and offered fact-based commentaries on Cooper's jump. Miss "Amazona" had no patience whatsoever with the forum's fools, and I think she would smile to know that I call her *One Tough Broad*.

Another formidable lassie was **Orange1**, whose insistence on sound discussion emanated from her home in South Africa. Orange is also fiercely protective of Tina Mucklow, and has challenged my efforts to make contact with this witness like a mother bear defending her cub.

Bob Sailshaw was a newcomer to the DZ, only posting in 2011 after reading about my Cooper investigations in the *Mountain News*. Sail had a unique position in the Norjak story—he may have lived with DB Cooper—having rented a room to prime suspect Sheridan Peterson in 1961. Sail was visited by the FBI in their 1971 sweep and asked about his relationship with Peterson. This encounter simmered for decades until Sail's retirement a few years ago, and one evening during an idle moment Sail perused the Internet, Googled Petey's name, and soon found the DZ.

Robert99, **MrShutter**, **Farflung**, **Hangdiver**, **SafecrackingPLF**, and **Meyer Louie** and many others have all been informative and good cyber company. But sadly, Meyer lost his cool one night and got kicked out in 2012. Same, too, for **Galen Cook** back in 2009.

As the DZ was writhing in its death throes in 2014, many Cooper sleuths broke away from the DZ and formed a new website, The **DB Cooper Forum** (www.dbcooperforum.com).

The forum is ably moderated by the above-mentioned Mr. Shutter, and features many subsections that make it easy to explore different aspects of Norjak.

Several new posters at the Forum have made significant contributions. The first to appear is **NMiWrecks**, a scuba-diving researcher of the unexplained, especially vessels that sink in the

Great Lakes. He lives in northern Michigan; hence his moniker. Nimi-Wrecks, as I call him, has introduced a new suspect: Dick Lepsy, a guy who went missing in 1969 from his home town of Grayling, Michigan. Although Lepsy's photo has some resemblance to Composite A, and he missed Thanksgiving dinner in 1971, not much else is a Norjak fit.

More important contributions come from a mysterious group of researchers who call themselves interchangeably: Moriarty, Reichenbach, or Lars Skoland. They have provided the FBI's initial crew debriefing interviews of Scott, Rataczak, Anderson and Mucklow in Reno; Hancock and Schaffner in Seattle, and a second follow-up with Tina in Trevose, PA, her hometown. They can be accessed at: thedbcooperforum.com/Cooper-Vault/.

However, such gems come with a steep price as Moriarty/Reichenbach/Lars Skoland are nasty cyber bullies who hacked my computer. How they got the debrief files is unknown, but it may also be a hack job. Fortunately, they ceased their unwanted activities towards me after I filed an "Internet Criminal Complaint" (IC3) record with the FBI.

Another open source for interesting Cooper commentaries is a blog managed by Marty Andrade (martinandrade.wordpress.com). It's basically a one-man show, but Marty's thoughts and insights are substantive. Plus, he explores topics others dismiss, such as novels on the skyjacking—in particular Max Gunther's *What Really Happened*.

The **Mountain News-WA** is my online news magazine that operates from Eatonville, Washington. It covers many newsworthy topics that are under-reported in this rural area, or digs a little deeper into stories that lay close to our hearts. One of those stories is DB Cooper because DB flew over our roof-tops on his getaway flight. Hence, the *Mountain News* is rich with Cooper material, and much of my in-depth Cooper reporting, especially the interviews, are posted there (themountainnewswa.net/category/db-cooper/).

Author Geoffrey Gray never posts on any of the above sites. Instead, he maintains his own website "Hunt for DB Cooper" (www.huntfordbcooper.com). Besides supporting his book, *Skyjack—The Hunt for DB Cooper*, GG's website also offers a calendar of events and blog-like postings that are original, substantive and fresh, even if they sound wildly outlandish from time-to-time.

Sluggo Monster, aka Wayne Walker, has followed the case since 1971 and is acknowledged as one of the most authoritative voices on Norjak. Besides being a frequent but selective poster on the DZ, he is also the curator of one of the foremost Internet depositories for facts on the DB Cooper case: (n467us.com/index.htm).

Chapter 15

Emergence of DNA as a Forensic Tool

One of the primary dynamics fueling the resurgence of the Cooper case has been the widespread use of DNA to evaluate suspects. Developed initially in the 1980s, DNA analysis was in full swing by the late 1990s, and with it came the ability to trump Cooper's careful efforts to mask his identity. In essence, DNA testing has re-opened the case, and the FBI has re-examined its top Cooper suspects.

However, not all sources of DNA are equal, which complicates its application in Norjak. Apparently, the best samples come from bodily fluids, such as saliva, which should be available from the eight cigarette butts retrieved in Reno but are now lost. Next are skin tissues, such as epithelial cells, which the FBI has. Last are hair samples, which were obtained from the head-rest cloth of seat 18-E. However, it is unknown if any hair samples have been tested for DNA.

As previously discussed, Carr confirmed not only that the eight cigarette butts are missing, but the Seattle FO never had possession of them and they had been stored in the Las Vegas FO. Why Carr and other Norjak case agents in Seattle did not have absolute authority to gather all pertinent evidence from all FBI field offices has never been explained. Nevertheless, the best source for DB Cooper's DNA is now officially missing.

But, were they ever tested for DNA? Carr posted a cryptic message at the DropZone on December 18, 2007 that suggests they might have been. Carr stated that the FBI had possession of the cigarette butts for at least a period of time and had "processed" them. Does that mean analyzed? Carr isn't available to clarify this, but his veiled post at the DZ was in response to a question from 377 and Smokin99 about the fate of the cigarette butts:

> Still looking for the cigarettes, after they were processed in the lab they were sent back to the field. So they are somewhere between Washington, DC and Seattle or disposed of.

Additionally, Carr told me in 2008 that epithelial cells found on the clasp of the clip-on tie were being used to extract the DNA to compare Cooper suspects. Carr acknowledged that the skin samples on the clasp could be DB Cooper's, or any number of people who have handled the tie since the recovery in Reno. Also, the FBI has collected DNA samples from other spots on the tie, possibly the fabric, which further complicates the issue.

"The DNA could be Cooper's, or not," Carr told me, acknowledging the unreliably of this sample. In fact, Carr posted a disturbing truth at the DZ on December 13, 2007, "Yes, there were multiple male donors on the tie."

Along those lines, PIO Ayn Dietrich-Williams has confirmed that the tie sample has DNA from three different males.

Adding more concern to the chain of custody issue of whose epithelial cells are on the clasp, the tie was four days late to Seattle, held somewhere by somebody over the Thanksgiving holiday weekend. As discussed previously, the leading suspect for this gaff is Las Vegas SAC Red Campbell, who led the evidence retrieval team in Reno.

Carr also told me that the DNA sample the FBI had from the epithelial cells was a "partial," and could be used only to rule-out suspects, not necessarily prove DB Cooper's identity. This element of "partiality" remains a controversial aspect of Norjak. Specifically, *how* partial is the sample, and what are the exact limitations of the sample?

Additionally, information from the Formans puts this dilemma into an even darker light—the best DNA samples went missing just as their contributions were called upon to solve the case. The Formans say the FBI did have the Reno cigarette butts tested, based upon a TV news broadcast they viewed in 2001 or 2002, which described how the FBI had profiled Cooper's DNA derived from dried saliva. The Formans say they learned this from the nightly news of NBC Seattle affiliate, KING-5, reportedly delivered by Dennis Bounds, the longtime news anchor. Here is one of several emails the Formans sent to me on this subject.

> The KING 5 news story we heard was before 2003. We both remember Dennis Bounds reporting that the FBI now had DNA from the Raleigh cigarettes. We remember it because we were excited that we could finally prove that Barb was Cooper. Barb was still alive at the time. We also saw articles back then about the FBI doing comparisons to the DNA from the Raleigh cigarettes.

> We apparently missed the 2003 story that the cigarettes were lost and there was a partial from the tie. We found out about that much after 2003.

To confirm the Formans' story I enlisted the help of "Linda" at KING-TV, who searched the stations' archives. She found nothing on the cigarette butts, but recommended that I also contact KIRO-TV, as the two stations are often confused for each other. Hence, I spoke with a "Sharon" at KIRO, who diligently searched her archives but could only access back to 2004.

I also contacted Chris Ingalls, a long-time KING-TV news reporter who has covered the DB Cooper case in-depth. He graciously responded to my request for clarification on what he knew about Norjak DNA:

> I've spoken with Dennis Bounds. He's our main news anchor, and he has not produced any DB Cooper stories. However, he introduced several of the stories that I reported, so that may be where the confusion lies.
>
> The bottom line is that we have not reported that saliva was taken from the cigarette butts.
>
> In 2003, I reported that a weak sample of DNA was retrieved from Cooper and it was now considered somewhat usable for ruling out a suspect.
>
> In 2007, I reported that Agent Carr said that this DNA came from the tie clasp and tie clip recovered on the plane.
>
> I don't know that I ever reported it, but I have been told by at least a couple of FBI agents that the cigarette butts were lost at some point.

Further, the possibility of a TV broadcast on DNA from cigarette butts suggests that the FBI had developed a press release to assist journalists in developing their story. So, where is that press release?

The Formans heard the broadcast just as they were beginning the research on their Barb Dayton book, so they fully expected that the documentation would be available to them as investigators. Hence, they were shocked in 2006 when Special Agent Jeremy Blauser told them that it wasn't, which suggests that documentation on the cigarette saliva DNA tests is also missing.

I sought the assistance of Dietrich-Williams in locating any FBI press releases that could confirm the testing of saliva from the cigarettes. However, her answer not only set new levels for opaqueness, she officially slammed the door on any future efforts to assist open-sourced journalists investigating Norjak:

> I'm sorry to disappoint you, yet again, but it would not be appropriate at this time for me to provide details about the investigation.
>
> As you are aware, there was a time when the FBI's Seattle Division answered media questions and proactively sought coverage. At that time, the FBI thought it might be beneficial to the investigation to share information publicly.
>
> The FBI's (current) media policy prohibits discussing ongoing investigations unless a release is specifically thought to have potential benefit to the investigation.

Following further investigative efforts, the FBI in the fall of 2011 determined that media coverage of the case was more detrimental than helpful. We've found that media coverage generates considerable new interest, which is not proportional to where we are in allocating resources to this investigation.

I understand your continued interest in our investigation and apologize that I will not be able to share additional information to answer your questions.

So, the cigarettes remain a mystery, and apparently will remain so until a breakthrough occurs at the FBI. But related questions linger: is anyone looking for the cigarette butts, and if not, why not? Plus, where is the paperwork that surely was developed when the cigarette butts were tested? In effect, we have two missing pieces of important evidence—the cigarette butts and its documentation.

Unfortunately, these investigatory kerfuffles exist in a larger environment of questionable practices at the FBI's Forensic Science Research and Training Center in Quantico, Virginia and its crime lab at its Washington, DC headquarters.

In the late 1990s, the FBI's National Crime Laboratory (NCL) was subjected to an 18-month investigation by the Inspector General of the Department of Justice, triggered by a decade's worth of allegations and persistent whistleblowing by one of the NCL's former supervising agents, Dr. Frederic Whitehurst. Beginning in 1986, Whitehurst charged that the NCL was compromised by corruption, incompetence, and conflicts of interest—most notably the hiring of special agents without scientific degrees to do lab investigations, thereby insuring a prosecutorial bias. At its worst, though, Whitehurst charged that the lab had falsified, altered or suppressed evidence in thousands of cases.

In April 1997, the Inspector General released a 517-page report of its investigation, and according to the *New York Times* it confirmed Whitehurst's assertions of "testimonial errors, substandard analytical work and poor practices at the lab's chemistry-toxicology, explosives and material analysis units."

But it found no criminal wrongdoing. Nevertheless, an over-sight panel recommended forty changes for the laboratory. Since the IG's report only examined three of the FBI's 21 lab divisions and confined itself primarily to Dr. Whitehurst's allegations, the US Congress launched its own investigation, titled, "A Review of the FBI Laboratory: Beyond the Inspector General's Report."

The findings are shocking. Decades later, convictions are reportedly still being overturned due to the evidentiary errors revealed by this process. *The Atlantic* magazine published a review of the *Washington Post's* investigation of the IG's findings, stating:

'Nearly every examiner in an elite FBI forensic unit gave flawed testimony in almost all trials in which they offered evidence against criminal defendants over more than a two-decade period before 2000,' the newspaper reported, adding that 'the cases include those of 32 defendants sentenced to death.'

The article notes that the admissions from the FBI and Department of Justice "confirm long-suspected problems with subjective, pattern-based forensic techniques, like hair and bite-mark comparisons, that have contributed to wrongful convictions in more than one-quarter of 329 DNA-exoneration cases since 1989."

PBS-TV broadcast a special documentary on these travesties, and the chief producer, John F. Kelly, in conjunction with Phillip K. Wearne, wrote a book about his discoveries: *Tainting Evidence—Inside the Scandals at the FBI's Crime Lab.* Below is one example of how egregious an FBI agent performed at the National Crime Lab—the infamous Special Agent Thomas N. Curran.

> In February 1975, an internal FBI investigation into the activities of Special Agent Thomas N. Curran, an examiner in the FBI lab's serology unit, revealed a staggering record of perjury, incompetence and falsification.
>
> At the trial of Thomas Doepel for rape and murder in Washington, D.C. in 1974, Curran testified under oath that he had a bachelor and masters degree in science, that both Doepel and the victim were blood type O and that the defendant's shorts bore a single bloodstain. In reality, Curran had no degree in anything; Doepel, on re-testing, turned out to be blood type B; and the shorts evidenced two, not one blood stain.

Further, Kelly and Wearne show that these kinds of problems at the Crime Lab were widespread and ignored by supervisors:

> Curran's aberrations... were systemic. Curran had issued reports of blood analyses when "no laboratory tests were done"; had relied on presumptive tests to draw up confirmatory results and written up inadequate and deceptive lab reports, ignoring or distorting tests results.
>
> 'The real issue is that he chose to ignore the virtue of integrity and to lie when asked if specific tests were

conducted,' concluded Cochran's report to the then head of the FBI laboratory, Dr. Briggs White.

It was an early warning of what could happen at the FBI lab. Tom Curran turned out to have lied repeatedly under oath about his credentials and his reports were persistently deceptive, **yet no one, FBI lab management, defense lawyers, judges, had noticed. When they did, there was no prosecution for perjury**. (Emphasis added.)

Kelly and Wearne also reveal that the biggest and most persistent problem at the FBI's crime lab has been documentation. Perhaps it's the culture of cops working as forensic scientists and focused on convictions rather than evidentiary facts. Nevertheless, it has a direct connection to the on-going issue with the cigarette butts and DB Cooper's DNA. Kelly and Wearne state:

> Documentation is a case in point. Examiners have proved remarkably loath to write up their bench notes in any adequate scientific manner. No names, no chain of custody history, no testing chronology, no details of supervisory oversight, no confirmatory tests, no signatures—such omissions are quite normal in FBI lab reports.

> What they do contain is obfuscation and overstated conclusions written in an often-incomprehensible style that some experts have termed 'forensonics.' Terms like 'match' or 'consistent with' are common; chronicled scientific procedures and protocols to justify them are not.

Another issue that Kelly and Wearne address is the insufficient effort given by the FBI to preserve its evidence, and a system-wide failure to insure adequate protection of the rights of the accused, including irresponsible inaction by the Supreme Court.

> An obligation to preserve evidence would seem to be at the heart of the *Brady* decision (the ruling by the Supreme Court that a defendant has the right to evidence that can show their innocence). If evidence, specimens, reports, or bench notes are destroyed or discarded, how can anyone determine what was exculpatory? But on two separate occasions the Supreme Court has declined to interpret the *Brady* ruling as including a duty to preserve evidence. Startling amounts of evidence—bullets, blood samples, hair—are routinely trashed at the FBI and other crime labs.

> ...At the FBI lab, an even larger amount of paperwork, reports, bench notes and charts—has been lost in a filing and record retention system no one, including management, seems to be able to rely on.

Hence, the loss of DB Cooper's cigarette butts seems in line with how criminal evidence in the United States is often handled, even by the FBI.

Competency at the FBI Crime Lab, and elsewhere in the nation's 400 state and local crime labs, is also highly suspect, especially regarding fingerprint analysis.

Kelly and Wearne reveal that proficiency exams and national certification boards for the forensic sciences are determining that professional expertise is highly variable. In fact, up to 20 percent of evidence has been shown to be misidentified at the local and national level, as indicated in a recent survey of fingerprinting experts:

> In... more than one-in-five instances 'damning evidence would have been presented against the wrong person' noted David Grieve, editor of the fingerprinters' magazine, *The Journal of Forensic Identification.*
>
> Worse still, examiners knew they were being tested and were thus presumably more careful and freer from law enforcement pressures.
>
> Calling for immediate action, David Grieve concluded: 'If one-in-five latent fingerprint examiners truly possesses knowledge, skill or ability at a level below an acceptable and understood baseline, then the entire profession is in jeopardy.'
>
> The same must be true of every suspect in the country, the vast majority of whom never get a fingerprint expert onto their defense team or any chance of a re-examination. Many crime laboratories routinely destroy fingerprint evidence.

Perhaps the greatest example of evidentiary malfeasance is shown by the impact of the Innocence Project. Since its founding in 1992, the Innocence Project has used DNA analysis to exonerate over 300 individuals wrongfully convicted, including twenty from Death Row. Although DNA testing gets the praise for these exonerations, the Innocence Project estimates that half of those convictions overturned were due to "unvalidated or improper forensic science," such as hair microscopy or bite-mark comparisons. The average length of unjust incarceration at the time of release was 14 years.

Of course, these acts of injustice occurred nationwide in state and local prisons besides federal penitentiaries, but such a broad view gives us a deeper appreciation of what may have happened to the physical evidence in Norjak.

Chapter 16

922 Confessions

Another dynamic fueling the resurgence of the Norjak investigation is a torrent of confessions since the mid-1990s, including several deathbed outcries. Over nine hundred people have reportedly confessed to being DB Cooper, and this aspect of the Norjak investigation gives pause about the lure of Cooper *and* the mental health of our nation.

Regardless of the psychological implications for our country, the confessions—estimated by Galen to be 922—are certainly curious. Of course, they need to be investigated, such as the one reported by the aforementioned Jo Weber, in which she says her husband, Duane, claimed he was "Dan Cooper" while lying in his hospital bed gravely ill from kidney disease. Jo, in turn, has become an investigatory zealot to learn the truth of her deceased husband.

As for the factual nature of the 922, I've sought unsuccessfully for corroboration of this heralded number. But here is what I've gathered about this unusual Norjak phenomenon.

First, I've learned that the confessions are often supported by family members, sometimes vigorously—just look at Jo and Duane. Clearly, there is something about the Cooper case that can grip a family and not let go. Why do so many people want their loved one to be DB Cooper? Does this mean that the 922 confessees and their families come from a societal stream surging with psychological disorders? Or are all these people desperately lonely, so hungry for attention that they are willing to admit to a felony? Is this another element of the Cooper Vortex—sucking in the needy?

Or more troubling, do a percentage of the 922 actually believe they are DB Cooper? Are we looking at the tip of a psychiatric iceberg shimmering in a haze of multiple personalities claiming to be DB Cooper? Does the Vortex scoop up *really* crazy people?

In 2010, I went looking for answers, and emailed Ayn Dietrich-Williams. Not surprisingly, she said she was unable to shed any light on the subject of confessions since Norjak was an open case, even though it is not active. Seeking something more substantive, I endeavored to contact Special Agent Ralph Himmelsbach.

In January 2011, I was passing through Himmelsbach's home town of Woodburn, Oregon on my way to see Tina Mucklow's convent, and I wondered if I could approach the retired FBI agent and ask about the 922 confessions. However, Ralph had decided early in our relationship that he didn't want to talk to me on the phone, so I couldn't set up an appointment. Serendipitously, his buddy Jerry Thomas called me just before I left for Oregon, so I asked him what Ralph might do if I appeared unannounced.

"I'm sure that would be fine with Ralph," Jerry told me. "He's a great guy." So, I stopped at Ralph's home. It's easy to find, as his address is featured on Google and his property boasts a six-foot sign in his driveway proclaiming: "HIMMELSBACH."

Ralph lives on forty acres just east of the Pudding River, and his muddied land looks just like the river's namesake. His expansive house, a mini-mansion really, sits on a hillock in the middle of his farmlands, which I later learned are leased to a local tulip grower. To reach his house I had to drive down a causeway that made me feel like I was crossing the moat of a medieval castle. This knightly feel is further enhanced when one arrives at Ralph's compound. The house is an elegantly designed stone structure with multiple levels, and has several out-buildings. Coupled with exquisite stone and chrome interiors, it feels like the home of a modern-day Moorish squire.

I was just getting out of my pickup when Ralph marched out of his house to learn who had just entered his kingdom. He had a grim look on his face, so I evoked the magic of Jerry Thomas.

"Ralph," I called out. "My name is Bruce Smith, and Jerry Thomas said it would be okay if I just dropped-in on you to talk about the DB Cooper case. I hope that's okay." After hearing Jerry's name, he brightened. "You're a friend of Jerry's?" he asked.

I shrugged.

"Well, sure; c'mon in. We can talk for a few minutes, but I'm in the middle of putting the laundry into the washer, so let me finish that, first."

Ralph was clearly in his 80s, but looked fit and trim. His hand-shake was strong and he walked easily without any noticeable hitch, despite his reported back trouble. I explained my relation-ship with Jerry as we walked towards the front door. "I've talked with Jerry a bunch on the phone and we've emailed each other a lot, but we've never actually met," but Ralph wasn't really listening.

As we reached the front door Ralph opened it, and I handed him my business card. "I'm a newspaper reporter and we've talked before, Ralph," I announced. "I called you a couple years ago."

"Ah, yes, I remember. We exchanged a couple of emails, too," he said.

"No, never any emails, but I've sent you a snail mail packet on what I've been working on." Ralph waved his hands indicating, *no matter...*

"You house is beautiful, Ralph," I declared as we walked inside.

"Thanks. We like it," he replied.

Heading towards the open-spaced kitchen Ralph introduced me to his wife Joyce, who was chopping celery for a family dinner. "This is a friend of Jerry's," Ralph called out.

"You're a friend of Jerry's?" Joyce said joyfully, "It's wonderful meeting you."

"A pleasure meeting you as well," I intoned.

Joyce and I bantered in the kitchen as Ralph headed to the washing machine. "You sound like you're from Back East," she quipped.

"Yup, New York," I said. "Just got back this week after spending three months there taking care of my mother. I think my accent really deepened from being back there."

Joyce smiled and talked about her own upbringing in Massachusetts. "Yeah, my family's got that whole 'pahk-tha-cah-in-Havahd-Yahd thing," she said, laughing. After a few moments she begged-off from any more socializing since "the kids" were expected shortly for a Sunday dinner. I saw four place-settings at a small, round table adjacent to the kitchen area.

Ralph returned and ushered me into the nearby living room area, motioning me to sit in a large blue leather recliner. He stretched out in the adjoining couch, also made with the same turquoise-toned leather. "So what are your questions?" he posed.

"I understand that 922 individuals have confessed to being DB Cooper," I said. "Is that true?"

"I don't remember if that is the exact number, but it was a lot."

"Hundreds?"

"Yes, hundreds." Ralph then shared his perspective on why so many people have confessed to the skyjacking, saying that each had an individual motive but most were ex-cons in state prisons. Ralph posited that most state prisons are generally pretty crummy places, and he surmised that the Cooper confessions were an attempt by the confessees to be charged with the federal crime of skypiracy, and thus be placed in the better accommodations of a federal penitentiary.

"These ex-cons were looking for an upgrade?

"Yeah, you could say that. An upgrade." Ralph chuckled.

Chapter 17

Confession of Barb Dayton

Despite the hundreds of bogus confessions from convicts, a handful of others have risen to the level of serious consideration. Barb Dayton's in 1978 was one of the first. Her confession is also remarkable because she claimed to be "Dan Cooper," not DB Cooper, and her admission is featured in *The Legend of DB Cooper—Death by Natural Causes*, penned by Ron and Pat Forman of Puyallup, Washington.

According to the Formans, Barb made her announcement after months of dangling tantalizing tidbits in conversations about the case. One night, she delivered a detailed account of how she performed the skyjacking to a roomful of fellow pilots from Thun Field.

The story is so outrageous it may simply be a precisely stitched fabrication created by a lonely woman who was fascinated by the case. Or it's the real deal. But either way it gives us a detailed look at how the DB Cooper skyjacking *could* have been done.

To evaluate her confession, we need to explore her background and then examine the details of her confession. Barb Dayton first met the Formans in 1977 at Thun Field when Ron Forman, an Air Force mechanic stationed at the near-by McChord Air Base, bought a used Cessna 140. Barb Dayton, a top-notch mechanic and an owner of her own Cessna 140, pitched in to restore the Formans' new plane.

Although Barb was socially reserved to the point of being a near-recluse, her love of flying allowed her to build a guarded-but-warm relationship with Ron and Pat. Nearly every weekend for the next few years, Barb and the Formans flew in their 140s to myriad Pacific Northwest airfields, and cemented what was to become a lifelong, but uneven, friendship. Other Cessna 140 pilots from Thun would often join them in a kind of informal flying club.

The Formans say that during these weekend fly-ins, Barb began sharing snippets about the skyjacking. Typically, a cynical newspaper report touting how Cooper must have died would trigger Barb to offer a robust defense of DB Cooper, saying, "Well, he could have jumped over the flatlands of Oregon and not the wooded mountains of Washington. That way he could have easily survived."

During one of these friendly debates Ron shouted to his friend, "Yeah, I know Barb—you're DB Cooper!" and laughed.

This joke landed flat with Dayton, who gave Ron a "look that could kill," according to Pat, and the huddled pilots hastily finished their coffee and retreated back to their planes.

Crossing the tarmac, Barb sidled-up to Ron and announced in a low, no-nonsense tone of voice, "Ron, I don't want you to ever, *ever,* say that again. Not even as a joke."

The Formans say that shortly after the "flat joke" incident Barb admitted to them and a group of Thun pilots that she was "Dan Cooper," the name the hijacker actually used when he bought his ticket.

Dayton said she very easily survived the jump because she parachuted—not over the supposedly rugged terrain of Washington's Cascade Mountains where the FBI says DB jumped—but above the flat hazelnut groves of Woodburn, Oregon. The apparent discrepancy with the FBI's LZ-A derives from how to assess the floppy behavior of the aft stairs in flight. The FBI says the biggest bounce occurred over Ariel, Washington, presumably triggered by DB Cooper jumping off the bottom step and causing the stairs to spring sharply upwards.

However, the Formans say Barb told them she descended to the bottom step over Ariel to ascertain where the glow of Portland's lights were in the cloud cover. That glaze of light became her primary beacon, and then she climbed back up the stairs to await Woodburn, and the stairs bounced as she retreated.

After passing over Portland, Dayton said she waited eleven more minutes until she saw the strobing lights of Aurora State Airport, and then from the safety of the top step she dove into the rain-soaked sky. After a free-fall of 9,000 feet and counting the seconds to ascertain her altitude, she pulled the ripcord at 1,000 feet and guided herself to a soft landing by the now-visible lights on Interstate 5. Barb said she landed just off the highway in a hazelnut farm outside of Woodburn, a place where she had once worked as a field hand. Ironically, it was a spot only about three miles away from where Ralph Himmelsbach now lives.

Once Barb stashed her chute and money in an underground cistern, she walked to a motel where she had registered the day before. There she cleaned-up, donned her wig and dress, and took a bus back to Portland airport where she picked up her car and drove home to West Seattle. The Formans say they never completely believed their friend, but took notes surreptitiously once the flying was over and they'd retreated to the privacy of their home.

As for the money at Tina Bar, the Formans say Barb may have planted it in 1980 after having a dream in which the ink on the money began to "float away." After telling the Formans of her dream, Barb mysteriously skipped the next weekend's flying. The Formans believe she may have retrieved the money from

Woodburn, because when she rejoined the flying club the following weekend she announced that she had "taken a trip south" during her absence.

"Knowing Barb the way we did," the Formans say they believe that their friend re-deposited $5,800 of the ransom in a mud bank along the Columbia to "keep the story going." They also say the FBI never found the remainder of the money because Barb never spent any.

In fact, the skyjacking was not done for the money, apparently, but for therapeutic purposes because the sex operation was fraught with difficulties. The Formans says that Barb Dayton's "gender-reassignment surgery" was physically painful, and she had to sit on a special cushion for the first couple of months. Then the agitation she had felt all her life—that she was more a woman than a man and thus needed a woman's body to properly experience herself—was only partially lifted. Clinical records from the period just before the skyjacking indicate that Barb Dayton was depressed, suicidal, and broke.

Yet her psychiatrist, whom she was seeing regularly for several years after the 1969 operation, reported a few months after the skyjacking that Barb had experienced an inexplicable mood shift and was noticeably happier and more content with her life. In fact, a month after the skyjacking Barb landed her library job at the UW, a position she held for many years. As wacky as it sounds, the notion of skyjacking a plane to lift a suicidal depression fits the larger personality profile of Bobby/Barb Dayton.

The information the Formans have been able to collect from Barb's family reinforces their own observations that Barb Dayton was an individual who constantly needed to challenge herself, as if she was absorbed in an epic quest for self-worth. She indulged in high-speed car races down country roads, challenged authority relentlessly, and flew fearlessly—even to the point of recklessness. Jumping out of a plane at night while wearing loafers was the kind of daredevil stunt Barb thrived upon. The Formans say that when Barb Dayton's brother Billy heard about the skyjacking on TV the night of the crime, he remarked, "That's the kind of thing Bobby would do."

After the period of self-disclosure to her friends, Barb learned the Department of Justice, literally at the last hour, obtained a "John Doe" indictment for the DB Cooper skyjacking, bypassing the statute of limitations. This meant Barb would remain on a legal hook forever and she quickly refuted her claims of being Dan Cooper.

Nevertheless, Dayton had plenty of other wild stories to tell her fellow pilots. Besides fighting with head hunters during WWII and being chased by a grizzly in the Yukon, Barb also told tales about bar room brawls, earning a black belt in karate, and adorning her body with tattoos.

Do you really believe this stuff? Barb's friends would ask each other. *Is Barb really DB Cooper?*

On one hand they never fully believed her, but on the other they were also paralyzed with fear. *What if Barb was telling the truth—would the FBI consider them accomplices in the skyjacking if they didn't turn her in?* As a result, the Formans and the several other pilots who had received Barb's confession remained silent.

So, when Barb Dayton died of pulmonary disease in 2002, Ron and Pat decided to investigate their old friend's stories. Through extensive research that has included military and medical records, and numerous conversations with Barb's family, the Formans have been able to prove all of Barb's stories are true except for one, and for that they need the FBI to release the DNA profile of DB Cooper. For reasons that are unclear, the FBI has not publicly revealed the

188 Bruce A. Smith

DNA analysis of Cooper that they have been able to gather—either from the cigarette butts or the clip-on tie.

However, when Special Agent Jeremy Blauser met with the Formans in 2006, he asked them for hair brushes and envelopes that might contain Barb's DNA. A few days later, the attorney for the Formans, Ed Hudson, delivered a number of items from Barb and her family to the FBI. Blauser's request is noteworthy because he was very skeptical of the Barb Dayton confession initially. However, during their two-hour interview he became a "true believer," according to Pat, who meet with Blauser in the company of her attorney Hudson and her daughter, Tammy Oughton, as Ron had became ill at the last moment. Oddly, Blauser met them in a nondescript-but-strange federal office building in Tacoma, not the FBI's HQ in Seattle.

"The building was like a scene out of 'Get Smart,'" Pat told me. You could hear your shoes squeak as you walked down the aisle, and you could hear doors closing behind you, "BOOM," just like in the old TV show. Plus, there was no 'FBI' sign on the office door where we met with Blauser, either, but only a little sign plate like you'd see on a desk once you got inside." Nevertheless, that was the last time anyone saw Special Agent Blauser.

In 2008, I went searching for him, but he was no longer working in the LA office and his FBI-issued cellphone had been disconnected. I spoke with the PIO in Los Angeles, but she could not say where Special Agent Jeremy Blauser had gone—only that he had once been a field agent there. "I guess I've reached a dead-end, haven't I?" I said.

"Yes, I think you have," she replied.

The Formans say they never heard a word back from Blauser, nor anything from the FBI about Barb's DNA. In fact, the personal effects from Barb, such as the hair brush, are now missing. In 2008,

I asked Larry Carr where the Dayton material was, and the Cooper case agent claimed he had no idea. He also said that the FBI had not evaluated Barb's DNA and would not in the future, so in response the Formans paid for their own assay.

I also asked Carr to describe Blauser's role in the Norjak investigation, and Larry seemed tongue-tied—able only to say that Blauser had been "on loan" from the LA field office and assisting in the DB Cooper case.

Despite the federal fog, the Formans persevered and compiled a lengthy evidence list on their friend. The Formans say Barb's drink of choice was Bourbon, and Cooper downed at least one Bourbon and water. Supposedly, the feds have the glass that held the drink, plus its fingerprints, and another sixty or so sets from the cabin area. The Formans say the government has Bobby's prints from his lengthy service in the Army and Merchant Marine, but the Bureau has not revealed if there is a match or not.

One of the last things Larry Carr said to me, with a chillingly dismissive tone of voice, was that "nothing the Formans have presented fits anything in the case files." He specifically mentioned Barb Dayton's stated height on her military record of 5'8" as grounds for dismissing her as a suspect.

Yet, Larry never offered an explanation why he would need an FBI agent from California to assist him in researching an individual who matches "nothing in the case files." Nevertheless, in Carr's defense Barb's official height of 5'8" definitely clashes with the eyewitnesses who say Cooper was around 6'0", although some have said 5'10". However, pictures the Formans have of Barb at Thun Field indicate she was a bit taller than 5'8" and was probably closer to 5'10".

Further, Barb was a sharp pilot and parachutist, plus she knew how to rig dynamite charges. Those are the basic skills for doing the Cooper caper. Plus, she was reckless enough or sufficiently depressed to jump into the November night sky wearing only thin clothes. This leads to a closer examination of the FBI's quick dismissal of Dayton.

Carr told me the FBI "intensely investigated" the skydiving and private pilot communities of the Pacific Northwest in the days after the skyjacking, considering at the time that pilots and skydivers were prime suspects. The manager of Thun Field, Bruce Thun, says the FBI scrutinized the skydiving community at his airfield, so how did the feds miss a 45-year old pilot minutes away from Sea-Tac who did stunts in a rinky-dink Cessna, even if she was possibly a few inches too short?

Furthermore, the Formans say Dayton knew from years of flying over Washington and Oregon that instructing the Northwest Orient pilots to fly to Mexico City at 10,000 feet would automatically put them in Victor 23, and as such would place her directly on top of I-5 at Woodburn. Plus, Dayton was a Raleigh chain-smoker and Cooper left eight Raleigh cigarette butts on the plane.

In addition, Dayton routinely wore loafers even while flying, and Ron Forman says he never saw her wear any other kind of shoes. Also, Dayton held a well-known grudge against the FAA for regulations that prevented her from becoming a commercial pilot. Hating authority in general, she flew without a valid pilot's license and refused to get medical clearances, which led to her having a heart attack in the air and once forcing Pat Forman, who is not a licensed pilot, to take control of the aircraft. Plus, Barb was known famously for her disregard of money, on at least one occasion draining the fuel from her Cessna 140 to put in her car so she could drive home to her apartment in West Seattle.

The Formans say that on the night Barb confessed to a group of pilots, they took a Polaroid of her done-up as DB. Ron says the resemblance of the picture compared to the published FBI composite sketch was so uncanny that one individual freaked-out, tore up the picture, and fled the house.

In addition, a newspaper article from the University of Washington *The Daily,* dated November 21, 1979, describes a Cooper scenario virtually identical to the story Ron and Pat now tell. Written by two undergraduate reporters named Clark Humphrey and Brian Guenther, *The Daily* says they got the story from two secretive sleuths who used psychic powers to uncover the truth.

Weird? Yes, but was Barb planting a story at *The Daily* while she worked at a library across campus? Further, *The Daily* reported that the FBI had been contacted regarding the story and that the feds considered the information "credible." Is that true? Did the FBI know of the alleged Woodburn landing and the Cooper-sex-change angle in 1979?

Regardless of whether or not Barb Dayton failed to register on the FBI's radar screen in the early 1970s as a crackerjack pilot, or got on it in 1979 with the UW publication but then inexplicably dropped off it again, why doesn't the FBI want to investigate Barb Dayton now?

Lastly, I met with Rena Ruddell, Barb's daughter, and I asked her if she thought her father was DB Cooper. "I asked him once, out-right," Rena told me. "But he was evasive, saying simply, 'Whoever that was must have been a very brave person.' My father didn't tell lies. He was pretty much on the up and up." After a pause, Rena continued, "Much later, I asked my mother if my father was DB Cooper and she said, 'He could be. He had the mind for it.'"

Pausing again, and then taking another breath, Rena stated, "So, yes, I really, truly believe my father was DB Cooper."

Chapter 18

Deathbed Confession of Duane Weber

W hile lying in a hospital bed eleven days before he died of kidney disease, Duane Weber, like Barb Dayton, confessed to being "Dan Cooper." Duane gave his confession to his wife, Jo, and as he spoke he drew out the first syllable of the last name, "Cooooooper." The soon-to-be-widowed Jo says she didn't know what Duane was talking about, and looked quizzically at her ill husband. Frustrated, Duane burst out: "Oh, fuck it, let it die with me."

After Duane's tirade a nurse rushed in, but the two women heard nothing more about Dan Cooper. The nurse did not hear any confession, and apparently Jo is the only one who did.

Whether the confession of Duane Weber is true or not, Jo's subsequent investigation to learn the truth of her husband resembles religious zealotry. Her efforts can be considered the beginning of a re-invigorated Norjak investigation, as she helped build chat rooms on the Internet, interviewed many principals in the case, and bludgeoned the FBI and media with her story. Simply, Jo Weber is the godmother of the resurgent Cooper investigation.

However, despite pumping a lot of time and energy into the Norjak case she has yet to prove that her husband was DB Cooper. Further, she has yet to put Duane aboard Flight 305 or show that he had any parachuting experience. But Duane certainly had criminal credibility. He was arrested twenty-six times and spent at least sixteen years in prison, including one stretch when he was incarcerated under a second identity, John C Collins.

Jo says the FBI told her in 1998 that their fingerprint analysis ruled out Duane as a suspect, and they confirmed this again after DNA testing in 2007. Nevertheless, Jo steadfastly holds out for Duane, and her arguments have some merit. At the very least, Duane was familiar with the topography of Cooper Country. Plus, he did confess to being "Dan Cooper," not DB Cooper.

Also, we know that the FBI's DNA samples are flawed and at least one FBI agent says the fingerprints retrieval was botched. Further, Ralph Himmelsbach is quoted by journalist Douglas Pasternak in a *US News and World Report* piece that Duane Weber "is one of the best suspects he's come across."

Additionally, Jo offers intriguing bits of information, most notably her account of a road trip she and Duane made through the Cooper LZ in the autumn of 1979. She describes it as "The Sentimental Journey," and feels Duane's strange behaviors during the odyssey indicate he was DB Cooper, as they only made sense to her sixteen years later when Duane made his confession.

The car trip began around the beginning of October, and took them from their home in Fort Collins, Colorado to Duane's insurance agents' conference in Seattle. Along the way, Duane made a few side trips along the Columbia Gorge, presumably visiting familiar landscapes from his younger days. But Jo also says that Duane left unannounced for up to six hours at a time, never telling her where he had gone when he returned. Once, in The Dalles of Oregon, she says Duane returned to their motel room with his clothes dirtied, as if he had been digging.

Duane displayed other bizarre behaviors on the trip, such as surreptitiously throwing a small paper sack into the Columbia River from a riverfront promenade. She now speculates that this was the $5,800 that was found a few months later by Brian Ingram a few miles downstream. Duane also drove to a few dead-end streets along the river, parked, and then told Jo to stay in the car while he retrieved something from the trunk. He then walked towards the Columbia and returned a few minutes later, but Jo is unable to say what Duane did or why.

The most memorable moment occurred in Camas, Washington, where Duane pointed to a spot in the woods along the north shore of Lake Camas and told Jo, "That's where Cooper came out of the woods." Jo said she replied, "How would you know?"

"Maybe I was his ground man," Duane answered, according to Jo. This exchange refutes Jo's initial claim to me, which she has reiterated many times on the DZ—that she had never heard of DB Cooper until Duane made his confession in 1995.

But both of these accounts can not be true, which begs the question: is Jo Weber lying? Or is she simply a distraught widow lost in her grief? I confronted Jo on this discrepancy and she artfully backtracked from her claim that she had never heard about DB Cooper until her husband's confession. I am unsatisfied by her explanations, and I feel deceived.

Jo Weber is certainly an odd case. She is cranky and whiny, needy and lonely. She obfuscated much of what she wrote on the DZ, cloaking details in gibberish. Or she clammed up, claiming she needed to protect her sources. As a result, Jo Weber is easy to dismiss as a BS-artist. Yet she is no dummy. She has a profound knowledge of the case and seems to have plenty of Norjak contacts. Jo converses freely with all the principals. Often, I wonder if she is somebody else's eyes and ears, monitoring Norjak's cyber sleuths.

Further, she is a skilled investigator, or appears to be one, and was the first researcher to find Tina Mucklow. She did this while Galen Cook, Geoffrey Gray and I were frantically seeking the elusive flight attendant.

In fact, Jo was instrumental in helping me discover Tina's whereabouts. Looking closely at her remarkable finding, the mystery intensifies because Jo says a critical piece of information came to her in an email from an anonymous source she calls "Robbie Clampett." Jo says this individual told her the county and state where Tina had received a divorce in the mid-1970s, and from that Jo says she was able to determine Tina's current address using many of the skills she learned as a real estate agent perusing public records.

But who is Robbie Clampett? When pressed at the DZ, Jo said it was a "high government official." After that, Jo clammed shut.

Further, Jo says that she has called Tina several times and has spoken with her once, briefly in September 2003. Recounting that conversation, all Jo will say is that Tina announced: "He (Cooper) was a very sad man." Since then, Jo has become very protective of Tina, and harshly criticizes my efforts to speak with Ms. Mucklow and her family.

In addition to her claims of multiple contacts with Tina Mucklow, Jo has direct and substantive access to Tina's sister, Jane. I know, because when I was talking to Jane's husband, Lee Dormuth, he told me Jo had a lengthy phone chat with his wife the night before.

Similarly, Jo says that Ralph Himmelsbach has invited her to dinner at his home, which I consider to be a coup since Himmelsbach generally won't talk to anyone without cash up front.

In addition, Jo contacted a Special Forces vet and author, SgtMaj Billy Waugh years before I did in 2009, and I required

Snowmman's assistance to find him. Billy has valuable insights into how commando operations in Vietnam may have given DB Cooper his skills, and when I spoke with Billy he hoped I wasn't like "that crazy Weber lady." Billy certainly remembers the encounter: "The lady is suffering from delusions. (She) bothered the hell out of me..." he wrote in a note for me.

Further, when I began corresponding with Jo via the DZ in 2008, she talked extensively about JMWAVE, the largest CIA covert operational base on US soil. Prior, I had never heard of JMWAVE, and still have only a foggy idea of what they did there. Nevertheless, Jo researched her husband's possible involvement in their activities as a prelude to Norjak.

These findings cause me to wonder—is she that good a sleuth? Or is Jo being fed information from somebody? Is she the beneficiary of a Norjak puppet master? Or does she just weasel information out of everybody by her incessant needling? Her behaviors cast her in a suspicious light, amplified by her frequent phone calls to me that are veiled fishing expeditions. Is she keeping tabs on frisky investigators like me? Why?

In a later chapter we will explore the intriguing possibility that Duane was part of a ground team and Norjak was a group effort. After all, if DB Cooper made it how did he get away with his loot?

Chapter 19

Confession of Kenny Christiansen

Kenneth Christiansen did not directly confess to being DB Cooper when he was alive, but his brother, Lyle, thinks Kenny might have attempted to do so on his deathbed. Lyle Christiansen says that as Kenny lay dying of cancer in 1995, he motioned for his younger brother to come closer. Kenny whispered, "There is something that I have to tell you..." but he never finished the message before hovering family members gushed words of encouragement and faith.

Lyle didn't make any connection to DB Cooper until much later, and now feels the mysterious deathbed statement was Kenny's endeavor to admit he was the skyjacker.

In 2005, Lyle launched a crusade to learn the truth of his brother, and he contacted a New York City private investigator named **Skipp Porteous** to help him tell his tale.

That association led to author Geoffrey Gray's involvement, and a profile on Christensen followed in 2007, published in *New York* magazine and titled, "Unmasking DB Cooper." Subsequently, Gray followed up his magazine piece with *Skyjack—The Hunt for DB Cooper,* which is one of the major works in the Cooper literature.

Lyle's outreach also spurred Porteous to co-author a separate work with **Robert Blevins** on Christiansen, and together the two writers created *Into the Blast—The True Story of DB Cooper*. Adding to this interest, the History Channel based a Brad Meltzer's *Decoded* episode upon Blevins' and Porteous' writings. In fact, Blevins appeared briefly in the telecast. However, Porteous dropped out of the picture in 2014 due to health reasons, and currently Blevins is sole torch bearer for Kenny Christiansen.

The written works on Christiansen seem to be based on solid research—certainly Gray's—but they offer only circumstantial evidence. Their central theme is that Ken Christiansen had a lot of money after 1971 but no obvious means of generating the funds. For example, Blevins reports that Ken bought his house in Bonney Lake, WA in 1972 for $16,500 in cash despite earning only $215 per week working as a purser for Northwest Orient Airlines. At the same time, Kenny loaned an additional $5,000 to a friend.

Further, at his death Kenny reportedly left an inheritance that included a stamp and coin collection valued at over $300,000, a checking account with nearly $25,000, and a savings account with $186,000. But, his tax returns reveal that he never claimed over $20,000 in income. As a result, these pronouncements of financial bounty are now questioned.

Several sleuths at the DZ, such as Mr. Shutter, Robert 99 and Georger, soundly rebuke Mr. Blevins for his wildly inaccurate reporting of Christiansen's wealth, and have proven that Christiansen did not pay cash for his house but used a conventional mortgage.

In the wake of this heightened scrutiny, Blevins has recalculated Christiansen's wealth and reduced the value of the stamps and coins 90 percent, to $30,000, and acknowledges that Christiansen did not buy his house for cash.

Despite these controversies, Blevins and Lyle Christiansen continues to believe that Kenny was DB Cooper. They said he used the $200,000 ransom as seed money to buy property, and reaped the customary rewards of land development. However, few, if any in the Cooper firmament share that belief.

What is not disputed, however, is that Ken Christiansen was a former Northwest Orient mechanic and flight attendant, and flew routes to the Orient exclusively. Additionally, he had been a paratrooper in WWII, was by most accounts a loner, and had lived alone in the Tacoma suburb of Bonney Lake. Blevins claims that these facts are enough to peg Christiansen as Cooper.

However, Christiansen had a disturbing side to his personality that casts a harsh shadow—he invited runaway boys to stay at his home in Bonney Lake for extended periods of time. This was revealed by Gray and confirmed by Blevins.

Gray interviewed one of the young men, now an adult, who said that Kenny was generous with his money and returned from his travels with gifts. He also said that Kenny would treat him to meals in restaurants. Despite Christiansen's questionable parenting skills, the young man who stayed at Kenny's home told Gray, and Blevins in a follow-up interview, he had never been abused by Kenny in any way, and knew no one who had.

Nevertheless, it is unclear what kind of supervision these at-risk kids received when Kenny was flying to Asia. Certainly, these behaviors do not rule out his candidacy to be DB Cooper, but they seem a more plausible explanation for a deathbed tête-à-tête with Lyle than stealing an airplane.

As for the skyjacking, Gray wrote in his magazine article that Florence Schaffner had claimed the photograph he showed her of Christiansen "was the closest in resemblance to Cooper than any of the suspects she's ever seen." But no one has been able to corroborate Gray's claim of what Schaffner has said because Flo refuses to talk to any researchers since Geoffrey's announcement.

Casting more doubt, Christiansen was another guy at 5'8", and although reported to be 170 pounds in 1971, he appears heavier in pictures. He was also pale-skinned and did not possess the "olive" skin tone reported by eyewitnesses. Additionally, his eye color was hazel and not the piercing brown, as reported by Florence.

Nevertheless, Blevins writes that Kenny's best friend, Bernie Geestman, worked at Boeing during the late 1960s when they conducted skydiving exercises with 727s, and the author suggests that this is how Christiansen learned the parachuting metrics for the airplane. He also places great importance on Christiansen's WWII airborne stint, but Kenny's letters home to his mother convey a fear of jumping.

Adding to the uncertainty, Blevins interviewed a number of Christiansen's close associates for *Into the Blast* and they seemed to be covering up some secret, especially Bernie. But Kenny and Geestman were each other's alibis for missing Thanksgiving Day dinner in 1971, and their whereabouts have never been explained. Nevertheless, Blevins and Porteous espouse that Bernie was the getaway man to Kenny's skyjacking.

Curiously, Christiansen remained at Northwest Orient after the hijacking for over twenty years, flying NWO routes twice-monthly to Asia—mostly Tokyo, Hong Kong and the Philippines. Blevins maintains that employment at NWO was a clever place to hide, but it's a scenario that seems ludicrous to most researchers.

But Tina Mucklow disputes that notion, indirectly. In 2012, Tina gave an interview with the Eugene Weekly—not about DB Cooper—but about her NWO experiences in general, and she said she flew Northwest routes to Asia until 1981. This suggests she would have met her ersatz hijacker sometime during that period.

Also, Kenny did not seem to be a guy who could convincingly convey his threat to blow up an airplane. "He'd never hurt anyone," Lyle told me, adding that his brother "was a sensitive kid," and loved to pull weeds in the garden with his mother.

Larry Carr was quite blunt in his dismissal of Kenny Christiansen as DB Cooper. On December 4, 2007, he posted the following on the DZ:

> **Christiansen was dismissed because the only part of his physical description that matches Coopers is that he is male.** There were other items as well, one of them was that he was a Northwest flight attendant. It does not fit (for me) that a NW stew would hijack a flight associated in his area of operation. The chance someone would recognize him immediately would be too great. On top of that the chance someone that works for Northwest would have said, "Cooper looks like that guy I work with, you know Kenny?" Which never happened. (Emphasis added.)

Nevertheless, Blevins maintains that the Bureau has not rejected his suspect. Besides Carr's post, the FBI has not made any public statement regarding Kenny Christiansen as the skyjacker. But they do not seem to be conducting any substantive investigation of this suspect.

Chapter 20

Family Confession of Wolfgang Gossett

Like Kenny Christiansen, another near-confession comes from the family of William "Wolfgang" Gossett, whose sons say that he confessed to being DB Cooper in the 1990s.

One of the sons, Greg Gossett, expanded upon this claim in 2009 on Coast-To-Coast radio, calling the show during a broadcast on DB Cooper that featured Galen Cook. The younger Gossett told the radio audience that his father had shown him keys to a safe deposit box in a Vancouver, BC bank where he said the $200,000 was stashed. However, the son does not know where those bank keys are presently. As with all the other confessees and suspects, no one has produced any concrete evidence that links Gossett to Norjak. But the clues that do exist are tantalizing.

William "Wolfgang" Gossett was a former Marine, career Army officer, and highly skilled paratrooper. He possessed all the basic skills and physical appearances of Cooper—5' 10", 185 pounds with brown eyes and short, dark hair parted on the left. Gossett even drank bourbon and smoked cigarettes.

In addition, Gossett was stationed in Ft. Lewis, adjacent to McChord AB and just south of Sea-Tac Airport, when he left the Army in 1973. Further, Gossett had been stationed in Brienne la

Chateau, France during the time that the *Dan Cooper* action comic books were available, plus Gossett could read and write in French.

Even though Galen has been a long-time Cooper investigator and has touted other suspects as the hijacker, these days he is championing Wolfgang Gossett.

Although Galen and I discuss Norjak frequently, we do not talk much about Wolfgang and I think the reasons are twofold—one, Galen is keeping the juicy tidbits for his own book, and secondly, I'm not too ga-ga over Gossett. In fact, I'm not too enthused over any single suspect, as no one, including Galen, has shown me how their suspect gained the top-secret level of knowledge of the 727s that DB Cooper possessed. So, I believe that when the DB Cooper case is solved and we hear Dan Cooper's real name, we'll say, "Who's that?"

Nevertheless, Galen has told me that the FBI has not eliminated Gossett as a potential suspect in the case, and in many important ways Galen functions as a co-investigator with the FBI on Gossett, such as providing Wolf's DNA samples.

Galen has talked extensively about Gossett with a journalist named John Craig, who has published his account on a Yahoo "Voices" website: jcocktail.wix.com/d-b-cooper-suspect.

As a result, much of what I know of Gossett as the skyjacker comes from Mr. Craig and his Yahoo postings. Further, Galen has asked me not to interview any of Gossett's family members, and he welcomes my use of Craig's writing. Hence, here is what I know of William "Wolfgang" Gossett via Craig:

Gossett was born in San Diego in 1930, making him 41 on the date of the skyjacking. While in the military, he was decorated for action in Korea and Vietnam, and was a trained survivalist. In the second half of his life, William

Gossett legally changed his name to Wolfgang Gossett, and preferred being called "Wolf." He died of natural causes at 73.

Craig says that Gossett often spoke of the DB Cooper sky-jacking to his friends and family, and reportedly told one of his four (possibly five) wives that he could "write the epitaph for D.B. Cooper." Despite his many marriages, Cook says Wolf was a loner.

At the time of the skyjacking, Gossett was recently divorced and worked at Weber State College in Ogden, Utah as a ROTC instructor. The details of his whereabouts on that Thanksgiving holiday weekend of 1971 are inconclusive, as he was scheduled to be on campus but there are no confirming records.

Additionally, Galen has claimed that Gossett confessed to the skyjacking to a close friend, a retired Salt Lake City judge. John Craig gives the following account:

> The judge told Galen Cook: 'In 1977, he walked into my office and closed the door and said he thought he might be in some trouble, that he was involved in a hijacking in Portland and Seattle a few years ago and that he might have left prints behind. He said he was DB Cooper. I told him to keep his mouth shut and don't do anything stupid, and not to bring it up again.'

When Greg Gossett initiated the contact with Galen, he provided basic information about his father but also shared a personal assessment of his father's motivation to hijack an air-plane. Greg claimed his father was always strapped for money and had a gambling problem, yet his father showed him wads of cash just before the Christmas of 1971, only weeks after the skyjacking. Greg believes his father squandered much of his loot at Las Vegas casinos. Similarly, on a Coast to Coast radio show in 2011, a woman claiming to be William Gossett's niece said she also remembered her uncle having an unusually large amount of money at Christmas 1971.

But in the *Strange Twist Department,* Gossett became a private detective after his military service and specialized in money fraud, exposing cults, and finding missing people. Most notably, he was commended by the FBI for his help in rescuing a woman from the Bhagwan Rajneesh's compound in Antelope, Oregon.

However, at the same time Gossett also began hiding his identity. First, he changed his name to Wolfgang, and then began wearing a goatee and mustache. In 1988, he even became an "Antioch" priest in the Old Catholic Church of the Salt Lake City Diocese. He further obfuscated his persona by never telling his fellow ROTC instructors that he had served ten years with the Marines, nor that he had parachute training. These are accomplishments most servicemen would be proud to acknowledge, and in addition, he never wore his jump wings on his uniform. However, late in life he stitched his wings to a headband that he wore while jogging.

Wolf also manifested lifestyle changes. He left the military life and became an expert in the paranormal. He even hosted a call-in radio show on the subject on KCGL in Bountiful, Utah.

Clyde Lewis, the current host of "Ground Zero" talk radio, says that Wolfgang Gossett was not only a skilled paranormal investigator, but was also his mentor. "He was my Obi Wan Kenobi," Clyde told me in 2012 at the Ariel DB Cooper festival. "Everything I know about investigating the paranormal and doing a talk radio show, I learned from Wolfgang Gossett."

Clyde also characterizes Wolfgang as "one of the best bullshit artists I've ever met," but Clyde also told me that Gossett could be very deliberate, and his work investigating missing persons was stellar. "He was a remarkable guy," Clyde told me.

Wolfgang was also very psychic, according to Lewis. His Obi Wan accurately forecasted a life-threatening illness for Clyde. Clyde also told me that Wolfgang had a "dark side" to his personality and could be foul-mouthed and moody. Also, his gambling addiction worsened later in life.

Surprisingly, Clyde crossed paths with Wolf a second time in Oregon. After they last saw each other in Utah in 1996, Gossett moved to Depoe Bay on the Oregon coast, and eventually Clyde took his radio show to Portland.

After Wolfgang's death, Clyde searched for information on his old friend, learning that Gossett had been living in Depoe Bay for many years and was known there as a guy who could blow $500 a night in machine poker games. "He was a bad gambler, they told me," Clyde said, clearly saddened.

But was he a good skyjacker?

Chapter 21

Early Suspects and the Cooper Vortex

Besides the hundreds of confessions, there have been over a thousand suspects investigated in Norjak. Geoffrey Gray pegs the number of suspects at 1,100, and has amusingly shown that vast numbers of them were the result of a romance gone off the rails. Gray intimates that many women thought a felonious accusation was cheaper than a divorce—or better payback.

However, as we examine Norjak suspects we find something similar to the confessors—a psychological pressure from the families to have their loved one be DB Cooper. It's a pull so strong that people who would be repelled normally by a criminal investigation actually welcome it. It is as if the fame and glory of Norjak warps people's judgment, fuzzes their memory, and distorts their perceptions. It's one more manifestation of the "Cooper Vortex."

Despite the torrent of leads from angry ex-lovers, the FBI focused more on ex-cons than spouses in the early stages of the investigation. Two felons garnered sharp attention. The first was John List, and he was a doozy. List murdered his entire family—his wife, three kids and an 82-year old mother. In addition, he stole $200,000 from his dead mother's bank account, which generated the initial suspicion from law enforcement. List was arrested for the murders and theft in 1989, and admitted to these crimes, but he denied any connection to the skyjacking. He died in prison in 2008.

The second felon was Bryant "Jack" Coffelt, a prisoner who died in 1975, but had an uncanny knowledge of the Cooper skyjacking, which he shared with a fellow inmate named James Brown. In turn, Brown has tried to peddle the Coffelt-was-Cooper story several times to major media sources.

Las Vegas Sun journalist Jack Sheehan has written the Brown story, and claims that Coffelt jumped near Mount Hood and had a getaway car parked there along with an accomplice. He also says that pictures of Coffelt reportedly received an excited response from Florence Schaffner.

Nevertheless, Coffelt was dismissed by the FBI. "We were certain that Coffelt was not Cooper, and that an opportunist was trying to score without any basis in fact," writes Himmelsbach in *NORJAK,* giving early notice to the presence of the Vortex.

However, one early suspect has lingered to this day, Ted Mayfield, who enjoyed a revival in 2006 when two Oregonian sleuths, Matt Meyers and Dan Dvorak, drew sharp attention to Ted.

Mayfield was a former Special Forces trooper, skydiving champion, and pilot. He also owned a skydiving school, Pacific Parachuting Center, and had an impressive criminal history. In 1994, he was convicted on two counts of negligent homicide stemming from the deaths of a pair of his skydiving students, and equally troubling is a report that Mayfield's Pacific Parachuting school had thirteen skydiving fatalities during his tenure.

Earlier, he had been found guilty of transporting a stolen airplane across state lines, plus he lost his parachute rigging certificate from the FAA for packing improprieties. In 2010, Mayfield got tagged again for flying without a proper license. Lastly, as a young man Mayfield had been convicted for the armed robbery of a grocery store,

According to Ralph Himmelsbach, Ted Mayfield had been such a bad egg that he was allegedly fingered as DB Cooper by six different callers to the FBI on the night of the hijacking. In fact, written notes from NWO's George Harrison reveal that Mayfield was targeted while Flight 305 was still winging its way to Reno.

More impressively, Mayfield was already well-known to Himmelsbach because Ralph had a "run-in" with some of Mayfield's skydiving staff at the Aurora State Airport.

This small airport southeast of Portland is where Himmelsbach parked his private plane, and at issue was the failure of Mayfield's people to comply with proper procedures and causing unsafe conditions.

Astonishingly, Mayfield called Himmelsbach the night of the skyjacking to offer his assistance, making Himmelsbach, in effect, his alibi. However, the agent also turned to Mayfield for some level of assistance in the Cooper investigation. In his book *NORJAK,* Himmelsbach praised Mayfield for being "most helpful," although it is not quite clear what contributions Mayfield made to the FBI. But, later Himmelsbach did describe Mayfield as assisting him in identifying certain skydivers being put forward as Cooper suspects. Himmelsbach specifically stated that Mayfield was helpful for his "comments that night, and other conversations we had later when he assisted us in the investigation."

But such pronouncements make me curious. Why did Ralph maintain a relationship with an ex-con like Mayfield, particularly since he already had bad business with him? Couldn't Himmelsbach get a more trustworthy skydiver to identify local jumpers? Seeking answers, I called Mayfield at his Oregon home in November 2009. When I identified myself, however, he hung up on me—but not before saying, "No thanks. I always get wracked over the coals every time when I talk about this stuff."

Digging more deeply, I interviewed a Seattle-area skydiving official in 2013, Bill Jeswine, the former manager of the Issaquah Sky Sports center. Jeswine told me that he was summoned to help run the Pacific Parachuting Center when Mayfield went to jail, and he described the conditions at the facility as "horrible."

But the similarities between Mayfield and DB Cooper were all behavioral. Physically, Mayfield was too short and seems to have little of Cooper's bodily characteristics. Plus, Mayfield was in his twenties—much too young to be the skyjacker. In addition, his attitude was so pugnacious that in YouTube clips he walked with a strut reminiscent of Danny DeVito's character in "Other Peoples Money".

Perhaps Ted Mayfield had been buffeted by the Cooper Vortex long enough that he had chosen to decline its embrace. Nevertheless, Ted Mayfield died in August 2015 from injuries suffered while working on a vintage aircraft at his Sheridan, Oregon airport.

Ted was 79 years old.

Chapter 22

Jailed Suspect—
Don Burnworth

One of the most remarkable suspects of the DB Cooper case has been Don Burnworth, and his story reflects the power of the Vortex in a dramatic fashion. It is also a tale that is unique to the Cooper literature, replete with an eight-day incarceration that was reportedly part of a Norjak interrogation. This story has never been told before and only came to light through the efforts of Snowmman and Galen Cook.

In 2009, Galen was contacted by a flight attendant who flies for Delta about a fabulous DB Cooper story she had heard from a passenger, claiming that he had worked with Cooper just prior to the hijacking. The passenger got in touch with Galen, who referred him to me as I am considered to be receptive to "the really far-out stuff." The passenger has requested anonymity, but he does post snippets of his story on the Internet using his title, "Captain," based on his ownership of a vessel named Grey Goose. Here is the gist of the "Captain's" story:

In the early 1970s, the Captain worked as a pilot for a whole-sale seafood company in Salt Lake City, Utah named Sailfish. In the late summer or early fall of 1971, another pilot joined Sailfish to fly the company's new and huge DC-7C, a top-of-the-line cargo prop plane. The pilot was a recently unemployed United Airlines pilot, a captain named Don Burnworth.

For the next several months, the Captain says he flew this DC-7C with Burnworth on runs to Alaska, transporting fresh fruit and vegetables north, and seafood south, especially crab and salmon. "When the fish piled up, the price became very attractive and we would buy fish to re-sell," said the Captain, who estimated that they flew two round trips per month.

The Captain says their last flight together was a run to Kodiak in early November 1971, and they ran low on fuel and had to make an emergency landing in Homer, Alaska. With "two engines turning and two engines burning" they landed with uneven thrust, putting an awkward torque on the tires. One blew upon landing, and because Homer lacked the necessary equipment it took several days to replace. "It was a real drill," the Captain said.

By the time they returned to Salt Lake City, the schedule had become so disrupted that Sailfish told the crew to take a vacation for a week or so, and return to work after the Thanksgiving holiday. The Captain says he never saw Don Burnworth again. However, when the Captain returned to work on the Monday morning after the Thanksgiving weekend he was met by three federal officials. "They introduced themselves as 'Inspector This and Inspector That, and Special Agent So-and-So,'" the Captain said. "The FBI agent held up an artist's sketch and asked me, 'Do you know who this is?'"

"'Yeah, it's Don Burnworth,' I told them, but the agent said it was a drawing of DB Cooper. I just said 'Oh, My God.'"

The Captain said that later sketches of Cooper looked less like Burnworth. "They lost something in the eyes," the Captain told me.

But, when I asked the Captain about the details of the federal interview he became uncharacteristically circumspect, and refused to reveal specific information. "I'm not even going to go there," he announced to me. "It's all of a confidential nature that

I'd like to withhold for obvious reasons." However, those reasons are *not* obvious to me, and they do cast doubt on the Captain's truthfulness.

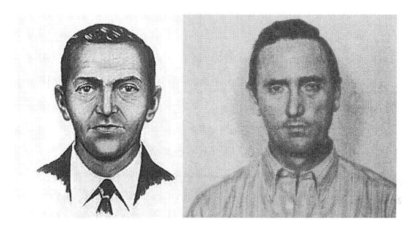

Picture of Don Burnworth provided by the San Mateo County jail Comparison with Composite B provided by "The Captain."

Shedding more doubt on the Captain, he also said that the federal agents described Burnworth as having extensive military experiences, which is not true.

But everyone agrees on one aspect of Don Burnworth—he was a crackerjack pilot. Besides the tricky landing at Homer, the Captain says Burnworth saved them a second time in Seattle when the DC-7 was overloaded and Don was able to avoid an eight-foot fence on takeoff at Boeing Field.

"He was an extremely skilled commercial pilot, and very calm under pressure," the Captain told me. "He could fly a DC-7 right to the edge and keep it in the air. He had amazing natural flying ability."

The Captain also said that Burnworth called the midwest home. "I can't remember exactly where in the midwest, but it was someplace like Indiana or Ohio," he claimed. He also stated that Burnworth had told him that he was going through a bad divorce.

Fortunately, with Snowmman's assistance I was able to locate Don Burnworth at his home in Arizona, and over several phone conversations in 2010 I was able to corroborate some of the Captain's story. Sadly, as I prepared this chapter for publication I learned Don Burnworth had passed away from cancer in June 2012. He was 82 years old.

Don denied serving in Vietnam or having any combat experiences. Rather, Don said he had been an electronic technician in the Air Force during the Korean War. However, he did confirm that he had flown for Sailfish for a short time, but told me that he had made only one run to Alaska. Prior, and then later when he was reinstated, he had been a pilot for United Airlines. In fact, he served most of his flying career as a UAL "check pilot," a captain assigned to test other United pilots on their flying skills.

Don emphatically declared that he was not DB Cooper and stated that he had been living in Germany with his three daughters at the time of the skyjacking. Nevertheless, Burnworth had extensive connections to the Norjak case.

First, Don knew the 727 supremely well, and was the patent holder on several improvements to the aircraft's electrical and sensoring systems. But more importantly, Don certainly looked like DB Cooper, and acknowledged being a likely suspect.

Additionally, Don had some legal troubles that led to an interrogation by the FBI regarding his whereabouts on November 24, 1971. As mentioned previously, Don was in the midst of his divorce at the time of skyjacking and had taken his kids—three girls aged 2, 5 and 7—to Germany without their mother's consent. This later aspect landed him in the county jail for eight days on a "Contempt of Court" ruling when he returned to the United States. But Don felt the unusually lengthy jail time was actually a ploy by the FBI to pressure him into a Norjak confession, perhaps by spilling the beans to his cellmate.

Don also claimed a unique association with the hijacking, and insisted the DB Cooper skyjacking was engineered by his ex-wife, a woman named Bernice Lucille Day Burnworth Bruno, who found a look-alike to perform the hijacking in order to frame Don, and regain custody of the children. Don said his ex was a mafia princess and fully capable of conducting such a stunt.

It's a wild tale, but the marital disputes were real. Before fleeing to Germany, Don said he saw his kids bruised and crying routinely, and on at least one occasion he said he saw one child with a broken bone and another was "starved nearly to death." He also claimed that his kids had been sexually molested by a lover of Bernice's.

After multiple appeals and hearings, Don received a 30-day temporary custody grant, but he felt he couldn't get any real help from the courts long-term so he began crafting an escape plan to Germany. "It was a matter of life and death," he told me.

In the summer of 1971 and prior to Cooper' skyjacking, Don obtained a leave of absence from UAL and fled to Germany with his girls. They lived near Heidelberg for nearly a year, but in early August 1972, United demanded that he resume working and Don returned alone to the United States.

However, when he arrived at his operational base at San Francisco Airport, local sheriff's deputies arrested him on the child custody violations. Lieutenant Ray Lunny of the San Mateo County Sheriff's Department has provided me with Don's arrest file and photos, which corroborate this aspect of Don's story.

When he was first taken in custody, Don was interviewed by Special Agent Collopy of the FBI and questioned about DB Cooper.

"They asked me about my whereabouts last Thanksgiving," Don said. Apparently, they were satisfied he wasn't DB Cooper, at least overtly, and there was no official follow-up.

Eventually, Don relented to the judge's demands and arranged for the girls to be brought home. Upon their reunion with their mother on September 1, 1972, the court released Don from the San Mateo jail.

However, UAL fired Don shortly thereafter, ostensibly for bringing "bad publicity" to the company. He then went to fly for Sailfish, but after the one trip to Alaska he quit.

"They stiffed me," he told me. "They offered me stock options, but they were worthless. So, I left."

Eventually, UAL rehired Don after a lengthy National Labor Relations Board lawsuit, and he flew for United for the remainder of his career.

As for the incredible claim that his ex-wife had arranged the skyjacking to obtain full custody of the kids, Don said his ex-father-in-law, Charlie Bruno and his family were responsible, especially his ex-mother-in-law, Dorothy Bruno, using mafia connections via their relationship to the Bruno crime family of Philadelphia. However, I have not been able to find any corroboration of the existence of a Bruno crime family in Kansas City, involvement with the Bruno family in Philly, nor any criminal activity by Don' ex-wife.

Regarding the skyjacking, Don said that he had followed Norjak intensely since his incarceration, and he clearly held some strange views. Besides the mafia-look-alike angle, Don claimed that DB Cooper didn't jump. Rather, he said that Cooper hid in a small side compartment in the stairwell that was covered by a cloth and Velcro flap. As proof, Don said these cloth covers were replaced throughout the 727 fleet shortly after the Cooper skyjacking.

However, the Vortex is particularly fierce at this point because Don also declared that DB Cooper deplaned at Sea-Tac and had a getaway car waiting at the end of the runway. Don didn't say how he knew this, and these statements certainly make his Norjak story suspect.

But, the Cooper Vortex swirls around more than just Don Burnworth and includes other members of his family. One of his daughters, "Meg," is so enthralled by the Vortex that in 2010 she told me that she hoped her father was DB Cooper. "It would be so cool," she said. When I reminded her that if her father was proven to be DB Cooper he might go to prison for the rest of his life, she became distraught and muttered, "Oh, no. No, no. no, no.........."

But, Don's allegations of sexual abuse by Bernice's family were partially substantiated by Meg. In our 2010 interview, Meg told me that her mother's new husband in 1972 was a "monster," and when I informed her of the sexual molestation allegations by her father, she replied, "Think of an abuse and he (the new husband) did it."

Don had also told me that Bernice died in 1977 from injuries sustained in a horseback riding incident. Don claimed that she had been murdered by Earl Hughes, the man Bernice married soon after the girls returned from Germany in 1972, and Hughes had sabotaged Bernice's life-support system in the middle of the night.

But subsequent conversations with Meg muddled these aspects of the family story. In our second interview in 2013, Meg countered her father's account of these events and told me that her mother married Earl Hughes in 1977, not 1972.

Further, she said that her mother died in 1985, and that the "plug was not pulled." Meg contends that her family and she were at Bernice's bedside when her mother died.

As for the Cooper-look-alike allegations, I had asked Meg in 2010 if she thought that her mother's family, particularly her grandmother Dorothy, whom Don described as the true power in the Bruno household, could concoct the skyjacking to discredit her father. "I wouldn't put it past her," she told me. But in 2013, Meg reversed her story and said that her mother's family was not involved in any criminal activity, and had no connection to the DB Cooper case.

As for Don and his incredible—and conflicting—stories, I feel he told the truth as he knew it. I assume he had a psychological impairment that was triggered by our discussion of DB Cooper and Bernice. As for the possibility that Don Burnworth may be connected to DB Cooper, I see no compelling sign other than an uncanny photographic resemblance.

Clearly, the Vortex is strong.

Chapter 23

Ideal Suspect—
Sheridan Peterson

In 2009, Snowmman developed a computer model of the ideal Cooper suspect, and it signaled smokejumpers as prime candidates. Since smokejumpers are skilled skydivers and resourceful under pressure, they were also ideal for secret airborne missions in Southeast Asia, which added further to their skyjacking potential. The CIA's Air America used 727s to drop supplies and agents into combat, it's possible that Cooper could have been a former smokejumper working in a 727 squadron.

Snow's efforts triggered a closer exploration of the military and CIA operations in Vietnam. First, we examined individuals in Vietnam who drew attention to themselves by their skydiving skills and "grudge" attitudes.

At the top of Snowmman's list was Sheridan Peterson, a former Forest Service smokejumper who fought forest fires in Montana during the 1950s. Peterson was also a former WWII Marine, had spent seven years in Vietnam working for the State Department as a refugee specialist, and had skydived with ARVN officers—even gaining international notoriety from the US Parachuting Association for his unauthorized use of home-made "bat wings."

But Peterson was not only pegged by Snowmman, Sheridan was also cited by the FBI as a prime suspect, and they investigated him twice—first in 1971, and then a second time in 2002 when DNA testing had become readily available.

On paper, Sheridan Peterson is the perfect DB Cooper. "Petey" as the DZ called him, has got it all—height, weight and skin tone, and enough "grudge" to fill a room. When Petey served in Vietnam with the State Department, he was "invited" to leave Vietnam by the US Ambassador because of his strident advocacy of the South Vietnam nationals under his care. Petey also voiced loud accusations of American combat atrocities, and apparently needed to seriously "chill out" after Vietnam, moving to a mud hut in Nepal for years to write his account of what he saw in the war.

Besides being kicked out of Vietnam, Peterson had also been incarcerated by the FBI for a short time in Mississippi during the mid-1960s for his work in the Civil Rights movement. So, he is clearly a strange mix of rebel and bureaucrat.

Petersen says he was 44 years old at the time of the skyjacking, and most intriguingly, he worked at Boeing in the Manuals and Handbook Group in the 1960s when the 727 was being tested for its parachuting capabilities.

Petey also belonged to the Boeing Employees Skydiving Club, and in the late 1960s he performed a skydiving stunt for Boeing by jumping in a business suit and toting a fifty-pound sack of flour strapped to his legs. The latter is an element of the Cooper jump that mystifies investigators because the $200,000 weighed nearly twenty-two pounds and was a destabilizing factor in a free-fall. Nevertheless, Petey made it to the ground successfully with his a-symmetrical load.

The FBI's initial investigation of Sheridan in 1971 was deemed inconclusive, and when the Bureau came knocking a second time in 2002 and asked to take a swab of his saliva for a DNA comparison, he readily agreed because the two agents were *very* attractive women. In fact, Petey regaled them for two hours with tales of his exploits in Vietnam, Nepal, Saudi Arabia, Iran, China and Papua New Guinea.

In Petey's defense, who wouldn't want to give up the goods to a special agent named Nicole Devereaux, especially when she was a "long, tall glass of water, if you know what I mean," according to her partner, Special Agent Mary Jean Fryar.

Fryar, now a real estate agent in Santa Rosa, California, told me that Petey was the "most fascinating suspect" she had ever interviewed during her FBI career. But Mary Jean smelled a rat, or at least a quirky intelligence officer, and came back a second time claiming she needed fingerprints. She used her additional interview session to grill Petey about his extensive travels throughout Asia, hopping among political hot spots without a plausible means of financial support. Nevertheless, she couldn't find any wrongdoing, and the Bureau told her that Petey's DNA wasn't a match, so she cut Peterson loose.

Whether Sheridan Peterson is DB Cooper, a retired CIA agent, or just a free-spirited individual with a flinty attitude is unknown, as he currently resists any substantive contact with journalists. But Petey likes to write about himself, and Snowmman found plenty of autobiographical postings from Sheridan. Snow shared links to Sheridan's writings on the DZ, and we dug into them. Here are two of the primary sources we reviewed:

1. "Homecoming," an autobiography written in the third-person to support his candidacy for the Windsor, California School Board Election in 2006 (www.smartvoter. org/2006/11/07/ca/sn/vote/petersons/paper3.html).

2. "Where Have You Been Hiding, DB Cooper?" in the July 2007 *Smokejumper* magazine.

Although reticent, Petey is far from a recluse, and we were able to contact him in Santa Rosa, California. Following our outreach, Petey came to the DZ to see what we were saying about him, and he warily joined the conversation for a short time. In addition, Petey is a savvy tech guy, and besides posting on the DropZone he has also maintained a presence on Facebook and Twitter. Yet, he won't answer direct questions about how he did what he says he's done in Asia.

Nevertheless, Sheridan has written a 300-page "lightly" fictionalized account of his experiences in Vietnam. It is a gripping and graphic condemnation of American atrocities in Southeast Asia, and his account of a massacre of a corrupt American Special Forces unit by the South Vietnamese *Nung* commandos they betrayed is searing.

Petey engaged several of us intermittently with a series of email exchanges, and over a two-year period I received about a dozen. During this thaw Petey told us he had been a teacher of English and journalism at Lake Washington High School in Kirkland, Washington. Towards the end of our email correspondence, though, most of his missives were harsh ramblings peppered with paranoia. Petey often called me a CIA dupe or worse. We haven't had any contact since the spring of 2012.

But we continued investigating, and as we learned more the doubts mounted as well. I could not find any publishing credits for Petey at any major newspapers or magazines despite his claim to be a journalist who had worked extensively at universities in Asia as a writing instructor. In fact, a fellow high school teacher from Kirkland, Russ Hulet, told me that he and Petey had worked at the *Eastside Journal* in Bellevue, Washington, but Peterson only covered light stories, such as high school sports. "He only did little, inconsequential stories—like for pocket change—nothing major," Hulet said.

Along these lines, my opinion of Pete's writing, as presented on the Internet, did not impress me as being at a level where he could get a job at the drop of a hat anywhere in the world. In addition, the content is so extraordinary that it borders on the implausible.

Here is a snippet of Peterson's writing, as presented in his "autobiographical" third-person account, "Homecoming."

In 1987, he (Sheridan) and Ginger (his daughter) went to Tianjin, China, and he taught technical English at the Civil Aviation Institute of China and lectured the faculty on methodology. The next year he transferred to the College of Economic Management in Beijing and taught English geared to the global market. He participated in the students' democratic movement at Tiananmen Square marching with the Tibetan students and witnessed the June 4th massacre at Muxidi, some four kilometers west of the square. From beneath a bridge, he saw the slaughter of over a thousand peaceful protesters. He wrote an eyewitness account of it for a bilingual magazine in Japan.

He and Ginger traveled throughout China sailing down the Yangtze River on an old freighter, riding horseback in the Mongolian grasslands and skiing at Shangzhi in Heilongjiang Province which was once part of Siberia. He explored the vast network of caves in Yan'an. It was the final destination of Mao Zedong's historic 8,000 km Long March in 1934. It is rumored that Peterson's father, Captain Chauncey Peterson, had been a military adviser to the Chinese troops there in the late '30's.

In 1989 Sheridan and Ginger returned to Japan and he got a job managing the Tesco International ESL Company (*E*nglish as a *S*econd *L*anguage) with over eighteen schools spread throughout Japan's four major islands. In 1991 Peterson was writing coordinator for the Tokyo branch of the U.S. University of Rio Grande. Next he taught English in Nagano, Japan's famed ski resort town. He skied every morning, teaching in the afternoons and evenings. At sixty-five he became a proficient down-hill skier.

Nevertheless, we tried to corroborate what Sheridan was saying and endeavored to find plausible answers to how Peterson and his family were able to roam over Asia for thirty years. During that time they visited numerous political hot spots, such as Saudi Arabia, Iran and Iraq, in addition to China.

First, we talked with family. Snowmman provided me with the contact information for Sheridan's older brother, Alden, who lives in the Sacramento area with his wife, Barbara. Alden was astonished to hear that anyone, let alone the FBI, would consider his brother a candidate for the DB Cooper skyjacking. Nor could he shed much light on Petey's Asian adventures.

"I take a lot of what he says with a grain of salt," Alden said. He also said that he didn't think that his brother was a great writer, either. But, he did confirm that their childhood was tough, even brutal. Sheridan's allegation that their father beat him to the point of unconsciousness is correct. Alden was also able to clarify the status of Sheridan's personal family, confirming two marriages. Sheridan writes extensively about one of his wives, a Philippina who lived with him in that mud hut in Nepal. They had two children, the previously mentioned Ginger, and a son named Sheridan III.

However, Petey's first wife was an American and allegedly lived in Bakersfield, California. The FBI questioned her in 1971. Prior, the Petersons had lived in the tri-cities area of Washington. Sheridan had three kids with this woman, named Claire, and they had one boy and two girls. Sheridan has identified this son as "Mark," and says he lives in Boise, Idaho, but I was unable to reach anyone by that name despite Snowmman's extensive help.

After those explorations and Sheridan's stonewalling, my interest in Petey faded. However, it reignited in an unusual manner: a *Mountain News* reader named "Bob Sailshaw" contacted me and said he had lived with Sheridan Peterson. Sail has a fabulous story to tell.

Sail and his wife had rented a room in their Seattle home to Sheridan Peterson in 1961. However, after a month they had to evict "Dan," as in Sher-i-*dan*, for non-payment of rent. Ten years later, they were reminded of "Dan" when an FBI agent knocked on their door asking for information on Sheridan Peterson. According to Sail, the agent said that Dan's ex-wife was living in Richland, Washington and had given their address as the only one she had for her ex-husband.

All she could offer was a ten-year old address for the father of her three kids?

The FBI's claim does not jibe with what we knew from Petey's writings, so I wondered if they were investigating Sailshaw as well as Petey, since both had worked at Boeing. Sail is a retired electrical engineer from Boeing and has found kindred spirits at the DZ and the *Mountain News.*

In fact, Sail is now leading a crusade to prove that Sheridan Peterson is DB Cooper, and in that process he has established a "salon" of study on Norjak that features periodic luncheons at the Seattle Yacht Club. Through his boating contacts Sail knows a plethora of retired FBI agents, skydivers and airline pilots, so the luncheons are lively and original. Because of Sail, my knowledge of the workings of the Seattle FO has greatly expanded.

In addition, Sail informed us that Boeing's Manuals and Handbooks Group, where Petey worked, was in the same building that the SST was being developed, Building 9-101. As a result, Petey had ready access to the bins of scrap airplane parts—including pure titanium, such as found by Tom Kaye—that were placed there for any employee to scrounge. Sail feels that the titanium found on DB Cooper tie could have come from these scrap tubs, and in the spirit of the resurgence Sail has begun lobbying Kaye and the Citizens Sleuths to take a closer look at this possibility. Here is a snippet of a recent email exchange that clearly frames the issue:

> Tom... The pure titanium you found on the DB Cooper tie and the very small machining curly-cues of aluminum were very likely from the Boeing Materials and Processes Lab in the 9-101 building main floor. The lab would place the scrap metals in tub-skids (4ftx4ftx4ft deep) that were kept in the alley ways inside and next to the lab. Sheridan worked in the Handbook and Manuals Group with offices just above the M&P Lab and he would have passed by the tub-skids three to four times a day. People

would typically look through the scrap materials for neat stuff they could use. I used titanium alloy metal for parts on my sailboat as an example. If Sheridan looked into the tub-skid, his tie would have hung down into and touched various scrap parts including powdered pure titanium that we were trying out on the leading edges of the SST airplane. We were flame spraying the pure titanium on the leading edges as it had better properties (temperature and abrasion) than the leading edges that were made of titanium alloy.

So, the titanium you found on the DB tie was an actual pointer to the 9-101 building lab at Boeing with Sheridan working just above in his office.

Sail has also told us that he had many engaging conversations with Dan in the evenings, who often mused about creating "The System to Beat the System," a phrase that appeared later in one of the many letters the FBI and newspapers received in the days following the skyjacking.

Now, Sail is pushing the FBI to test the DNA of the stamps and envelope of this letter, known as Letter #3, and compare it to Sheridan's. There's no direct proof that Letter #3 actually came from the skyjacker, but it could blow Peterson's alibi that he was living in a mud hut in Nepal when DB Cooper jumped.

Also, when they lived under the same roof in Seattle Sheridan pumped Sail for information on how the aft stairs on a 727 performed in flight. Sail says that Sheridan rebuffed him when he told Peterson that he was unable to comment knowledgeably since he was working on the 737, Boeing's next generation of commercial aircraft.

In addition, Petey spoke frequently about his days as a smoke-jumper, and told Sail that he was never afraid of parachuting into forest or brush. "The only thing Sheridan was afraid of was cliffs and overhangs, where his canopy could get snagged and he'd be trapped," Sail said.

Casting more suspicion on Sheridan, Sail contacted Peterson by email in 2012, and Petey denied ever living in Sail's rooming house. But, why would Peterson lie? Petey also denied ever knowing skydiver Earl Cossey, even though both jumped out of the nearby Issaquah Sky Sports facility in the 1960s.

Braced by these tantalizing tidbits of information, I went looking for Sheridan in late 2011 at his last known address in Windsor, California. I found Petey's apartment in an assisted living community, but he had just been evicted a few weeks prior. Nevertheless, I spoke with plenty of his former neighbors, and a few of them told me they were glad to see him leave. They also gave me some leads on where he might have gone.

One suggestion led to a nearby neighborhood that had a Peet's coffee shop. Needing to re-focus my thoughts, I stopped for a cup of java and began kibitzing with a bunch of 60-something gals who were celebrating a girls-night-out in the middle of a Saturday afternoon. As we traded jokes and witty come-backs, I mentioned that I was looking for a guy named Sheridan Peterson. Lightning struck. One of the women volunteered that she worked with Sheridan in his new residential facility.

Although tightly constrained by confidentiality concerns, she agreed to deliver a basket of cheer to Petey that had been purchased earlier by 377 and given to me to deliver on behalf of all the skydivers at the DZ. She delivered the goods.

Pete was touched—in truth his heart melted—and that's when he began his season of correspondence. He also shared the names and addresses of several of his friends, and I developed a greater sense of his work in Vietnam. The friends that I spoke with clearly trusted Sheridan and honored him for his righteous political convictions. Further, none of the friends I contacted thought he could be DB Cooper. Additionally, no one thought he was a former CIA agent either, and half of them thought I was a creep for asking.

I don't think Sheridan Peterson is DB Cooper because most of what I know about him comes from his autobiographical essays and I doubt a skyjacker would write about his crime so publicly. Nevertheless, his story is filled with mystery and I sense that knowing Peterson better will educate us in fruitful ways. Besides, he *may* be DB Cooper.

So, I'm endeavoring to return to Santa Rosa and meet with Petey. He's got a lot of stories to tell and I'm eager to listen.

Chapter 24

"Most Promising" Suspect Uncle LD Cooper

Cooper World was jolted in the summer of 2011 when the FBI announced they were investigating the "most promising" suspect ever in the DB Cooper case—an Oregon man named Lynn Doyle Cooper, aka LD Cooper.

This shocking news came via a journalist named Alex Hannaford, writing a "40th Anniversary DB Cooper" piece for the *London Sunday Telegram* (UK) newspaper. Hannaford interviewed Seattle PIO Ayn Dietrich-Williams, who informed him of the "most promising" development. However, neither Dietrich-Williams nor anyone else in the FBI provided a stitch of solid evidence to support this blockbusting statement, which soon cast enormous doubt over the announcement and heightened scrutiny of the Bureau's investigation. After all, why would the FBI tell the world they had their most promising suspect if they couldn't prove it?

Regardless, the lead came to the FBI via the efforts of LD Cooper's niece, an Oklahoma woman named Marla Cooper. As events soon revealed, the FBI's claim was so lame that if it hadn't been for Marla it is most likely that the world would have never heard of LD Cooper. In short, Marla is a blonde bombshell, and on the DZ she is affectionately called "Twisty Butt." But Marla is much more than just a pretty face with a curvy figure—she is also a delightful mix of needy waif, religious seeker, and a top-notch storyteller. All these aspects, along with LD's imprimatur from the FBI, converged to place Marla and her Uncle LD on the front page of every English-speaking newspaper in the world in August 2011. It also raises the question: did the FBI use Marla Cooper to sell their "most promising" story for reasons that can only be speculated, such as conning the world to believe that Norjak was solved by mistaking DB Cooper for LD Cooper?

Marla's story is really a two-act drama—the opener in August, and a spectacular second act in November during the 40th Anniversary celebration in Portland, Oregon that was hosted by Geoffrey Gray. There, in front of a packed auditorium and a bank of TV cameras, Marla declared that Cooper case agent Curtis Eng had confirmed to her that he was "convinced" that her uncle LD was DB Cooper. Despite the worldwide headlines, Eng has wrapped himself in a cloak of inscrutable silence, and to date he has not spoken a public word about Marla or Uncle LD.

It's another complex Cooper story, so let's start at the beginning: In 2009, Marla Wynn Cooper was broke, in-between husbands and lovers, and working as an interior decorator in the greater Oklahoma City area. She was also in her mid-40s and openly wondering about the many turns her life had taken. With such vulnerability the Vortex seemed to engulf her fully, and she began exploring an old family story that one of her father's four brothers, Lynn Doyle Cooper, had been DB Cooper.

In the mid-1990s, Marla says she began recalling memories of an eventful family gathering at her grandmother's house when she was eight years old. Two of her uncles, Lynn Doyle, whom everyone called "LD," and his younger brother Dewey, showed up at her grandmother's house early on the Friday after Thanksgiving, 1971, and the two brothers looked disheveled and LD was injured.

Marla says that she remembers seeing Uncle LD folded into the passenger seat of Dewey's Triumph sports car, "looking like a bloody mess." LD couldn't walk, and Marla's grandmother refused to let her two sons into the house so they drove to Dewey's girl-friend, a woman named "Wink."

Such family kerfuffles were not uncommon in the Cooper household, and the morning's antics by LD and Dewey went with-out further notice during the Thanksgiving weekend. However, decades later Marla says that she now remembers family mem-bers commenting back then that their money troubles were over. Additionally, Uncle LD disappeared a year later during the Christmas holiday, and Marla never saw him again.

Her memories were stirred further in 1995 when she had a heart-to-heart talk with her father, Don Cooper. He was then divorced from Marla's mother and near death, and in the midst of this tête-à-tête, Marla says her father blurted: "Don't you remem-ber that your Uncle LD hijacked that airplane?" Marla also says that her mother reiterated the tale of *LD-is-DB* in a similarly weighty conversation in 2009, which solidified Marla's desire to unearth the truth of this family saga. However, Marla says her mother, Grace Hailey, "clammed-up" afterwards.

Nevertheless, in 2009 Marla told her story to a kindly old guy named Arden Dorney, who was remodeling his house and needed Marla's decorating services. Besides being a good listener, Arden was also attuned to helping a troubled sister of the faith. He was also a cop—a retired Elk City, Oklahoma detective—and he embraced Marla's quest to learn the truth of her Uncle LD. Dorney developed a dossier on LD Cooper, and helped Marla organize her investigation.

Arden became convinced that Uncle LD was DB Cooper, and for assistance in moving the case forward he approached a former law enforcement associate—a FBI agent who had been an undercover operative for the Bureau in their organized crime division, and had worked several cases with Arden and his department. Arden has refused to tell me the name of the special agent, and Marla says she doesn't know, either.

Nevertheless, this agent brought the case to the Seattle FBI office in 2009 or 2010, and then the dossier sat for awhile. Dissatisfied with the FBI's inaction, Arden told them that he and his Bureau buddy were going to FOX-TV with their story, including Seattle's inactivity. Arden says the threats prompted the FBI into action, and by June 2011 the Seattle office had launched an investigation of Uncle LD.

When I asked Arden why he thought the Bureau had finally began pursuing LD Cooper, he replied, "The FBI respects their own."

About this time, Hannaford visited the Seattle FO for his 40th Anniversary DB Cooper article, scheduled to appear in print by mid-summer. Alex received a two-hour interview with Dietrich-Williams, the Seattle PIO who specializes in the Cooper case, and she told Hannaford that the FBI had recently received its "most promising" lead in the case, courtesy of unnamed sources. Dietrich claims she did not tell Hannaford the name of the suspect, "LD Cooper," or that an undercover FBI agent was instrumental in bringing the information forward. Hannaford wrote his "most promising" piece without the names, and it published on Saturday July 30, 2011.

The story went viral immediately, and the *Seattle Post-Intelligencer* ran a piece on the "most promising" angle that weekend, quoting Dietrich-Williams at length. Additionally, the names of Marla, Uncle LD, and his getaway driver, Dewey, mysteriously surfaced within hours, suggesting serious leakage to the media by the FBI.

However, the FBI hadn't bothered to get any DNA samples or fingerprints of Uncle LD, apparently. It is as if the Vortex blew through Seattle and whipped the Marla story into a tumult before anyone thought to procure the evidence.

Predictably, the media tore into the story, and soon a bevy of holes were discovered besides the lack of direct evidence. Most notable was the absence of fundamental facts on the suspects, such as height, weight and distinguishing marks or tattoos.

Specifically, Arden Dorney had neglected to procure basic information, such as LD's driver's license, military records, or other official documents that would identify LD Cooper's physical characteristics.

Seeking clarification about the actions of the FBI agent in the LD Cooper matter, I sought information on the unnamed FBI agent from the Organized Crime Division (OCD). In September 2015, I spoke with the former Director of the OCD, Tom Fuentes, but he was unable to give me any details on the identify of this agent.

In addition, he was unable to offer any substantive insights on how an agent from a distinguished unit of the FBI could fail to provide source information on the suspect, nor procure vital documents. Yet, the Seattle FBI believed their colleague from the OCD, and Curtis Eng allowed his PIO to announce their "most promising" finding. Clearly, at every step Marla and law enforcement failed. So, how did this happen, and what does it mean?

To fully understand this dimension of the Marla saga, we need to explore related events that were happening in Cooper World during August 2011.

A week after Marla's story broke, Geoffrey Gray's *Skyjack—The Hunt for DB Cooper* was released. The timing of Geoffrey's book was intriguing because it came after many months of delays, as if powerful interests were waiting for a more propitious time to put his book into the public consciousness. Remember, Geoffrey had unprecedented access to FBI files and evidence, and I wonder if the price Gray had to pay was to help the Bureau spin a new DB Cooper narrative. The similarities in the names, *LD Cooper* and *DB Cooper*, imprinted in the publics' mind that the skyjacking was solved, and that the iconic figure was dead and buried.

Were Marla and Geoffrey all part of a scheme by the FBI to dispose of the DB Cooper case psychologically?

Adding to this possibility, Geoffrey also organized the Portland Symposium and he invited Marla, whose presence played as one last gesture to bury DB Cooper in the publics' mind. Many reporters and commentators, especially at the DZ, noted this incredible coincidence. Seeking answers, I chased Geoffrey through half of Portland trying to elicit an answer from him on why his book was released just after Marla's appearance on the world stage. To this day, he dodges the issue whenever I broach it with him.

Other occurrences added to my suspicions. In particular, Hannaford had interviewed me for his *Sunday Telegram* article and during our conversation he displayed an uncanny knowledge of DB Cooper. In fact, I complimented him on his grasp of Norjak. Alex was appreciative, and said he had gained his elevated knowledge by reading an advance copy of Geoffrey's book. I was shocked. I openly pondered if Hannaford and Gray were working as a team.

After concluding with Alex, I called Geoffrey and asked him if he had given the British writer a copy. GG laughed and assured me that he had not, nor had he schooled him in the nuance of Norjak. Geoffrey said that Hannaford must have gotten an electronic copy via his publisher in New York, Crown Publishing.

As for Marla, I queried her on the timing of the release of Geoffrey Gray's book and the "most promising" news from the FBI.

"It must have looked shocking to you," she told me bluntly, but denied that there was any collusion. In later comments she told me that "Geoffrey was blindsided" by the FBI's announcement. Nevertheless, I asked if she perceived any orchestration in these events.

"I feel there is Divine Orchestration," she replied. Marla told me that she has "faith in God's timing and his plan to get this story out to the world," adding, "God wants me to tell this story."

The agenda of the Almighty notwithstanding, the events of August and November 2011 suggest another possibility—a concerted effort to bury DB Cooper psychologically in the tomb of LD Cooper. I have no hard facts to support this theory, just a preponderance of circumstantial evidence, and the key ingredient is the FBI-induced fog that enveloped the Marla Cooper drama.

To wit: After the nudge from media, the FBI tested items from LD and determined there were no fingerprint or DNA matches, although the details of the exact tests and findings are hazy. Marla said at the symposium in November that the FBI was still involved in a multi-month probe of fingerprints, which wasn't expected to conclude until February 2012. She also claimed that the Bureau had investigated LD's DNA as far back as 2010, which seems to counter the Bureau's public comments.

Nevertheless, when the FBI declared in September they had no fingerprint or DNA matches, it deflated the mainstream media's interest in Uncle LD and Marla.

However, Marla told the symposium audience that even though Eng couldn't prove LD-is-DB conclusively, he was going to shut down the investigation in February 2012. "He (Eng) told me that he will be closing down the case after the (fingerprint) findings are reported regardless of whether they find a match or not," she said.

Over the next week, Marla continued to make the media rounds with this story, and in response reporters chased after Marla and her family for more details. The FBI remained stone-cold silent, which also contributed to the tumult.

Fortunately, I was able to talk with Marla at the Symposium. At that time, she gave me the name and contact details for Arden, which was information that had not been released publicly. She also provided contact information for other family members, and by early December 2011, I had spoken with most of the principals of the Marla saga, except for the undercover FBI agent.

Although Eng has never publicly commented on any aspect of Marla's story, and his PIO, Ayn Dietrich-Williams, has not delivered any definitive response on LD, either, I pressed Ayn to confirm or refute what Marla was saying. Specifically, I asked her three questions: did Eng meet with Marla, was Eng certain LD Cooper was the skyjacker, and was he shutting down the case? Ms. Dietrich replied via email:

> I can confirm that the case agent meets with various people, as necessary to fully pursue investigative leads. We do not divulge the particulars of those meetings, though. I know it must be disappointing that I cannot answer questions you ask me, but I appreciate you understanding that we are not discussing the details of this pending investigation.

Unsatisfied, I pressed for more details and Ayn responded with continued opaqueness:

> I appreciate your continued interest in gaining an accurate understanding of information you hear. I can only assure you that we continue to pursue credible leads accordingly. This does include testing any additional personal items of Lynn Doyle Cooper that we may be able to secure.

Additionally, in my phone conversations with Marla she reiterated that Eng did not feel the need to have fingerprint confirmation, but claimed that Eng had told her that *if* the fingerprints *did* match, "that would be enough to convict." But they don't, apparently, so the question remains—why did the FBI continue to investigate LD Cooper? Marla addressed this issue, and told me that she felt the FBI would actually close the case soon due to a preponderance of evidence. "Curtis Eng told me that he sees no reason to pursue any further leads," she said.

Over time, she told me why. First, Marla said that Eng had received a positive ID on LD Cooper from Tina Mucklow. Expanding on that shocker, Marla said Eng reported Mucklow as saying, "This is the closest picture of all the ones you've shown me over the years."

Disbelieving, I questioned Marla directly about this sketch claim and reminded her that this statement is virtually identical to what Geoffrey said about Florence and Kenny Christiansen. Marla then back-tracked from the Tina claim, saying she was not able to specify which member of Flight 305 had made the identification.

In general, though, Marla was undaunted. She expanded upon her original position and declared that Eng held his belief due to the large number of her uncle's incriminating behaviors. I was unclear what that meant, and pressed the issue.

Marla responded, "There were so many things about my uncle's life—he had no contact with his family after 1972, vanishing like that."

Marla also declared that her own demeanor had added to Eng's confidence. Specifically, Marla touted the fact that she has never changed her story, had passed an FBI polygraph test in January 2011, and had a first-person account of her Uncle LD being a bloody mess at Thanksgiving in 1971. She said that all these occurrences solidified her claim in Curtis Eng's mind.

Not convinced, I explored Marla's story further, and was able to weave a more comprehensive picture of the Cooper family and the events surrounding their Thanksgiving in 1971. By all accounts Marla's life, and by extension the Cooper clan, was chaotic, dysfunctional, and rift with alcohol. When he introduced Marla to the symposium, Geoffrey said that she had attended twenty-two different schools during her childhood. Later, Marla rattled off a number of towns in Cooper Country where she once lived, such as Centralia and Mount Lake Terrace, Washington, finally moving to Oklahoma when she was ten-years old.

What Marla remembers of the fateful night is brief, but specific. First, Marla says that she only saw LD sitting in the car when her uncles arrived, and he didn't get out. Afterwards, he and Dewey left quickly. However, Marla has expanded upon these descriptions, and at times has claimed that LD was bloodied, bruised, and unable to walk. Marla said that a cousin told her that Dewey had carried LD into the grandmother's house later that day, but this point was later amended and Marla now claims the two brothers had gone to Dewey's girlfriend.

Nevertheless, in the course of several conversations with me, Marla continued to clarify aspects of her story. She said that at one point she was told that LD had hijacked an airplane, and she also learned that Dewey had been his accomplice on the ground, picking him up in Washington and traveling the next day to the family homestead in Oregon.

Nevertheless, after the Thanksgiving incident, Marla and her family left the Pacific Northwest and traveled to New Mexico, settling two years later in Oklahoma.

This lengthy separation from the rest of the family put the skyjacking story on a kind of hiatus. As a result, Marla now has been seeking information from family members whose memories have been reawakened by her public announcements. To support that effort, Marla launched a road trip in the fall of 2011 to reconnect with family and hear their recollections.

First, she learned that LD remarried and had a daughter, whom the FBI discovered in Nevada. The feds retrieved a DNA sample from her to compare to their DB Cooper stock, but did not find a match with the skyjacker.

Nevertheless, Marla was unfazed and continued her search for family connections to Norjak. She learned that Uncle Dewey had worked at Boeing on the 727 assembly line, and from that experience she believes he learned how to parachute from the aircraft.

As for Boeing, they have confirmed that a Dewey Cooper did work for them "briefly" in the late 1960s, but what he did there is unknown publicly. When I pushed Boeing for details, their media relations officer got huffy and said, "That's all I can give you."

However, there is no evidence whatsoever indicating that LD Cooper had any skydiving experience.

But, Marla says that family members told her that Dewey had been questioned by the FBI shortly after the skyjacking. Then, immediately upon his release he grabbed his family and relocated to British Columbia, not even pausing at home to gather clothes.

In the process of these family discussions, Marla also experienced her own re-awakening. She began remembering other, long-buried memories, such as a pair of powerful walkie-talkies that her two uncles possessed in 1971. She now thinks that Uncle LD used them to link-up with Dewey after the hijacking.

But a big question lingers: If Marla had largely forgotten the 1971 Thanksgiving episode until her father reminded her in 1995, why did she wait until 2009 to further explore the possibilities?

"My life was chaotic then, too," she told me. "I was going through a divorce and raising three boys, so I didn't pay much attention to what my father was saying." In addition, Marla said that her father passed away a month later, and his death forced her memories more deeply into the shadows. But they re-surfaced again in September 2009, when her mother began talking about LD-as-DB. This time the memories stuck, and Marla took her story all the way to the FBI.

Reactions to Marla's story have been mixed. Many believe her, but most Cooper researchers don't, and scathe her for being an opportunist. After hearing Marla's pronouncements in 2011, long-time Cooper sleuth Jerry Thomas became outraged that Marla claimed the case would be closed. "That can not be done at the field office level," he argued on the DZ in 2012. "The decision to shut down a case must be made at a higher level, such as DC." Jerry also said that he had called Curtis Eng to confirm the statements being attributed to him by Marla, and even asked if LD was DB. Jerry says he received a less than crystal-clear answer from Eng: "Maybe."

Galen Cook was also miffed by Marla's statements. "How can Curtis Eng shut down the case before the fingerprint analysis comes in? How can the case be shut down when an open indictment still exists for DB Cooper?" Galen also questioned how organized the FBI is regarding their efforts to show LD Cooper's picture to the flight crew. Galen told me that Eng had asked him for the phone number of Florence Schaffner, so clearly no one in Seattle has been keeping up-to-date files on Norjak witnesses.

As the media scrutiny intensified, Marla began changing her tune, or at least her tone. She threatened to sue me if I contacted one of her ex-husbands, John Santore, Jr. This "Ex," in turn, contacted me, and with a dollop of irony said he would sue me if I didn't talk to him and learn all about Marla.

Not surprisingly the soap opera of Marla's life exploded on the stages of Norjak. Tales of her four marriages and a child out of wedlock spiced the DZ for days.

More importantly, legal issues began emerging besides the questioning of Marla's credibility. If Marla was correct about Uncle LD, would her family be in jeopardy for not telling law enforcement about the skyjacking? Specifically, did members of the Cooper family help LD and Dewey escape or stay hidden? If so, are they criminally liable? At the very least, pressures ensued when the family entered the media spotlight.

Nevertheless, Marla became furious with me for speaking to members of her family, and in the midst of an interview she hung up the phone on me, saying: "I'm done talking to you!"

Regardless, here are some highlights of my interviews with her family and her investigatory team.

Arden Dorney

When Marla gave me Arden's name she advised me that his "memory might be off." I was unfazed, as I have come to learn that such lapses are part of the Norjak story since so many of the principals are of an advanced age.

However, the most troubling aspects of Marla's investigation have nothing to do with memory. First, facts do not appear to be highly valued by Marla and her team. To wit: Marla didn't know what kind of cop Arden was. She announced to the 2011 Symposium that he was a retired member of the Oklahoma Highway Patrol, (OHP) but he is actually a retired detective from the Elk City, Oklahoma PD. Second, the second cop who assisted Arden was not another OHP officer, as Marla indicated in Portland, but an FBI agent.

Worse, no one—not Marla, her family, Arden or his FBI teammate—can provide details as simple as height and weight and build, or distinguishing marks. Despite such obvious failures, Arden has been happy to declare, "As a former investigator, I am totally satisfied that Marla is the niece of DB Cooper."

Dale Miller

Marla's support team is enlivened by "Santa Claus," a fellow named Dale Miller who works as a professional Santa from his home in Eugene, Oregon. Dale has the requisite kindly demeanor and snowy white beard to be a real-live Saint Nicholas, and Marla presented him at the Portland Symposium as a very good friend of Uncle LD.

Besides his Yuletide charm, Dale is also a self-styled pastor. He operates a small ministry for ex-felons in Eugene, and said that LD Cooper had been a resident during the 1990s. Over time, LD also became a good friend.

Dale added that "Lynn," as he knew Uncle LD, died at his ministerial compound in 1999 of pulmonary disease.

Even though Santa was very personable in Portland, he was difficult to pin down for a follow-up interview. His emails bounced back to me and Marla did not comply with her promise to give me his phone number. Nevertheless, I was able to track Santa via public records. Yet Dale did not return any of my initial phone messages, and I only spoke with him when he happened to pick up the phone on a Santa-related line.

He, too, did not know LD's physical characteristics. "I guess he was about 5'10", I'd say, give or take. I'm 6'1" and he was a little shorter than I am," he told me. "As for weight, hmmm, he was heavier now, of course, when I knew him at the end of his life, but I would estimate his weight (in 1971) to be about 175."

Equally mysterious is how Marla entered Santa's life. Dale told me that he was first contacted by a reporter, not Marla, which suggests that another player besides Marla is involved. "I'd heard about it (LD-as-DB) in the news, but the first thing that happened was a reporter called me," he told me in December 2011.

"How did the reporter know that you were connected with Lynn Doyle Cooper," I asked.

"I have no idea," Dale replied, laughing.

Dale says that Marla entered the picture shortly after that conversation, and he subsequently called the FBI to inform them he had some of LD's personal effects, which could be used to retrieve DNA samples. "The FBI told me, 'Yeah, we'll send somebody over next week to pick them up.' But an FBI agent showed up at my door within the hour!" Dale said.

This account suggests that someone other than Marla was orchestrating the LD Cooper scenario, alerting a "reporter" to the significance of Dale and LD, and lighting a fire under the feet of the FBI in Eugene. It suggests that an unknown somebody was setting the stage for Marla and Uncle LD to don the mantle of DB Cooper. Or the FBI was ahead of Marla in researching her uncle and found Dale Miller before she did. Dynamics like this lead researchers to suspect that an unknown DB Cooper "puppet master" is at work in Norjak.

Janet Cooper, Dewey's Widow

LD Cooper was not as "vanished" as Marla has indicated. In fact, Uncle LD was the best man at Dewey's wedding in 1981. I called Dewey's widow, Janet Cooper, now 73, in the aftermath of my haggling with Marla over whom in her family I could interview. She recommended Janet.

"I don't know how much I can tell you," Janet said softly when I phoned.

"Just tell me what you remember," I suggested. "Perhaps you can tell me a little about the family—their history or what they were like. What kind of guy was Dewey, or LD?"

"Well, as for LD, I met him," Janet replied. "He and Marcia (LD's last wife) stood up for me and Dewey in 1981."

Janet said that the five Cooper brothers split from their ancestral home in Sisters, Oregon soon after the skyjacking and didn't stay in touch. Nevertheless, by the late 1970s, Dewey began searching for his long-lost brother LD in phone books and found him in Sparks, Nevada. Soon after, Janet and Dewey traveled there to marry. "We stayed with them overnight in Sparks," she said.

Janet said LD and Marcia were a hard-working couple, and that she liked them. "But I never saw them again," she added, and said LD only called her once, in 1985, to offer his condolences when Dewey died of lung cancer.

I asked Janet if she thought LD was the skyjacker and Dewey his getaway man. "There were a half-a-dozen times when the topic of DB Cooper came up and Dewey just laughed it off," Janet said.

"But do you think Dewey was involved?" I pressed.

"I questioned him directly, once," Janet replied. "I asked him, 'Is this really a joke, or what?' And Dewey said it just a big joke."

As for family history, Janet didn't miss a beat. She told me the five Cooper boys—Clyde, Donny, Wendell, Dewey and LD—all graduated from Sisters High School, had multiple marriages, and loved to party. "They all liked to drink—they were all good ol' boys," she said. "They liked Cajun music, too," adding that Marla's father, Donny, tried to develop a professional career in music.

When asked about the details of the skyjacking, Janet was befuddled. "How the skyjacking came about, I have no idea. I never would have guessed they'd be involved. Dewey never showed that side to me."

"But is LD, DB Cooper?" I asked.

"I really think that LD and Dewey did it," Janet said.

Yet, she was obviously conflicted with the reality of what that statement meant. "But I wouldn't have stood for it. If he had told me that he had done it, I probably would have thrown him out the door... I probably would have turned him in," Janet stated.

As she mused, Janet said LD and Dewey "wouldn't ever go out and hurt anybody," inferring that the notion of her brother-in-law blowing up Flight 305 was not real somehow. "They were just a bunch of good ol' boys and full of mischief," she added.

As for her husband working at Boeing, Janet is unsure if he really worked there in the late 1960s, or what he did there if he had. "I really don't know. All I know is that he worked power line construction, out of the union here in Salem, and they'd send him all over—out of state, too."

Janet has strong feelings of affection for Marla's father, Donny Cooper, engendered by his caring for her husband when Dewey had cancer. "Donny came up and stayed with us when Dewey got very sick. Dewey was a big man, and Donny could turn him and take care of him."

Janet spoke of the Cooper clan with a note of wistfulness. "I love to cook, but the boys never had any family reunions or any get-togethers like that."

"And Marla?"

"She's the real deal."

"How about LD's widow, Marcia Cooper?"

"She wants no part of this. She's not talking to anyone. But she had two girls with LD."

There's one interesting side note: Janet told me she used to do a little flying and jumped out of an airplane three years ago, when she was seventy.

Grace Hailey

I located Marla's mother, Grace Hailey, via Grace's Facebook page before it was scrubbed clean in early December, 2011. When I spoke with her via the phone she was soft spoken, a little shy and uncertain, but generally gracious and warm.

"So what do you think of LD as DB Cooper?" I asked.

"I always had a hunch," she said, "but it was more like what they didn't say."

"What do you mean?" I asked.

"It was like they'd get real quiet when somebody would walk into the room. It was more of a feeling than anything specific."

Grace never revealed exactly what *she* thought, either. During our entire conversation she never said anything definitive, such as "Yes, I think LD Cooper skyjacked that airplane." Nevertheless, Grace cast a lot of light on the family dynamics.

"The last time I saw LD was the Christmas of 1972. After that he disappeared. He didn't even show up for his mother's funeral. The brothers couldn't find him." Grace added that Dewey was still living with his mother when she died.

Grace also gave some interesting insights into LD. "LD stayed to himself a lot," she said, describing how LD would go off into the woods and stay out there for extended periods of time. She also said that LD had long hospitalizations in the VA. "That's what the family told me, at least," said Grace. "But it was all hush-hush. The family didn't talk about it too much."

Grace said that after she and her husband Donny divorced in "about 1980," she lost contact with the Cooper side of the family.

When asked about LD's physical characteristics, Grace paused. "Well, Don was the shortest. LD was around, hmmm, 5' 9", maybe 5' 10", but he wasn't 6-foot. And Dewey, he was overweight. He was always pretty soft."

As for pictures of LD, the only one she had was the famous shot with the guitar strap that she had given to Marla. Additionally, Grace does not remember the details of the fateful morning in 1971. "Marla says she remembers that I was up at the restaurant, baking pies, but I don't remember. I'm not remembering too much from forty years ago," she said.

Published accounts from Marla add another version—Grace was in the house as the brothers drove up, and when Marla started crying at the sight of LD bloodied and bruised, her mother told her to stop crying and "go get your father."

When I asked Grace how she and the family were handling the publicity from Marla's revelations, she was nonplussed. "I'm not getting as many phone calls as you would think," she replied. She added that others in the family think "Marla is nuts," such as her son Dave.

Lastly: "It's hard to keep track of Marla," Grace concluded.

It seems that the FBI has let go of Marla and Uncle LD, as well.

Chapter 25

The Mysterious Al Di

As the Marla craziness rumbled through the summer and fall of 2011, an individual within the FBI—or closely associated with the Norjak investigation—emerged from the investigatory shadows. The person called himself "Al Di," and his insertion into the DB Cooper story may prove to be more significant than anything produced by the antics of Marla Cooper and her Uncle LD.

Al Di has put a spotlight on several letters sent to the FBI from "DB Cooper" in the days immediately following the skyjacking. Whether they are truly from the skyjacker or not is still unknown, but Al Di has created a very real Cooper mystery because his identity is unknown. In fact, Al Di may be more than one person, and I only assign him the singular masculine gender because the solo voice-over on his website is male.

It is widely rumored, especially from Galen Cook, that Al Di is Cooper case agent Curtis Eng conducting a private investigation—in effect doing an end-run around his own agency. In fact, Galen believes that "Al Di" is a play on "L. D."

However, I do not have any proof whatsoever as to Al Di's real identity. In addition, I don't have any explanation why Eng would conduct such an operation, unless he doesn't trust his colleagues at the FBI and somehow needs to work off the books.

Also unexplained—and not understood—is why Al Di chose the chaos of August 2011 to launch his operation. Galen and others have speculated that Al Di needed the Marla hub-bub as a smokescreen, shielding his activities from excessive scrutiny. But Al Di eventually went public with his findings: www.dbcooperdecoded.com, so this hypothesis is weak.

Nevertheless, Al Di launched a crusade in mid-August 2011 to investigate the letters sent to the FBI and media outlets in the early days of the Norjak investigation. Many missives had been mailed to the feds after the skyjacking, but four of these letters were signed, "DB Cooper" and appear to be part of a group due to their tone and content. They were generally unknown to the public until Al Di re-introduced them to the world.

Al Di claims, and it now appears corroborated—although denied by the FBI—that around August 1, 2011 someone in the FBI authorized the release of "Letter #3" to the Portland, Oregon newspaper that had originally received it, the *Oregonian*.

This letter was the third communication regional newspapers had received from "DB Cooper" in the days immediately following the skyjacking, hence its numeric identification.

Although the *Oregonian* had received Letter #3, they had not published it due to their agreement with the FBI to maintain public silence on evidence received. However, forty years later on August 1, 2011, Letter #3 was published at the *Oregon Live* website, the digital home of the *Oregonian:* oregonlive.com. It appears they did so at the behest of the FBI, or someone close to the Norjak investigation who had access to the DB Cooper files.

So, the publication of Letter #3 and the subsequent actions of Al Di indicate that very serious sleuthing was occurring during the latter part of the summer in 2011, and it took place far from the Marla fireworks.

Al Di intimates that he learned of Letter #3 from its public appearance on *Oregon Live* at the beginning of August. However, few outside of the FBI even knew of the existence of Letter #3, and my efforts to learn the how and why of its posting on *Oregon Live* have not clarified the matter at all.

In 2013, I spoke with a long-time reporter at the *Oregonian,* Stuart Tomlinson, who told me that he wasn't sure why *Oregon Live* posted it. Searching his memory, he theorized that the Marla flap had caused some *Oregonian* staff, possibly in the photo department, to examine their archival documents regarding DB Cooper. Apparently, they had a photocopy of the original letter and that was published on *Oregon Live.* Tomlinson also claimed that he had never heard of Letter #3 before I called.

So, somehow Al Di stumbled upon the *Oregon Live* website and found the photocopy of Letter #3 after someone at *Oregon Live* had stumbled upon it first. But the reverse seems equally plausible—that Al Di was part of a process that placed Letter #3 into the hands of *Oregon Live.* Why, is unknown. However, Galen is able to shed some light on this matter:

> I contacted the Portland *Oregonian* in 2010 and talked with a reporter who was interested in the DB Cooper case. I informed him about "Letter #3" addressed to the *Oregonian,* which I knew about from the news articles from the Reno *Gazette* in the November 1971 publications. He said it was all new to him, as he had never heard about any DB Cooper letter. He told me that he'd call me back later after he did some research. About a month later we talked on the phone again. He told me that he had called Ralph Himmelsbach and asked Ralph if he

knew about any DB Cooper letters sent to the *Oregonian*. Ralph told him that 'none were ever sent to or received by the *Oregonian*.' Then he told me that Ralph Himmelsbach also told him, 'Galen Cook is full of shit.'

Well, it appears that old RH was caught in a big lie. He knew that there was a letter sent by DBC to the *Oregonian*, but the FBI told the *Oregonian* not to publish it. The FBI kept it under wraps for all of these years, until recently. It was all a part of the effort by the FBI to catch DBC. But they never could. Sort of telling that they believed he might be alive, based on the fact that they tried to cover-up the letters.

Galen later identified the *Oregonian* reporter as Stuart Tomlinson, the same reporter I had spoken with. Hence, Tomlinson knew about Letter #3 in 2010, yet forgot that Galen had spoken with him before I called in 2011.

In addition, Galen told me that Al Di had sent him dozens of emails during this time period, and in one email Al Di admitted to speaking with Tomlinson—so this newspaper reporter forgot *two* important aspects of the Letter #3 story when I talked with him. It's too outrageous to believe.

Nevertheless, Al Di made a post at the DZ on September 8, 2011, announcing that he had deciphered Letter #3 and offered a link to his website, which reveals an extensive and well-crafted analysis of the letter.

Letter #3 is a cut-and-paste-job formed from letters found in a magazine, and reads:

Am alive and well in hometown P.O.

The system that beat the system

DB Cooper

In addition, the letter's envelope is hand-written in pencil and addressed:

Editor - Oregonian

1320 SW Broadway

97201

Al Di's "decoding" proved that all the lettering came from the June and July 1970 issues of *Playboy* magazine. How he deduced the connection to *Playboy* is mind-boggling, and Al Di has not revealed exactly how he did so, stating only that he "colorized" the black and white version that the *Oregonian* had posted. Once colorized, the unique characteristics of the background used on *Playboy* cover pages were apparent, thus revealing the source of some of the lettering. But not all.

How did he pick the remaining letters from within two different 40-year old girly mags? Did Al Di have help or just a lot of spare time on his hands? Had the FBI already decoded Letter #3 and Al Di simply re-discovered their findings? Al Di hasn't answered these questions directly, but he does float the idea that J. Edgar Hoover had ordered his agents to closely monitor *Playboy* magazine during the 1970s, and the Norjak team might have gotten lucky.

Additionally, Al Di says that there are two different types of communications that DB Cooper is transmitting to the FBI: a "first level" message and "second level" ones. Their status is determined from the ad copy or story text in which the letters are found.

For instance, Al Di says that the "w" in "**w**ell" comes from a clip-on bow-tie ad, and he makes note that the clip-on tie found on the plane was not common knowledge until 2007 when Larry Carr made its presence known to the public.

Similarly, the "p" for Coo**p**er comes from a pipe tobacco ad, and Al reminds us that the skyjacker was a smoker, albeit cigarettes. Al Di has identified many of these kinds of associations, and he calls them "first level" messages—basically a prompt by DB Cooper alerting the FBI that he had made a successful getaway.

The second level messages are much more subtle, and Al Di feels they are ploys by DB Cooper to tell the FBI of his real identity. However, I find Al Di's interpretations to be tea-leaf reading *in extremis*. Nevertheless, Al Di posits that the feature article in the July 1970 *Playboy*, "Anatomy of a Massacre," is a major clue, and that's intriguing. The piece is an in-depth article on the events that led to the My Lai massacre in Vietnam, and it details much of the notorious actions of the CIA's Phoenix program. Reading Al Di's commentary draws immediate associations to covert operations and the Special Forces—even Sheridan Peterson and his outrage at American combat atrocities.

In my judgment, Al Di delivers a superb job of sleuthing, even if all he really did was dust-off someone else's work from 1971. At the very least, his video presentation has excellent production values and the voice-over sounds as if a professional actor is reading from a well-crafted script. However, Al Di's full decoding is obtuse at best.

But, what is more compelling—and more difficult to determine—is Al Di's identity. My efforts to contact him via his email address have been unsuccessful, but Al Di was busy talking to other people, at least Galen Cook. From late 2011 to early 2012, Al

Di exchanged over sixty emails with Galen. In those correspondences Al Di revealed that he was studying Cooper postings at the *DropZone* and the *Mountain News*. (Thanks, Al!)

In addition, Galen told me that Al Di asked him many questions across the full spectrum of the Norjak investigation, including detailed queries about Jo and Duane Weber. They even discussed Wolfgang Gossett's handwriting. Galen describes Al Di as having a "superior" knowledge of the case, and Al Di shared details that suggested he had inside information, such as knowing the exact wording of communications between the pilots of Flight 305 and the ground crew at Sea-Tac.

Curiously, Curtis Eng was also emailing Galen extensively at the same time. Further, the emails from both Al Di and Eng ceased abruptly in June 2012.

Nevertheless, Al Di began visiting another Cooper cyber hot spot, www.websleuths.com, where he called himself "Idla," which is Al Di spelled backwards. Idla and another poster, the renowned Shutter, bantered over a rumor rampant in Cooper World that Al Di's email address was traceable to Redmond, Washington, the home of Microsoft. Intriguingly, Cooper case agent Curtis Eng is reportedly a former Microsoft engineer who lives in the Redmond area.

So, the Big Question remains: who is Al Di? I queried the FBI if they knew the identity of Al Di. I also inquired about the origins of Letter #3, and Ayn Dietrich-Williams addressed both issues in an email:

> I don't have any information on Al Di whatsoever. Also,
> I am not aware of any release of a letter in August 2011.
> I've reached out to the case agent to check if I missed

something but I can say with absolute certainty that we did not put out anything along those lines in an official and public manner—like an announcement to the media. Why is it that you think a letter was released last August?

In a follow-up phone call, Ayn specifically told me that Al Di was not an FBI agent and that he has no relationship with the Bureau. Nevertheless, Galen, who has had an excellent relationship with Curtis Eng and has met with him in person at least six times, told me definitively that the FBI released Letter #3 during its flurry of media announcements during "Marla Week" in early August, 2011. Al Di seconds this perspective on his website:

For undisclosed reasons, the FBI withheld a copy or picture of the letter (#3) until now. This letter was released in August of 2011.

Al Di also says he decoded the letter ten days after the FBI's release, which again implies the FBI gave it to *Oregon Live* in early August.

As for his identity, Al Di claims on his website that he is just an "average Joe" who is interested in the DB Cooper saga. But Al Di knows details about Letter #3 that only the FBI knows. So, if Al Di is a member of the FBI what is transpiring within the Bureau that compels one of their investigators to disguise his actions? Or, if Al Di is not a fed but knows of Letter #3 because he has ties to the Cooper case, is he keeping quiet because of a fear of retribution? But if that is true, wouldn't that be more reason to act in the open?

Additionally, the manner in which Al Di describes DB Cooper is intriguing, calling the skyjacker "brash... highly calculating" and an individual who "coolly executed" the hijacking. Echoing the elevated cultural status of Cooper, Al characterizes the skyjacking as "akin... to a James Bond movie." These are not the perspectives usually associated with the expressed views of the FBI, so Al Di might be a federal agent marginalized by his colleagues.

Another wrinkle was added in the summer of 2015 when a quirky group of DB Cooper researchers, using the monikers Moriarty and Reichenbach, joined the search for Al Di's identity. They have been unsuccessful, so far, but they hounded Galen for weeks. Intriguingly, Al Di's website, dbcooperdecoded.com, went dark when these investigators started probing into him.

Nevertheless, what does Letter #3 tell us about Norjak? The answer to that question is elusive, but Snowmman again has been able to offer an insight. Originally, Letter #3 was postmarked December 1, 1971, and had a northern Oregon—but not Portland—postal marking. Its origin is now believed to have been the town of Scappoose. The letter was received by the *Oregonian* editorial department on December 2, 1971, but instead of publishing it they sent it to the FBI.

However, Snowmman discovered that Letter #3 was published on December 3, 1971, in the Billings, Montana *Gazette*, but was buried on page 38.

Why Letter #3 was only published in Billings is unknown, but it is reasonable to posit that the FBI was trying to lure accomplices from the Paul Cini skyjacking. Remember, Cini landed in Great Falls, Montana during his hijacking adventures of November 11, 1971. Remarkably, the FBI acted with great speed. In the days before emails and ubiquitous fax machines, the FBI had to really hustle to get Letter #3 to Montana and into the *Gazette* within a twenty-four hour period. If there weren't top-quality digital transmission equipment at both ends, the FBI would have needed to take a photograph of Letter #3 and send it by air courier to the *Gazette*.

Nevertheless, for the next forty years Letter #3 remained hidden until Al Di drew our attention to it. By extension, Al Di's announcements in 2011 created interest in all the letters received by newspapers shortly after the skyjacking.

Additionally, what is the present response of the FBI to Al Di and the existence of all the letters? Are they checking the DNA of the envelopes and stamps? What are their conclusions from this evidence? It is unknown.

Cooper aficionado Bob Sailshaw is vocal in championing the examination of the letters for DNA, demanding that the FBI compare the samples with those of DB Cooper suspect Sheridan Peterson. Sail wants to know if Peterson's alibi can stand up to scrutiny—that he was living in a mud hut in Nepal with his new wife and two little kids at the time of the skyjacking. Sailshaw feels that the DNA contained in the saliva residues can prove whether Peterson was in Nepal or not. If the DNA on the stamps and envelopes is Petey's, then he probably wasn't in Nepal. Sailshaw acknowledges that a positive match won't prove conclusively that Peterson was Cooper, but it can tell us if Petey is lying.

Further, Sailshaw claims that a line from Letter #3, "The system that beats the system" is identical to a mantra Peterson uttered frequently when he lived in Sail's home in 1961. "The coincidence is just too uncanny," says Sailshaw.

In addition, Sailshaw announced on the DZ in April 2013 that the Seattle FO has developed its own DNA testing laboratory. As always, we await the FBI's findings.

In the meantime—and digging further—there are important similarities among the "core four" letters. First, they are short, pithy and smug. In fact, there is a haiku quality to them. Also, all the letters were sent to west coast newspapers in the week following the skyjacking.

Dissimilarities exist, as well: Letters #1 and #3 are cut-and-paste jobs, while Letters #2 and #4 are hand-written. However, all the envelopes are hand-written.

Letter #1 was postmarked on November 27, 1971 in the northern Californian town of Oakdale, and was received by the Reno *Evening Gazette* on November 29, five days after the skyjacking. Interestingly, Cooper's plane had landed in Reno for refueling. The first letter utilized lettering from the Friday, November 26 evening edition of the Sacramento *Bee* newspaper. Letter #1 reads:

Attention!
Thanks for the hospitality
Was in a rut.
DB Cooper

It was published by the Reno *Gazette* and then handed to the FBI.

Letter #2 was sent to the *Vancouver Province* newspaper in Vancouver, British Columbia, Canada. It was mailed sometime between November 30 and December 2, 1971, and was posted in Vancouver, BC. Its full length and complete details are unknown publicly, but it claimed that the first composite drawing of DB Cooper "did not represent the truth." Nevertheless, the following has been released:

I enjoyed the Grey Cup game.
Am leaving Vancouver.
Thanks for the hospitality.
DB Cooper

The Grey Cup game is the championship Canadian football game and in 1971 it was played in Vancouver on Sunday, November 28. Also, the repeat of the phrase "thanks for the hospitality" suggests that the person who wrote Letter #1 also wrote Letter #2.

Letter #4 was again mailed to the Reno *Evening Gazette,* and mailed December 1 from the Sacramento, California area. Like the *Oregonian* and its Letter #3, the *Gazette* did not publish #4 in accordance with the FBI's wishes. However, the *Gazette* did write a story about the letter's existence. It contained the following snippet:

Plan ahead for retirement income.
DB Cooper.

However, these four letters were not the only ones received by newspapers from people calling themselves "DB Cooper." Snowmman has discovered several others and he says that multiple media outlets received them, including the *New York Times* and the *LA Times*. Some were typewritten, too. These other letters are qualitatively different from the "core four," and one lengthy missive to the *New York Times* seems particularly pedestrian.

Sirs,

I knew from the start that I wouldn't be caught. I didn't rob Northwest Orient because I thought it would be romantic, heroic or any of the other euphemisms that seem to attach to situations of high risks.

I'm no modern day Robin Hood. Unfortunately I do have only 14 months to live. My life has been one of hate, turmoil, hunger and more hate; this seemed to be the fastest and most profitable way to gain a few fast grains of peace of mind. I don't blame people for hating me for what I've done nor do I blame anybody for wanting me to be caught and punished, though this can never happen. Here are some (not all) of the things working against the authorities:

I'm not a boasting man

I left no fingerprints

I wore a toupee

I wore putty make-up

They could add or subtract from the composite a hundred times and not come up with an accurate description; and we both know it. I've come and gone on several airline flights already and am not holed up in some obscure backwoods town. Neither am I a psycopathic [sic] killer. As a matter of fact I've never even received a speeding ticket.

Thank you for your attention.
DB Cooper

Another letter, written in block letters and in pencil, is also at odds with the four.

> I'm your hero, the great D.B. Cooper, the cool hijacker turned paratrooper, who bailed out with the cash, shed no blood, caused no crash, but sure left old John Law in a stupor. Viva Las Vegas ... D.B. Cooper

Are any of these letters from the skyjacker? How do they factor into the investigation? It's another unknown.

Chapter 26

Most Compelling Suspects, Commandos

Perhaps the most compelling suspects for the Cooper skyjacking come from the pool of Special Forces commandos who fought in the Vietnam War.

This angle of inquiry has only appeared recently as a result of the declassification of secret military operations in Vietnam in 2000. This has given many soldiers the freedom to talk about their wartime experiences, particularly members of the 5th Special Forces (SF) and their ultra-secretive unit, MAC-V-SOG. This later acronym is understood to signify Materials Assistance Command—Vietnam—Special Operations Group.

In Vietnam, SOG troopers were drawn from the ranks of the 5th SF, but were funded completely by the CIA, so they weren't officially on the Army's books. Their operations were so secretive that they had their own air wing, manned by South Vietnamese pilots, and they conducted missions exclusively outside of South Vietnam, specifically Laos, Cambodia and North Vietnam. Many of these soldiers have written books detailing their combat experiences, and they clearly illustrate that SOG troopers had the physical training, mental preparation, and tactical capabilities to perform the Cooper skyjacking.

In fact, there is compelling—but not conclusive—evidence that some commando groups used 727s as their jump and resupply aircraft. Hence, DB Cooper may have learned how to parachute from a 727 in Vietnam, and on the taxpayers' nickel.

The most original sleuthing by open-sourced parties occurred in our search for Cooper suspects who had fought in SOG. Again, Snowmman led the way on this effort, and he and I reached our greatest heights of partnership. Besides feeding me numerous addresses and phone numbers of SOG soldiers and their families, Snowmman spent months helping me track down one of the most intriguing Norjak suspects to come out of Vietnam—**Sergeant Ted B Braden.**

To date, I know of no FBI investigator to comment on our work. Not even Larry Carr has discussed our discoveries from the Vietnam War. Recently, I asked retired Special Agent John Detlor how extensively the Norjak team investigated soldiers from the Special Forces and he became noticeably tongue-tied. After he cleared his throat, Detlor confirmed that the FBI did interview paratroopers in the early days of the investigation, but he offered no details.

SOG trooper Rex Jaco confirmed to me that he had been interviewed by the FBI in regards to DB Cooper, and said he had been questioned at Fort Bragg after his rotation out of Vietnam in the early 1970s.

"I guess they put all the airborne guys in a computer and my name was one of those that got spit out," Rex said.

To begin our search, Snowmman and I reviewed the writings from two key SOG warriors—**Sergeant Major Billy Waugh**, and **Major John Plaster**. Waugh has penned a memoir of his fifty years in combat: *Hunting the Jackal,* while Plaster is the author of several SOG books, most notably: *Secret Commandos: Behind*

Enemy Lines with the Elite Warriors of SOG, and *SOG: The Secret Wars of America's Commandos in Vietnam.*

Both men say that the aforementioned Sgt Ted Braden was widely rumored to be DB Cooper.

Waugh told me that he has no factual proof that Braden was Cooper, but he said that Ted's looks and behavior match the skyjacker's. "Bradon (sic) had 'nads' as big as watermelons," Waugh wrote me.

But Ted wasn't as tall as Cooper. At 5'8" Braden was several inches shorter than Cooper's reported six-foot or so. Plus, Braden's eye color was hazel whereas Cooper's eyes were brown and piercing. Yet, Braden had the Cooper smirk in spades, along with his cool, confident demeanor. Further, Braden disappeared from Vietnam in late 1966, after a mission that both he and his men survived. So where was he in 1971?

I interviewed SOG troopers who had served with Braden, and Snow and I looked for Braden himself. As we searched, I wrote and posted my findings on the DZ and the *Mountain News,* and this in turn generated more information from retired military personnel who had served with Braden.

First, I learned the soldiers of SOG were elite, perhaps more so than Army Rangers or Green Berets.

Plus, they were absolutely gung-ho, and totally secretive and closed-mouth. Sergeant Major Billy Waugh served over seven years in Vietnam, and he was still running recon for the CIA in Afghanistan in late 2001 when he was in his seventies. As for Ted Braden, when he vanished he had just completed twenty-three consecutive months of covert jungle warfare in Vietnam, Laos and Cambodia.

I was astonished to realize how much these guys loved combat and thrived in the brotherhood of soldiering. Billy Waugh has earned eight purple hearts during his career, and in his book he tells the story of leaving his hospital bed at Walter Reed Medical Center in Washington, DC to return in secret to Saigon so he could hang out with his SOG buddies in their favorite downtown tavern.

In fact, Waugh suggests that one of the most compelling reasons for a SOG trooper to do the Cooper skyjacking was resentment within the SOG force that the Vietnam War was winding down before victory had been achieved. SOG was disbanded in March 1972, leading Waugh to retire from the US Army after 24 years of service. Soon afterwards, he was hired as a private contractor for the CIA.

In Vietnam, the primary mission of SOG was to "run recon." This meant conducting reconnaissance missions "across the fence," which was the euphemism for crossing the boundaries of South Vietnam and fighting in the neighboring countries of Laos, Cambodia, and sometimes even North Vietnam. Not only was this strictly covert, it was also widely seen as illegal, or at least unauthorized by the rules of engagement established by the American government. Opponents of the conflict championed these operations as proof of sordid American activities, worse perhaps than the cursed Phoenix program.

Not surprisingly, SOG troopers had been forbidden to talk about their activities until recently, and one SOG trooper, Bill Kendall told me that there were several levels of secrecy, with some actions of MAC-V-SOG still closed. "I could tell you stories, but I won't," he said to me in 2009. "I signed four pieces of paper that said I wouldn't divulge secret information, and I won't."

But Waugh did discuss some of the specifics of SOG operations. He said that SOG never ran recon in North Vietnam specifically, as it was too problematic politically for American leadership—who were hounded by the press on the issue of extra-legal combat missions. As a result, combat operations in North Vietnam were relegated directly to CIA operatives, which supposedly was a more palatable option politically. However, SOG teams did enter North Vietnam to rescue downed pilots. Billy sent me the following missive to clarify the extent of SOG activity in North Vietnam:

> SOG Bright Light (Rescue) Teams crossed into North Vietnam occasionally for "rescue of downed pilot missions," but intentional SOG Recon Teams did not specifically land for reconnaissance inside North Vietnam to conduct these reconnaissance missions. SOG Teams surely sat down on the borders of North Vietnam, inside Laos; especially adjacent to the Mu Gia Pass where traffic by the North Vietnamese Military to the South was especially heavy... Our very best teams fringed the border of North Vietnam.

However, this claim is directly refuted by a SOG trooper named Don Duncan, who later became an outspoken opponent of the Vietnam War and an investigative journalist for *Ramparts* magazine. Specially, Duncan writes in *Ramparts* that:

> SOG dropped long-range teams into North Vietnam, (OP-34) as well as Laos. Most of these have been remarkable for their lack of success. OP-35, 'Shining Brass,' Braden's group - was more successful. Most of this group's operations were short-range jaunts into Laos and North Vietnam.

Author's Note: OP-34 and OP-35 were mission designations.

Running recon was tough work. These units did more than just gather information—they interdicted Viet Cong and North Vietnamese troops along the Ho Chi Minh Trail on a regular basis, destroying command and material centers.

MAC-V-SOG was very good at its job, and was subject to intense countermeasures from the communist forces, including sabotage within the ranks. By the late 1960s, SOG felt certain that details of their operations were being relayed to the Viet Cong and North Vietnamese by ARVN liaison officers who were embedded within US Special Forces command centers. As a result, casualties were very high for recon units and forced a change in tactics.

Originally, recon units were inserted into operational areas via helicopters flown by ARVN Air Force pilots aboard helicopters, the H-34 "Kingbees." However, by the late 1960s SOG began to experiment with direct HALO jumps from 14,000 feet from regular US Air Force jump ships. HALO means, High Altitude, Low-Opening, and is a parachuting maneuver that had mixed results for SOG—troopers got to the ground safely, but had difficulty in linking with each other in a timely fashion. Braden was considered a master HALO jumper, and is reported to have trained ARVN paratroopers in HALO jumps as early as 1965. Obviously, HALO jumping was great training for anyone who wanted to skydive from a 727.

Other changes were also mandated. In particular, the recon units were beefed-up in size to increase their safety and efficiency. Originally, a SOG recon unit was composed of only three American soldiers and a handful of South Vietnamese volunteers, but at this time the role of indigenous soldiers was expanded to fill their ranks, especially from the *Montagnards,* the semi-autonomous people of the highlands of Vietnam. These troopers were able fighters and called "Yards" by their SOG compatriots. On occasion, the recon units also drew upon another indigenous group, the *Nungs*, an ethnic Chinese people who lived in Vietnam.

As a result, the recon units were multi-cultural, which was at great variance with most American combat units in Vietnam. In fact, DB Cooper suspect Richard McCoy drew distinction to himself during his tours of duty in Vietnam as being one of the few US helicopter pilots to volunteer to fly rescue missions to retrieve beleaguered ARVN troops. Usually, it was an optional task and US chopper pilots who refused to help ARVN troops did so without reproach.

In addition, the SOG troopers had to become increasingly self-reliant, as they were most vulnerable when they exited hot spots. One SOG trooper, Tom Smith, described his extensive preparation: "We were cross-trained in everything—weapons, radio, and demolitions—all the specialties."

SOG units were known as Recon Teams (RT) and given code names drawn from the states of the union. Ted Braden's unit was called "RT Colorado." Structurally, the boss of an RT was called the 1-0, pronounced "The One-Zero," the next in command was the 1-1, and the radio operator was the 1-2.

As for researching Ted Braden, we had some help from him directly. In 1967, a well-written and purportedly autobiographical account of Ted's disappearance surfaced in *Ramparts* magazine, along with a supporting commentary from the aforementioned *Ramparts* writer, Don Duncan. Duncan was a former SOG colleague of Ted's and went on to journalistic fame by writing a scathing account of his experiences in Vietnam, which has earned him great enmity from many SOG troopers. Duncan describes Braden as possessing the mannerisms of a cold-blooded assassin:

The similarities between Braden and the arch-prototype of the modern mercenary, Germany's infamous Kongo-Muller, are many," Duncan writes. "They can laugh about the most gruesome things; both display an obvious *machismo* syndrome; they share the habit of using their well-manicured hands in little gestures, which detract attention from their eyes."

Duncan trained with Braden in the specialized HALO jumping, and Duncan describes Braden as a major thrill-seeker. In fact, Duncan calls Ted, "Mr. Low Pull," and says that he observed Braden "pulling (his ripcord) well below 1,000 feet." Duncan adds:

With no safety restrictions on jumping in Vietnam, he (Braden) had a ball. Similarly, on operations deep in NLF (National Liberation Front) territory, he wandered away from his team on at least two occasions, the better to seek trouble.

Duncan continued:

He (Braden) also shares the cynicism common to the professional soldier in Vietnam. Idealism makes him uncomfortable and like the rest, he gives it lip-service only for public consumption.

Braden's story also appeared in the *Stars and Stripes* newspaper soon after it was published in *Ramparts*. In these publications, Ted acknowledged that he left Vietnam because of money and a lack of gratitude. In Vietnam he was making $800 a month, but he sought the bigger money and glory of fighting as a mercenary in the CIA-backed civil war raging in the Congo.

When Ted showed up in Africa, however, the CIA was not thrilled to see him and hauled him off to the stockade at Fort Dix, New Jersey. Allegedly, a deal was brokered to free Ted in exchange for keeping his mouth shut about the sensitive subject of American troops fighting across the fence.

By all accounts Ted was an *über* warrior. Generally disliked by his superiors for his quirky and reckless behavior, he nevertheless brought his men home, always. Ted is also reported by the men who served with him to have extensive associations with the CIA, often drinking with agents at their hangout in the Caravelle Hotel in Saigon. He even told his squad, "If you see me in Saigon wearing civilian clothes, you don't know me."

Further, Braden is widely described as mentally unstable. "Yeah, I saw him go 'schizo' several times," said fellow trooper, JD Bath, who also respected Braden's soldiering skills and spent a year in RT Colorado as the 1-2.

After I posted my SOG interviews on the *Mountain News,* I was contacted by several retired military personnel. One was the aforementioned Tom Smith, who had three tours of duty in Vietnam and had served with Braden. He also knew Billy Waugh and Don Duncan. "I worked with Ted in SOG in '66 and I agree with the likeness," Tom wrote me in 2011, and revealed that he was following the Braden-DB Cooper story. "There are other unique things that fit, as well," he told me. Perhaps the most telling were Tom's personal recollections that he shared in a 2011 phone conversation.

Ted took risks, yes, and others were more, (pause) *sensible*. Ted always went a step beyond in taking risks, but he was not crazy. I knew the suspicions (Braden being Cooper), too. But I liked Ted. We had conversations, such as when Ted would talk about how he served with the 101st Airborne in Bastogne. It wouldn't surprise me one bit if Ted was DB Cooper... Ted would be one of the few to make the jump with confidence.

Author's note: The defense of Bastogne, Belgium during the Battle of the Bulge was a heroic event and earned the 101st Airborne a unit citation from General Eisenhower.

Tom continued: "Ted had the technical skills, the personality, and the psychological make-up (to be Cooper)."

However, some of the comments I received from Braden's SOG buddies were quite harsh. Jim Hetrick, the 1-1 on Braden's RT Colorado and now the leader of the national Special Operations Association, was scathing: "I don't like the man. I have no use for the man—no respect for the man—and he came close to getting us whacked by doing a lot of dumb-assed stuff."

Jim said that he knew Ted long after the time of Duncan, whom Hetrick doesn't care for either. "He's (Duncan) not welcomed around here or with the SOG guys—he's a real bullshit artist."

As for Braden, Hetrick said Ted was just out for himself, and was dangerous in the field. "He was a piss-poor leader," Hetrick said. "We did a lot of trail-walking," which Jim described as non-purposeful roaming in the jungle that exposed the unit to enemy fire instead of staying safe in a concealed, observatory position.

"I disliked the man tremendously," Hetrick said one more time.

Hetrick also said that when RT Colorado came back from a mission, Braden would go to Saigon alone for the debriefing, unlike all the other recon teams that would debrief together. "He'd fly back in a CIA airplane and it would waggle its wings to let us know that Braden was back and that we'd have to go down and pick him up."

Hetrick said that Braden liked to "hang with the embassy-types" and that he often wore a short-sleeved white shirt and tie, and would "hang in the CIA bar in Saigon," reportedly the Caravelle. "He could have been building deep-cover. Who knows?" said Hetrick. "You can make up any story about Ted Braden and it might just be true."

After Ted disappeared, Hetrick said that another SOG vet saw Braden sitting four rows ahead on a train in Thailand. He said Braden turned at one point and looked the guy straight in the eye but never acknowledged him.

"Maybe Braden was running drugs," Hetrick speculated, and described a more criminally-minded soldier than that of any other SOG trooper. Hetrick said that just prior to Ted's vanishing act, Braden was charged with "the murder of an RFP" (local Vietnamese police officer) in Hue and was placed under house arrest. According to Hetrick, Braden was subsequently transferred out of SOG into another unit but was eventually absorbed back into SOG.

Prior to that incident, Hetrick said that their commanding officer, Colonel "Bull" Simons, had begun to suspect that Braden was falsifying his after-action reports so he assigned a Navy Seal to "run" in RT Colorado. Hetrick said that the Seal, reported to be Gary Shadduck, proved Braden's accounts were false, and Ted was discredited.

In addition, Hetrick said that Braden was rumored to have passed a lot of bad checks before he left Vietnam. Further, Hetrick described Braden as highly provocative and argumentative, even violent. He said that Braden once spit in the face of the company commander, and the two had to be physically separated. "He was bad news when he was drinking,' said Hetrick. "I know. I used to be a drinker myself, but Braden was different. He'd get squirrelly. He was a wild man when he was drinking."

Hetrick continued. "He (Braden) was a crazy man. One of my friends was surprised to see me still alive after we had been away from camp for awhile—he was so sure Braden was going to get me killed."

Lastly, "I don't think Ted Braden was DB Cooper," Hetrick said. "He didn't look at all like the sketches I saw of DB Cooper."

Much of what Hetrick told me is refuted by the 1-2 of RT Colorado, JD Bath. "Ted was good for the team, especially with the 'Yards.' We had a cohesive team," he told me in 2009. JD added that he thought the falling-out between Hetrick and Braden had to do with Ted's use of bribes to motivate the indigenous troops. Bath described Hetrick as doing things by the book, while Braden was "more creative."

"Ted made sure things got done," Bath said. "He had a flair for the unorthodox, but he always knew what he was doing and he always got us out safely." As for DB Cooper, JD feels Braden could be the skyjacker.

"Ted could have done it—the Cooper thing. He was certainly capable of doing it.... He planned things out and was very thorough and very calm. Ted Braden was a cool-headed team leader... he never panicked or got wild-eyed... He was one of the best team leaders that I served with in Vietnam, and I learned a lot from Ted."

Yet, JD saw a disturbing side of Braden, and told me that he once saw Ted point a weapon at his men during a melee with Vietnamese civilians in Hue, during which Braden also called JD a coward. "Ted suffered from combat fatigue, PTSD or whatever you want to call it. He was in combat too long," JD said.

But Bath also has a deep affection for Ted, and he said it was widespread. "Ted was one of the old hands, and you never heard any of the old hands talk down about Ted Braden. Most of them were in Korea, so they understood Ted. They'd tell me to tell Hetrick to tone it down about Ted."

In a neat twist, JD conducted a HALO jump recon with Billy Waugh in 1971, just before Billy retired. JD's picture is even in Waugh's book, as their team posed for a unit photo.

When Ted disappeared from Vietnam, he supposedly left directly from Saigon during a CIA debriefing immediately following his latest recon. When he exited the country, Ted adopted the identity of a recent SOG KIA, Joseph Edward Horner, according to his account in *Ramparts*. However Major Plaster says the only similarly-named deceased SOG trooper during that time period was a William Horner, a fact also confirmed by Bill Kendall.

The story picks up from there via accounts from Lieutenant Colonel (retired) Hank Bertsch, who told us about Ted's incarceration at Fort Dix. Lt Col. Bertsch contacted us after reading about our findings at the DropZone. Simply, Lt Colonel, then Captain, Bertsch was the Commanding Officer of the stockade at Dix and reports that Ted walked away from confinement when US Army Chief of Staff, Harold K Johnson specifically ordered an end to all court martial proceedings against Braden.

That revelation earned us more reports. A retired paratrooper named Allan Tyre told us about serving with Ted in Germany prior to his deployment to Vietnam, and revealed that Ted had a strong relationship—both personal and professional—with the renown General, then Colonel, John Singlaub.

Singlaub is notable for his participation in the OSS during WWII, the predecessor to the CIA, where he distinguished himself by parachuting into France in 1944 to assist the French *Maquis* fighters against the Germans. In Vietnam, according to John Plaster, Singlaub commanded MAC-V-SOG from 1966–1968. After the war he became a principle in the Iran-Contra affair.

"Singlaub was the only guy Ted socialized with freely, and he was personally warm towards him, too," Al told me in 2011 regarding what he observed in Germany between the two old friends.

This information triggered another response from Bertsch, who told us an intriguing story about Ted after he left Ft. Dix.

In August, 1967, I was released from active duty and began my Army reserve career. In late June or early July, 1974, while on annual training at Fort Jackson, SC, I met an active duty Army Major who was the Assistant Inspector General (IG) on the post. Since Fort Jackson also had an SPD (Special Processing Detachment) and prisoners in the stockade frequently complain to the IG, I struck up a conversation with him about unusual cases each of us had experienced with SPD personnel.

I described the Braden case without ever mentioning Braden by name and the Major said "you are talking about Ted Braden aren't you?"

I was initially stunned, but replied, 'Yes.'

The Major then said, 'You were had. Braden was a CIA plant in the Congo and he was recognized so he was arrested to save face with the Congolese government. The entire Fort Dix episode was staged as part of the cover up. I saw Braden in Vietnam last year and he is now a Sergeant Major (Grade E-9).'

Braden was a Sergeant First Class (Grade E-7) when he was discharged in 1967 with a bar to ever re-entering the military. Now, according to the Major at Fort Jackson, Braden by 1973 had not only reentered the Army but had been promoted twice.

At this point at least I had closure on what had transpired in the Braden case. With what the Major had told me at Fort Jackson everything about the Braden case seemed to make sense and I sort of filed the whole matter away.

In October, 2011 I again thought about the case and wondered whatever had become of Braden, so I did a Google search on 'Braden,' which led me to the DropZone website. Via that site I got linked to Bruce Smith, Al Tyre, and Tom Smith. In a phone conversation with Al Tyre he told me he saw Braden in a truck stop in Bowling Green, KY in 1973, and had a lengthy conversation with him. I was stunned because this directly contradicted what the Major at Fort Jackson had told me in 1974. Why the Major lied to me I do not know, but it just adds another element to the strangeness of the entire Braden case.

Tyre expanded upon the truck stop episode. He told us that he had met Braden serendipitously at a trucker's lunch counter on I-65 in Bowling Green, Kentucky. "The last guy in the world I expected to see was Ted Braden," said Tyre, who was on his way to an exercise at Fort Benjamin Harrison in Indiana. "I hadn't seen him since Special Forces training at Fort Bragg in 1964." Tyre says that he stopped for a meal and discovered Braden finishing his. Al said they talked about old times, and Ted freely discussed his life as a long-haul trucker—and did not seem unhappy with his fate.

But was he just a truck driver? Al sent me the following email in 2011:

> When I saw Ted at the truck stop, I was thinking in my mind that he was working for the CIA, and I was very careful what questions I asked. I am still not 100 percent sure that I was incorrect... At the time, the CIA was supposedly involved in bringing in drugs from South America by road and air into this country.

While I explored the trucking angle, Snowmman found a woman named Pauline Braden in western Pennsylvania. When I called, she told me that years before she had been married to a Vietnam vet named Ted Braden. Intriguingly, Pauline claimed that her Ted was arrested by the FBI in the early 1970s for his involvement in a trucking scam. Apparently Ted would abandon his rigs and claim they were hijacked, but in fact they were simply being robbed by accomplices. Pauline says that the feds told her Ted stole $250,000 worth of goods, but Ted seems to have been released shortly after the FBI visit.

So, did Ted get a pass on this crime because he had a "get-out-of-jail-free card" from his SOG work, or was he part of a sting operation for law enforcement? As for being DB Cooper, Pauline told me between coughs and gasps for breath: "Honestly, I did... think he could be... him. I remember thinking that... at the time it happened."

Searching further, Snow and I were able to track Braden to Stroudsburg, PA, and found a DUI conviction for a driver named Ted B. Braden in nearby White Haven. Lastly, this Ted Baden died in 2007 in Stroudsburg. However, was Ted Braden the Pennsy trucker also the same Ted Braden that ran recon as RT Colorado's 1-0? Snow and I struggled to confirm this conclusively.

We continued to pursue Pauline and her kids from the rural community of Ellsworth, Pennsylvania down to their new homes in central Florida, but we were unsuccessful in contacting them.

Nevertheless, in 2013 we finally obtained a complete set of Ted B Braden's military DD-214 forms, replete with social security numbers. Thus, we were able to confirm that the Ted B Braden who ran recon in Vietnam was also the Ted B Braden who died in Stroudsburg.

Rest in Peace, Ted.

Chapter 27

The CIA and MKULTRA

The exploration of the Vietnam War as a source for suspects also reveals other intriguing elements, particularly the pervasive role of the CIA. Since SOG ops were financed directly by the CIA, having a SOG veteran commit the Cooper skyjacking may have triggered a CIA request to the FBI to derail the Norjak investigation and prevent the world from learning about the CIA's funding of combat troops throughout Southeast Asia.

At the very least, SOG operations "across the fence" put the government in a precarious political position. If DB Cooper was a SOG vet, he might have been too problematic to bring to justice.

Digging further, we find the possibility that soldiers' capabilities were enhanced with pharmaceuticals, such as amphetamines. During some of my conversations with SOG troopers, I caught inferences that some of the guys running recon took drugs to remain hyper-vigilant. Would the military seek to keep this information hidden from public view?

Along those lines, historians are giving us a broader view of the use of amphetamines in combat. The following is a distillation of the history of meth from the "Foundation for a Drug-Free World" and "meth-kills".org:

Amphetamine was first made in 1887 in Germany and methamphetamine, more potent and easy to make, was developed in Japan in 1919. The crystalline powder was soluble in water, making it a perfect candidate for injection.

Methamphetamine went into wide use during World War II, when both sides used it to keep troops awake. High doses were given to Japanese Kamikaze pilots before their suicide missions. After World War II, intravenous meth abuse in Japan reached epidemic proportions due to the fact that the Japanese military had large amounts of the drug stockpiled and had made it available to the public.

The United States military has used amphetamine in every war since World War II. In the Vietnam War, American soldiers used more amphetamine than the rest of the world did during World War II.

Hence, if drugs were valuable for combat, what else was utilized to enhance the fighting abilities of soldiers that might need to be kept secret? Could mind-control, such as the behavioral conditioning processes of MKULTRA, play a role in preparing soldiers for combat, such as diminishing their fear. Could it also play a role in preparing a soldier for special missions, such as stealing an airplane? Would all of this have to be protected from public scrutiny?

For those not familiar with MKULTRA (pronounced M-K Ultra), it was a clandestine CIA and military research program from WW II until the 1970s, and its mission was to develop mind control techniques akin to those popularized in the "Manchurian Candidate" movies. Specifically, MKULTRA was based in Fort Detrick, Maryland and employed surgical, pharmaceutical and clinical techniques to gain control over another's mind, mood and behavior.

Mind-control is crazy stuff, but it's real. MKULTRA was a top-secret CIA operation that was on-going during the same time period as Norjak. In fact, MKULTRA was a huge clandestine operation, and the purported goal was to learn the secrets of brain-washing techniques endured by captured American soldiers during the Korean War. However, the genesis of MKULTRA was probably in WWII as an effort to develop more effective interrogation techniques.

MKULTRA was purportedly shut down by Congress in the 1970s after congressional hearings revealed a host of nasty truths, such as the rampant abuse of test subjects, many of whom were psychiatric patients seeking legitimate help.

"Treatments," such as sleep deprivation, electroshock, and the dispensing of dangerous chemical cocktails like LSD and other mind-scramblers were commonplace. These processes were conducted by MKULTRA's nominal leader, Dr. Ewen Cameron, at the nefarious Allan Memorial Institute in Montreal, and many other psychiatric centers across the United States. Afterwards, Cameron went on to become the president of the American Psychiatric Association.

These kinds of abuses by the medical community have been confirmed by psychiatrist Colin Ross in his searing account of official malfeasance, *The CIA Doctors—Human Rights Violations by American Psychiatrists*. In a follow-up book, *Military Mind Control—A Story of Trauma and Recovery,* Ross describes how torture, rape, and sexual abuse were allegedly used to fracture a target's mind, making them malleable to their minders. Fortunately, Ross also delivers an inspiring account of how he aids those traumatized by MKULTRA programs.

Supporting Ross' charges is Cathy O'Brien, who details in *Tranceformation of America* how she was raped and physically abused by her father and trusted members of her community in an orchestrated efforts by MKULTRA to gain control of her personality. The goal, O'Brien says, was to transform her into a CIA courier who could deliver messages in one persona, and after the mission have her personality switched back without any recall of her previous actions. Therefore, if she was ever caught she would not be able to reveal her activities or contacts to her captors. Additionally, O'Brien testified before Congress as part of their investigation of MKULTRA in the mid-1970s, helping to put an end to this terrible excess of government power.

Although incredibly harmful and violent, MKULTRA was a huge program for much of its existence, encompassing 6 percent of the CIA's budget, as reported in John Marks' *The Search for the Manchurian Candidate: The CIA and Mind Control.*

Yet, despite its sordid and covert nature, MKULTRA entered the cultural landscape in two famous movies, "The Manchurian Candidate" in 1962 starring Frank Sinatra, and a remake in 2004 starring Denzel Washington. The Hollywood treatments revolve around psychological, surgical and pharmaceutical efforts to create a mind-controlled presidential candidate. However, the term "Manchurian Candidate" is also widely used to describe the development of intelligence operatives whose inhibitions can be switched-off to perform any infamous deed, such as a political assassination.

In addition, author Naomi Klein in *Shock Doctrine* shows that the current usage of water-boarding and psychological torture during interrogations at Abu Ghraib and Gitmo started with MKULTRA.

Although the military was ordered to stop its MKULTRA activities in the 1970s, they continue, apparently, by morphing into new ventures, growing beyond sexual abuse and mind control. Tragically, the level of sophistication has also evolved. Journalist and documentary film maker Jon Ronson details in *The Men Who Stare at Goats* how the military is now attempting to weaponization of mind-over-matter techniques. These efforts include biofeedback processes and other aspects of the science of consciousness, and Ronson claims they have been on-going since 1979. Specifically, Ronson describes a secretive unit at Fort Bragg that endeavored to kill their enemies by envisioning them dead. To practice, these soldiers stared at goats and mentally focused on stopping the animal's heart until the animal expired. Sadly, Ronson reports they have been successful.

Reportedly, the military has been keenly interested in these kinds of capabilities, and another one of the reported goals of these new program was to create super-warriors. Ronson reports that the military was utilizing exercises similar to the Goat program to see if soldiers could train their minds to heal their wounds in battle, thereby reducing the need for medics. Similar programs existed to train soldiers to need less food and survive for longer periods of time in combat. With all of this on-going in our military, is it that far-fetched to consider that MKULTRA and DB Cooper are connected somehow? Could the possible use of MKULTRA in Vietnam trigger a governmental white-wash? Consider: was DB Cooper an MKULTRA graduate and ordered to hijack a plane for some political reason, such as raising the public's awareness of inadequate safety aboard airplanes? Or were groups of individuals blitzed by MKULTRA to form getaway teams or be Cooper copycats, or even making people believe that they were DB Cooper? Could some of the 922 confessees and the alleged 20 or so Cooper copycats be part of some kind of Manchurian Candidate scenario? Or are all of the confessees woefully needy people, and the copycats are just run-of-the-mill wacko skyjackers?

Yes, the idea that anyone was brainwashed into hijacking a plane is highly improbable. But could some of the Cooper Confessees, such as Duane Weber or Barb Dayton, have been the subject of laboratory efforts to see if they could be made to believe they were DB Cooper? Yes, this may all be wild speculation, but let's probe more deeply into the candidates' psychological make-up and see if we can gain any hint of a link between DB Cooper and mind-control.

Starting with Cooper-esque skyjacker Richard McCoy, Richard Tosaw writes in, *DB Cooper—Dead or Alive?* that McCoy had a "mental breakdown with no warning whatsoever" in the fall of 1971, just months before his skyjacking.

Tosaw says that McCoy was admitted to a psychiatric hospital and determined to be suffering from "a delayed stress syndrome, confusion and disorientation," presumably from his two tours in Vietnam. Yet, he was back at his normal routine within days, casting doubt upon a diagnosis of PTSD, which usually has long-lasting effects and is resistant to treatment. If not PTSD, was he receiving a dose of MKULTRA? Further, Tosaw writes that McCoy's buddy, Robert Van Ieperen, is at a loss to explain why McCoy did the skyjacking. Van Ieperen told Tosaw:

> It couldn't have been for the money, because that was never important to him. I think he saw it as an adventure, like it was a personal challenge. He enjoyed the excitement of testing his skill, and the more dangerous the situation the better he liked it.

More confounding, Tosaw writes that at the time of his skyjacking McCoy was shouldering a heavy load of law enforcement classes at Brigham Young University, and had already taken a qualifying test for the Utah State Patrol, scoring first, state-wide.

Are these inconsistencies a sign of mind-control, or just another tragic example of a warrior wrestling with demons brought home from Vietnam?

Another behavioral clue that pops up with the Confessee-Copycat Crew is that many of them had serious relationship and behavioral issues: Dayton experienced both genders, Christiansen harbored runaway boys, while Gossett had five wives and Weber had six or seven—his widow Jo doesn't know for sure—plus a common-law marriage to make a possible total of nine marital unions.

Further, many held multiple jobs. Dayton had over 150 and others had disjointed careers. Most pulled macho military stints, knew planes, and were paratroopers. Also, several were criminally minded: Weber had an extensive record, and McCoy escaped twice from federal custody after his skyjacking conviction, and died in a shootout with the FBI. Plus, the Formans tell us that Barb fantasized about performing the perfect crime.

A closer look at Barb Dayton's clinical record gives us a clue as to what may be going on. Specifically, Dayton had more than a sex-change operation—she also picked up a new personality. As a man, Dayton was a brawling tough-guy, but as a woman she was a quiet, witty librarian. Better yet, she could switch between the two personalities as if she was trained. Ron Forman says he saw her adopt her macho masculine persona at will. Did the CIA teach her how? Seeking answers, I asked Barb Dayton's daughter, Rena Ruddell, if she had any inkling of her father being a subject of a secret mind-control program.

"No," she said, but added that her father and her Uncle Billie, Bobby's brother, often went off to Mexico on prolonged vagabonding trips. "Maybe something happened to them in Mexico," she added. "My cousins sure think so, plus, Billie became schizophrenic later in life and was obsessed with UFOs. Maybe that's a connection."

As for Ted Braden, how did he manage twenty-three consecutive months of covert jungle warfare in Vietnam, Laos and Cambodia? Psychological enhancements? Remember, Braden was widely described as mentally unstable by his SOG troopers, especially his 1-2, JD Bath, and the 1-1, Jim Hetrick, but he always brought his men back from the field. Can a truly crazy person do that?

Chapter 28

Findings from the Richard McCoy Investigation

Perhaps the most troubling information that suggests MKULTRA-like influences were present in Norjak comes from Calame and Rhodes in their book, *DB Cooper—The Real McCoy*. To begin, Calame and Rhodes are convinced that Richard McCoy was DB Cooper performing a second skyjacking in April 1972, but their subsequent exploration of McCoy reveals a plethora of disturbing information about the DB Cooper investigation that implicates MKULTRA or something akin to it.

At the top of the list is their concern about the behavior of FBI agents involved in the Cooper evidence retrieval in Reno. According to Rhodes, a combined team of FBI agents from the Las Vegas and Reno offices, plus hundreds of local police, met 305 in Reno. After the plane landed the feds quickly ascertained that Cooper was gone.

But something very strange happened next—no one seems to be able to recall exactly who did what. Some agents on the primary evidence retrieval couldn't remember vital details when Rhodes interviewed them in the 1980s, such as who did the fingerprint gathering. Specifically, Rhodes found that some FBI agents thought the fingerprint dusting was performed by the Reno City Police Department and not the FBI, even though the feds had jurisdiction and better resources.

Further, Rhodes writes that the FBI crime lab in Washington, DC found the Cooper fingerprints too smudged to be of any value. Additionally, the FBI failed to retrieve any of the in-flight magazines that Cooper was suspected of handling during the hours Flight 305 circled Sea-Tac. Without the magazines or any other back-up material to examine for latent prints, the FBI was left without a vital body of evidence. How could so many agents botch the biggest case of their careers? According to Calame, whispers flew throughout field offices nationally gossiping how badly the Reno group screwed-up.

Seeking answers, Rhodes interviewed the four agents responsible for the evidence retrieval, Jack Ricks, John Norris, Alf Stousland and the aforementioned Las Vegas SAC Harold "Red" Campbell. Rhodes discovered that the recall of these agents were at odds with one another—Ricks remembers Stousland dusting for fingerprints, while John Norris said the Reno City Police Department did the dusting.

More disturbing, Rhodes found the memories of these key Reno agents to be profoundly impaired. When Rhodes asked them to recall what they did on the evening of November 24, 1971, he writes that Ricks, Norris, Stousland and Campbell acted **"as if (they were) victims of some strange posthypnotic suggestion."** (Emphasis added).

Specifically, not one of the FBI agents remembered retrieving, or even seeing, the clip-on tie and tie-pin. Yet, the tie is the most dramatic piece of evidence DB Cooper left on the airplane. Calame also reports that Tina Mucklow had *no* memory of the tie when he spoke to her in the 1980s. Therefore, we now have the eerie circumstance that *no one* who saw or dealt with DB Cooper's tie can *now* remember a thing about it.

In addition, Cooper's tie and clasp were not included in the initial evidence packet from Reno, but were sent to Seattle four days later. So, where was it? Did someone else pick up the tie?

Additionally, members of the larger FBI team outside the aircraft, such as perimeter security, had difficulty recalling exactly what they did that night. As Rhodes described it, the agents weren't purposefully forgetful but rather their minds seemed fuzzy. Rhodes was aghast, and interviewed the agents on two additional occasions in 1989 to see if their memories improved. They didn't. So, was the cognitive dysfunction of the federal team in Reno caused by hypnosis or technological means? Did their brains get blitzed by MKULTRA?

Further, Larry Carr told me that the FBI had sixty sets of fingerprints from Reno, but this does not jibe with Calame and Rhodes, who say the FBI/Reno police collected only eleven sets. So, where did the extra fifty come from, and when?

Sadly, I have been unsuccessful in speaking with Rhodes directly about these matters, and it seems that he is not talking to others, since even Geoffrey Gray hasn't been able to make contact.

Lastly, the evidentiary foul-ups continue to this very day. In 2009, Larry Carr confirmed that the eight cigarette butts disappeared from FBI custody in Las Vegas.

Beyond the disturbing history of Reno, there is the perplexing role of Richard McCoy in the DB Cooper saga. First, Calame and Rhodes believe that McCoy was Cooper, but the facts are stacked against that conclusion—McCoy was 29, too short, and had blue eyes. But McCoy did hijack an airplane akin to DB Cooper, so the question lingers if McCoy learned to do so from Cooper.

Plus, two over-arching questions hover over Norjak: first, is the possibility of an extraction team for the getaway, secondly, was there any coordination among the copycats?

Skyjacker Richard McCoy is a prime candidate for both scenarios. McCoy is one of an estimated twenty Cooper copycats—hijackers who performed their heist using the methods employed by DB Cooper—and McCoy is one of five known skyjackers to have parachuted successfully for their getaway.

I do not believe that Richard McCoy was DB Cooper, but the McCoy story suggests he might have been involved in Norjak in *some* manner. During the FBI's investigation of McCoy's April 1972 hijacking, he was discovered to have been in Las Vegas during the time of the Cooper skyjacking in November 1971, and later lied about it to the FBI. Here is the time line that Calame's team developed for Richard McCoy:

On Tuesday, November 23, 1971, he attended his last class at Brigham Young University before the holiday recess. The next day, Wednesday, November 24, the day of the Cooper skyjacking, McCoy was scheduled to be on duty with his National Guard unit, but wasn't. Instead, McCoy was far south of Provo, buying gas in Cedar City, Utah, which is 182 miles northeast of Las Vegas. The following day, November 25—Thanksgiving Day—McCoy bought additional gas at a Power Thrust station adjacent to McCarran airport in Las Vegas. Then, at 10:41 pm on Thanksgiving night he made a collect call from the Tropicana Hotel in Las Vegas to his home in Provo.

Hence, the burning question is: why did McCoy travel to Las Vegas on the Wednesday before Thanksgiving, and appearing there on the holiday itself? Calame wondered if McCoy was actually catching a flight to Portland on Wednesday to perform his *first* skyjacking—the DB Cooper caper—and using Las Vegas as an intermediary travel point, returning there on Thanksgiving Day on his way home.

Disturbingly, the Seattle FBI doesn't accept these findings and believes that McCoy was not in Las Vegas. Rather, they claim McCoy was home with his family for Thanksgiving, refuting their colleagues from Salt Lake City. Seattle has never explained their perspective.

But Calame adds to the muddle by not asking McCoy directly what he was doing in Las Vegas on the days in question. Further, Calame and his team never asked McCoy about the DB Cooper skyjacking for reasons that are insufficiently explained in the book.

More perplexing, if McCoy was simply abandoning his family on Thanksgiving to go gambling in Sin City, why not tell the feds? In addition, why is the Seattle FBI so unaccepting of Calame's findings if the only reason for McCoy to be in Las Vegas was to go honky-tonking? Lastly, if Richard McCoy was DB Cooper, or connected in some way to Norjak, why didn't he mention it as leverage to work a better sentencing deal after his conviction in 1972?

Nevertheless, Calame's team was unable to determine if McCoy actually flew to-and-from PDX at Thanksgiving since the airlines servicing Las Vegas' McCarran airport destroyed their flight manifests after four months, in this case, March 1972. More puzzling, Calame's team discovered that McCoy had another mysterious visit to Las Vegas on the evening of November 2, 1971, and was absent from his family for several days. Calame speculated that McCoy was flying round-trip to Portland on a scouting mission.

Digging more deeply, Calame and Rhodes found many similarities between the Cooper skyjacking and McCoy's hijacking of United Flight 855, finally concluding that McCoy *was* DB Cooper, and doing a second hijacking in April 1972. Many don't believe that hypothesis because of the aforementioned physical discrepancies, but Calame and Rhodes showed that McCoy performed a near-carbon-copy of Cooper, using methods identical to Cooper in his November skyjacking or demonstrating refinements.

Here are a few of the Cooperesque aspects of the Richard McCoy skyjacking: McCoy sat in virtually the same seat as Cooper—giving him the same tactical advantages for crowd control and supervising the ransom transfer and refueling. Also, McCoy demanded that the refuel trucks approach the 727 in the same manner as Cooper.

Additionally, McCoy used pre-written notes like Cooper and demanded their return. They both refrained from any direct contact with the cockpit crew, and used a flight attendant as an intermediary. Like Cooper, McCoy used the same phrase, "No funny stuff," and both wore wrap-around sunglasses.

Cooper and McCoy both used arcane aviation terminology, i.e.: "interphone" instead of intercom, "air stairs" instead of ramps, and they wrote "azimuth" in notes to the cockpit. Also, both groups of passengers were released in a common fashion, and the two skyjackers kept one flight attendant on-board, along with the cockpit crew.

Both hijacked their planes during a holiday period—Cooper on the eve of Thanksgiving and McCoy just after Easter—and both demanded four parachutes, even though McCoy carried his own on board. In fact, McCoy used the four chutes to decoy the feds, as he correctly anticipated they would contain tracking devices. As a result, several federal chase planes went on a fruitless search over the wilds of Nevada when McCoy chucked them out of his aircraft, clearly learning from Cooper's experience of having F-106s tail him through Washington and Oregon.

Another improvement over Cooper was McCoy's selection of a longer trip than Cooper's short hop from Portland to Seattle. McCoy switched 855's original destination of LA to San Francisco to thwart any pre-arranged sabotage of the refueling and ransom transfer, and gave the FBI plenty of time to procure the chutes and money before landing. It also kept the passengers in a calmer mental state rather than circling over Sea-Tac for two hours.

One more refinement was McCoy's asking for more money—$500,000—but in hundreds rather than twenties, which resulted in a similar weight. Besides the bigger sum, McCoy also carried the necessary rings and harnesses to attach the duffel bag he brought aboard for the money.

In addition, McCoy knew how to deploy the aft stairs, unlike Cooper. "McCoy did basically the same (as Cooper), but was better prepared," Rhodes writes. McCoy was certainly a crafty skydiver, too, and was able to evade detection on his way down even though 200 cops were looking for him. Shockingly, he landed about four miles from his home.

At this point, however, the McCoy caper fell apart and does not reflect the savvy nature of DB Cooper. McCoy's hijacking took longer than expected and he was late for his rendezvous with his getaway driver, his wife. As a result, she had decided to return home and McCoy landed alone in the scrub. He stashed his loot and chute in a highway culvert, and after walking to a nearby soda shop he found a young man willing to drive him home. The next day, McCoy and his wife returned to the area and retrieved the money and chute.

However, they were unprepared for the next chapter of their hijacking—they didn't know where to stash the money—so they shoved it haphazardly into a stove pipe in their home. Further, McCoy's cover story to family and friends didn't convince people sufficiently, and a friend of McCoy's from the Utah National Guard alerted the FBI. Calame and his team raided McCoy's home, quickly found the money, and arrested him.

McCoy was an unlikely skyjacker. He was a Mormon Sunday school teacher besides studying law enforcement at Brigham Young University, and applying for a job with the Utah State Patrol. Additionally, he was a helicopter pilot for the Utah Air National Guard, and ironically flew a reconnaissance chopper in a post-hijacking surveillance of his own LZ. Calame and Rhodes report McCoy had taken up skydiving in the months prior to the skyjacking. But how much did he have to learn about diving out of a 727 once DB Cooper demonstrated its potentials?

Essentially, how did McCoy learn all of Cooper's hijacking nuances? Did McCoy uncover all the details of the Cooper skyjacking from newspaper accounts? It's possible, but in perusing the newspapers of the day I have never seen specificity on all the fine details of the Cooper job—the note-taking, seat selection, and refueling positioning. Although it is possible that McCoy learned Cooper's tricks by astute research, or spent lots of time brainstorming in skydiving circles, there is no record that McCoy did so, and Calame does not report finding a "DB Cooper Skyjacking Study Guide."

Investigating further, Calame and Rhodes found that McCoy was suicidal in the fall of 1971, adding to the psychiatric history that Tosaw provided concerning a PTSD-like breakdown requiring a hospitalization. As for his experiences in Vietnam, McCoy served two very different tours of duty. In 1965, he was a member of the Special Forces and was an infantry instructor with ARVN troops, a similar role to the one being performed by Ted Braden at the same time. However, it is unknown if they ever met.

In 1967, McCoy returned to Vietnam as a helicopter pilot with American forces, where he served with distinction and received a medal for rescuing survivors from two chopper crashes. By the time of his second deployment he was married, and when he hijacked Flight 855 in 1972, he had two kids and his sister-in-law also lived with the family, so the domestic scene was crowded and tense. McCoy explained his skyjacking to authorities as a response to domestic pressures, but his best friend suggested to Tosaw that it was done for psychological reasons, basically the thrill of it all.

After his trial, McCoy was sentenced to forty-five years in prison. However, he escaped twice from federal custody and after his second scoot he was on the lam for several months. Finally, in November 1974, McCoy was killed in a gun battle with the FBI in Virginia Beach, Virginia, after which Bernie Rhodes purports that the agent who shot McCoy, Nick O'Hara, proclaimed: "When I shot Richard McCoy, I shot DB Cooper."

I called Nick O'Hara in 2013 to shed some light on these elements. He was quite open, and when I asked about McCoy in Las Vegas, Nick suggested that I talk with retired agents from Salt Lake City. "They know more about that aspect than I do. They're really into the McCoy connection," he said. O'Hara even offered to contact some of his retired colleagues from Salt Lake City. When I didn't hear from O'Hara for several weeks, I called him back, and he said that he hadn't been able to reach any of his buddies.

Similarly, when I last spoke with Russ Calame in 2009, he was still convinced that Richard McCoy was DB Cooper. However, most researchers dismiss the McCoy-was-Cooper hypothesis as McCoy didn't match the physical descriptions of DB Cooper.

But, what was the relationship between Richard McCoy and DB Cooper? Clearly, McCoy knew a lot about the Cooper hijacking, with details far beyond, arguably, what would usually found in newspapers. So, did McCoy know Cooper? Did DB Cooper teach McCoy how to hijack a 727? Or did a third-party tutor both individuals?

Or is part of Calame's and Rhodes' hypothesis partially true? Was Richard McCoy part of Norjak—but as a member of DB Cooper's getaway team—and was returning to Provo via Las Vegas on Thanksgiving Day as Calame has proven? This raises, again, the question of how DB Cooper got away with all his gear, and suggests that there might have been a ground team assisting Cooper—providing transportation and medical attention besides picking up all the stuff DB ditched from 305.

We have no concrete information indicating that Cooper had a getaway team, but we do have some tantalizing circumstantial evidence. McCoy had at least $8,000 in his bank account that was unaccountable, and he used it to take his family on a vacation to see relatives in North Carolina in late 1971. Did McCoy win it in Las Vegas over the Thanksgiving weekend? Or was it payment for being part of DB Cooper's getaway team?

In addition, we have an intriguing story offered by "Jake" in Geoffrey Gray's *Skyjack*. Gray states that as he was writing *Skyjack* a mysterious figure contacted him at *New York* magazine, claiming that he was part of a trained team of "transporters" awaiting Cooper on the ground. Jake says he is a former freelance covert operative who was one of five guys assigned to pick up a "middle-aged Caucasian male" in the environs of Amboy, Washington on the night of November 24, 1971.

Jake told Geoffrey the expected extraction point was to be along the Buncombe Hollow Road, off of Cedar Creek Road in Amboy. The former is the main road along the southern shore of Lake Merwin, on the opposite side of the lake from the Ariel Tavern, and presumably the bright lights atop the Merwin Dam would be homing beacons to the incoming skyjacker.

Jake also told Geoffrey that prior to his assignment he had been imprisoned in Walla Walla state penitentiary on fraud charges, and his transporter services would earn him his release. Gray writes that he has not been able to prove Jake's pick-up plan, but he does confirm that the individual that he knows as Jake was in Walla Walla on a fraud conviction and had been "furloughed" the day before the skyjacking, November 23, 1971.

If Jake's story is legit, then a slew of questions follow: Who were the other transporters? Was McCoy one of them? How were the five transporters selected? Did they work together in Vietnam? Were they a SOG extraction team? Was Norjak one big SOG op? Was Ted Braden involved? Did McCoy know Braden from Vietnam back in 1965? Plus, we have Duane Weber claiming that he was Cooper's ground man. Was Duane part of it, or hypnotized to think that he was? Were any of them involved with MKULTRA?

The matrix of mind-control, CIA, and SOG is heady stuff, and our means of unraveling it are meager. Yet, the gravitational pull of these dynamics draws our investigation in that direction. Shedding a glimmer of light on the role of the CIA in the Cooper case is Ralph Himmelsbach. He writes in *NORJAK* that Northwest Orient Airlines learned their 727s could be flown with the aft stairs deployed from the CIA and Boeing and that information comes from the CIA who used 727s to drop material and agents in Southeast Asia.

Further, I received anecdotal accounts from SOG troopers that suggest the CIA used 727s extensively in operations over North Vietnam instead of their regular Air America prop craft because the 727s had a better chance of escaping the North Vietnamese MIG-21s when they had to bail on a mission and *didi-mau* their way home.

Similarly, former World Airways pilot Everett Johnson told me that he heard a story from his World co-pilot, Tom Sailor, claiming that Sailor had flown many covert commando operations over both North Vietnam and Laos during the war using 727s. Johnson said that Sailor had made this claim while they were conducting CIA surveillance missions in Yemen with 727s during the post-Vietnam period.

Granted, this is a paper-thin connection, and despite many inquiries I have nothing concrete to report on any direct use of MKULTRA techniques with any suspects or confessees. Not even Dr Ross, the foremost psychiatrist studying the deleterious effects of MKULTRA, says he knows of any connection to DB Cooper.

But the actions of the copycats might tell us something, because McCoy was a very smart one. How did McCoy learn the tricks of the hijacking trade, and were other copycats similarly schooled? We will explore that issue in the next chapter.

Before that, though, I would like to add one last comment from Russ Calame. It is perhaps the sharpest insight I ever heard expressed by an FBI agent regarding DB Cooper:

> The longer this Cooper thing goes on without being resolved, the wilder the theories are going to get. That's how it goes with these kinds of investigations.

Chapter 29

Copycats

Besides the value gained by piercing the veils of conspiracy, we need to look more closely at the copycats if for no other reason than some in the FBI, such as Ralph Himmelsbach, consider DB Cooper to be one.

"You have to remember that Cooper was a copycat," he told me when I visited him at his home in 2011.

Himmelsbach claimed that the first skyjacker to demand a ransom and parachute was not Cooper, but a fellow he called "Gaylord."

Ralph is incorrect, though. The first skydiving extortionist was actually named Paul Cini, and he hijacked an Air Canada flight out of Calgary, Alberta two weeks before Cooper's caper.

But, was DB Cooper really a copycat of Paul Cini? Possibly, but DB Cooper's skyjacking established the template of how to do a skyjacking successfully: select a 727, use a parachute to escape, and jump into a rural area. Hence, the skyjackers that followed are known as Cooper copycats, not Cini wannabees.

Himmelsbach also claimed there were up to twenty Cooperesque skyjackers, which opens the door for thinking there might have been a collective effort at work.

"With each new skyjacking, the skyjackers improved their techniques," Ralph said, echoing fellow FBI agent Russ Calame's evaluation of McCoy's effort.

Himmelsbach also shared Calame's interest in McCoy.

"We did look at McCoy in the Cooper case, but he (McCoy) was in Las Vegas when the Cooper skyjacking took place," Ralph declared.

But Himmelsbach is not correct when he characterizes each succeeding skyjacking as a refinement over the previous one. Most of the Cooper copycats bungled the job—one even tried to use a 707, which doesn't have an aft stairs.

But there were improvements in some hijackings, so the bigger question remains—how did the advancements occur? Did every hijacker simply do his homework by studying the news media? Did the newspaper reveal that much detail? Or was something else going on, such as an orchestration or coaching of the skyjackers—at least a few of them? To answer that, we need to take a close look at the copycats.

First, how many were there? Himmelsbach has stated there were up to twenty Cooper copycats, and other published accounts say a dozen or so. After diligent researching I have been able to find fourteen.

Most authors talk about the five primary copycats: McCoy, Robb Heady, Martin McNally, Richard LaPoint, and Frederick Hahneman, all of whom made it to the ground safely. Even McNally, who had never parachuted before, was successful, which belies the proposition that the Cooper jump was too dangerous.

But the essential questions remains: how did they learn to be a skyjacker, and were they a group? Did any of them know DB Cooper or Paul Cini? Were they schooled in any manner? Lastly, did any of them have a ground team?

Frankly, there is not enough information publicly available to make any determination on those questions, and it reveals some of the limitations of open-sourced sleuthing. We just don't have enough muscle to unearth these kinds of facts.

Nevertheless, this line of inquiry received a shot of adrenaline from an unexpected source: the Washington State Historical Museum in Tacoma. In 2013, they opened a major exhibit on DB Cooper, and mentioned that DB Cooper had thirteen copycats. I asked the WSHM to provide me with a list of these Cooperesque hijackers, and they gave me a few names I had never seen anywhere else.

Their primary source was a website called "Skyjacker of the Day—a Hundred Days, A Hundred Skyjackers," a site originally developed to build interest in the June 2013 launch of the book, *The Skies Belong to Us—Love and Terror in the Golden Age of Hijackings,* by Brendan Koerner (skyjackeroftheday.tumblr.com).

Koerner's book is an overview of the entire skyjacking phenomena, and is wrapped within a narrative of the hijacking of Western Flight 401, performed by two fugitives named Roger Holder and Cathy Kerkow. It grippingly includes a juicy romance, Black Panther politics and a dicey escape to Algiers.

But one of the most intriguing aspects of Koerner's work is showing how many skyjackings were occurring in the United States in the early 1970s—hundreds—and how they often overlapped, with multiple hijackings in one day and even involving the same airport. I was astonished to learn that one of the Cooper copycats, Robb Heady, hijacked his plane on the same day as Holder and Kerkow—and flew into San Francisco International as the others were leaving for Algeria!

The following is a list of what we know about *bona fide* copycats—the proviso being that a Cooper copycat has to demand money and use a parachute to escape.

Copycats

1. Paul Cini	Air Canada 812	11. 13. 71
2. DB Cooper	Northwest Orient 305	11. 24. 71
3. Everett Holt	Northwest Orient 734	12. 24. 71
4. Billy Hurst, Jr.	Braniff 38	1. 12. 72
5. Richard LaPoint*	Hughes Air West 800	1. 20. 72
6. Richard McCoy*	United 855	4. 7. 72
7. Stanley Spreck	Pacific Southwest 942	4. 9. 72
8. Frederick Hahneman*	Eastern 175	5. 5. 72
9. "Lomas"	Ecuatoriana de Aviacion	5. 22. 72
10. Robb Heady*	United 239	6. 2. 72
11. Martin McNally*	American 119	6. 23. 72
12. Daniel Carre	Hughes Airwest 775	6. 30. 72
13. Francis Goodell	Pacific Southwest 389	7. 6. 72
14. Melvin Fisher	American 633	7. 12. 72

Asterisk, "" indicates the skyjacker made it to the ground successfully. The rest were apprehended by the FBI or flight crews before they could jump, except for DB Cooper, whose fate is unknown.*

There were dozens of other extortive skyjackers, but they didn't jump. Some flew to Cuba or sat on a runway waiting for their money and a plane to the Middle East, so none are copycats by my definition.

Starting with **Paul Cini**, we have the following account provided via postings on the DZ, mostly in the form of newspaper clippings and an overview by DZ poster Farflung.

On November 13, 1971, eleven days before Cooper, Paul Cini boarded Air Canada Flight 812, a DC-8 flying from Calgary to Toronto. He carried a 12-gauge shotgun tucked under his black overcoat and a forty-pound box full of dynamite. Cini also toted a bag that contained a parachute.

Shortly after take-off, he pulled down a ski hat with holes poked through it for eye holes, flashed the 12-gauge and announced he was hijacking the plane. For emphasis, he fired a blast into a cabin partition, and disclosed the box of dynamite.

He demanded $1.5 million and declared that he wanted to go to Ireland. In the course of the hijacking he claimed he was a member of the IRA. While airborne, however, Cini demanded the flight be diverted to Great Falls, Montana, where he was given $50,000 in cash. Impulsively, he ordered the plane to depart before allowing any of the 115 passengers to leave. They then headed for Regina, Saskatchewan, but again, Cini changed his mind and ordered the plane back to Great Falls. This time, he let the passengers depart but kept the six crew members on board, who insisted on refueling.

The plane loaded approximately 7,000 gallons of fuel before Cini ordered the aircraft aloft for the third time. The pilot, Captain Vernon Ehmann, convinced Cini they needed more fuel so they set a course for Regina, again. Fifteen minutes after departing Great Falls, Captain Ehmann called Cini on the airphone to say he was coming back to talk.

Cini consented, but said that he wanted to don his parachute. Ehmann assured the hijacker that he wouldn't interfere. However, as Cini set down his shotgun to pick up his chute, Ehmann grabbed him and they wrestled. Then the purser, Philip Bonney, ran back with a fire axe and hit Cini over the head. They secured Cini and headed back to Great Falls. The whole ordeal lasted six hours.

Farflung's and the newspaper accounts say that the plane Cini hijacked was a DC-8, and he had ordered it to be flown at 3,000 ft with the rear emergency door opened. But the escape hatch on the DC-8 is located on the side of the fuselage, and as a result a skydiver enters the slipstream immediately. In addition, the opening is very small. Worse, the rear stabilizer wings are very low and have a nasty reputation for striking skydivers. Hence, the DC-8 is considered to be a dangerous jump platform, and Cini had a very dicey exit if he had gone.

Hence, DB Cooper's selection of a 727 two weeks later was considered a vast improvement. However, Geoffrey Gray stated on the Diane Rohm radio show that Cini hijacked a DC-9, which is comparable to a 727 and possesses an aft stairs system, along with dual rear engines and an elevated stabilizer.

Nonetheless, Cini was twenty-seven years old and employed as a delivery truck driver when he skyjacked his plane. He had lived previously in the United States, but had gone to Canada five years earlier to live with his parents. According to Michael Newton in his "Encyclopedia of Kidnappings," Paul Cini was sentenced to life imprisonment.

Compared to Cooper, Cini was a bumbling fool and it's hard to fathom any connection between the two skyjackers. But was he a MKULTRA subject? It is impossible to say without more information.

After **DB Cooper**, the next skyjacker was **Everett Holt**. On Christmas Eve, 1971 Holt boarded Northwest Airlines Flight 734, a 707, in Minneapolis and bound for Miami. He presented a pistol and said his suitcase was filled with dynamite. He was twenty-five years old and a dropout from Indiana University.

Holt demanded the plane be diverted to Chicago O'Hare International Airport. He wanted $300,000 and two parachutes.

How he planned to exit the 707, which has no rear stairway or hatch, is not known. Nevertheless, in Chicago he allowed all the passengers to leave except one, along with the three flight attendants. However, all the flight crew escaped, too, leaving Holt with an empty plane and his one hostage. The FBI then rushed him, blinding him with bright searchlights and foiling the skyjacking without incident. The gun was only loaded with blanks and the suitcase was devoid of any dynamite, indicating that Holt was not a serious criminal. Additionally, Holt was a practicing Quaker and reported to be "a nice guy."

"It certainly couldn't be the same kid," one family friend said. Holt was committed to a mental hospital and released about three years later, in May, 1975. Again, the comparison to Cooper or the copycats reveals nothing substantial other than mental illness, and Holt certainly was not an improvement over Cooper.

Next was **Billy Hurst, Jr.**, on January 12, 1972. From Listserve (listserve.com/2012/10/27/top-10-us-airline-hijackings-of-the-sixties) the following is known.

Hurst hijacked Braniff Flight 38 from Houston to Dallas. Like Cooper's plane, it was a 727. Hurst was armed with a .22-caliber pistol, and allowed all 94 passengers to deplane in Dallas. However, he held the seven crew members hostage, and demanded they fly to South America. He asked for $2 million, parachutes, a .357 Magnum pistol and jungle survival gear.

Hurst never jumped from the aircraft, though. Before takeoff he was distracted by the package containing the parachute and the .357 handgun, which had been modified so it could not be fired. Like the Holt hijack, the crew secretly fled the airplane. With no hostages left on the plane, the police stormed the aircraft and arrested Hurst without incident. Although Billy was a man with a long history of mental illness, he was sentenced to 20 years in prison. Again, only a psychological disorder connects Billy to a broader skyjacking profile, and no refinement in technique is evident.

A week later, January 20, 1972, **Richard LaPoint** hijacked Hughes Air West Flight 800. His plane was a DC-9, comparable to a 727, and contained an aft stair system.

DZ sleuth Farflung provides copious information, and says that LaPoint was a paratrooper. However, this claim is disputed by a Denver Post reporter named Kit Miniclier. Nevertheless, all agree that LaPoint, 23, hijacked a Hughes Airwest airliner flying from Las Vegas to Reno by showing a flight attendant his bag and declaring it contained a bomb. He demanded two chutes and a sky-diving helmet; however, he only wanted $50,000.

LaPoint released his 56 passengers and two flight attendants in Reno, and with the crew as hostages they took-off for Denver. LaPoint eventually jumped over northeastern Colorado.

Like Cooper, the conditions of LaPoint's jump were extreme and his clothing was minimal—he was wearing only a shirt, slacks and cowboy boots when he made his winter jump from 12,000 feet. So, the people who say that Cooper died because he was under-dressed must explain how LaPoint made it to the ground successfully.

LaPoint was unaware of the tracking devices the authorities had installed in his chute, so the F-111s trailing the plane picked up his signal. He landed in a snow-covered field nearly devoid of trees, and his brightly colored Air Force parachute was spotted easily by fixed-wing aircraft called into action. Hobbling in the snow due to an ankle sprain suffered in the landing, LaPoint surrendered to local sheriff deputies as they approached his position.

LaPoint was sentenced to forty years in prison, but served less than eight and was paroled to a halfway house near his home of Boston.

Miniclier also reported that LaPoint had just gotten out of Vietnam but had never jumped out of an airplane before. She wrote further that LaPoint seemed to have cognitive deficits and an explosive temper. Along those lines, Farflung reports that LaPoint had been a car thief prior to the skyjacking, and was well-known to local law enforcement.

Compared to Cooper, LaPoint's lack of sophistication is striking, but PTSD may be at play as the skyjacker was a Vietnam vet.

On April 7, 1972, we had **Richard McCoy.**

Two days later, on April 9, **Stanley Spreck** hijacked Pacific Southwest Airlines Flight 942, a 727 flying from Oakland to San Diego. Spreck, 31, was armed with a pistol and hand grenade, and he demanded $500,000 and four parachutes. In San Diego, he released all of his 85 passengers. However, the FBI informed him that they could not gather the money in time.

In response, Spreck said he wanted to fly to Miami, and he walked off the plane when the FBI said they would give him some maps and other material. Five agents jumped him as he descended the stairs.

Speck was a National Merit scholarship winner and a Stanford graduate, but his academic brilliance was not evident. "He doesn't appear to be the smartest hijacker that I've heard of," declared one agent.

"He must have flipped his lid," Speck's mother says after his surrender. "I just can't understand it."

Psychological aberrations are apparent again, but there seems to be no other substantive comparison to Cooper, other copycats, or any improvement in *modus operandi*.

On May 5, 1972 **Frederick Hahneman** used a handgun to hijack Eastern Airlines 175, a 727, in Allentown, Pennsylvania and bound for Miami. He demanded $303,000. They flew first to Washington, DC, where the skyjacker released the 41 passengers. They then flew to New Orleans and swapped airplanes.

Hahneman eventually parachuted into the jungles of Honduras, his country of birth. However, a month later with the FBI in pursuit and a $25,000 bounty on his head, he surrendered to the US Embassy in Tegucigalpa, claiming that he was "afraid and wanted to return to the United States."

The *New York Times* also reports that Hahneman was forty-nine years old—similar to Cooper—and claimed to have fought in WW II, Korea and Vietnam. The *Times* also states that federal authorities said that Hahneman was an Air Force radar technican.

Reportedly, the ransom money has not been recovered and Hahneman has refused to say where it is. Besides having an age comparable to Cooper's, Hahneman also possessed a steady competence that enabled him to endure the many hours of his crime. This separates him from most of the copycats and puts him in league with Cooper and McCoy.

Next was a skyjacker only known by his last name, **"Lomas,"** who hijacked an Ecuatoriana de Aviacion turboprop airliner in Quito, Ecuador on May 22, 1972. The flight was headed to Guayaquil, Ecuador, but it sat on the runway at Quito for six hours while authorities negotiated with Lomas, who had demanded $40,000 and a parachute.

Eventually Ecuadorian commandos gained access to the craft via the cargo hold and ambushed Lomas, killing him. How Lomas had planned to exit the aircraft is unknown, but presumably he was going to skydive since he had a parachute.

On June 2, 1972 we had **Robb Heady**, 22. Robb made it to the ground with approximately $180,000, and a full description of his hijacking follows in the next chapter.

Several weeks later on June 23, 1972, **Martin McNally**, 28, hijacked American Airlines Flight 119, a 727 enroute from St. Louis to Tulsa. According to Tulsa newspaper reporter, Gene Curtis, the skyjacking was characterized by profound indecision.

McNally changed the route several times—first to Fort Worth as it approached Tulsa, then reversing back to its origins in St Louis where McNally released all but one of the 92 passengers. They then headed to Toronto, but switched mid-flight to JFK in New York. Eventually, he bailed out over Indiana at night with $502,000 in ransom, but apparently lost the money as he exited the aircraft. Nevertheless, he landed safely in a field near Peru, Indiana.

Curtis writes that the skyjacker was armed with a .45-caliber submachine gun that he carried in a trombone case. In addition, McNally demanded parachute instructions as part of his ransom, and was given lessons by two FBI agents disguised as airlines officials. The agents reported that McNally had trouble following their directions.

Even though he was in the custody of local police that evening, he was eventually released. However, an associate named Walter J. Petlikowsky turned him into the FBI several days later in Michigan, and McNally was arrested in a Detroit suburb. McNally was convicted and sentenced to two life prison terms. However, he was paroled from prison in 2010.

On June 30, 1972, **Daniel Bernard Carre**, 25, boarded Hughes Air West Flight 775 in Sea-Tac, bound for Portland, Oregon. One sketchy report claims he brandished a knife in front of a flight attendant. But another account claims he had been searched prior to boarding because he fit a hijacker's pro-file in both physical demeanor and behavior. Nevertheless, Carre commandeered the aircraft and demanded $50,000. Yet, he was apprehended upon landing at PDX.

The Skies Belong to Us offers a more detailed account. The author states that Flight 775 was bound for Salt Lake City, with a scheduled stop in Portland. After take-off, Carre announced to a flight attendant that he wanted to "jump out over Pocatello (Idaho)" and also wanted $50,000 and a parachute. He made no mention of a weapon of any kind. The pilot landed at PDX and ordered all the passengers off the plane. Carre then surrendered to the feds without incident. He was remanded to a mental insti-tution. His subsequent life is indeterminable, and no connection to the copycat crew is evident.

On July 6, 21-year old **Francis Goodell** hijacked Pacific Southwest Airlines Flight 389, Oakland to Sacramento. Goodell diverted his aircraft to San Diego and demanded a parachute and $455,000. Goodell released his 57 passengers in San Diego and demanded to be flown back to Oakland.

Despite his request for a parachute, Goodell also asked to have a helicopter waiting for him in Oakland. Upon arriving, he surrendered to FBI without incident. He was sentenced to 25 years in prison.

One week later, July 12, 1972, **Melvin Martin Fisher** hijacked American Airlines Flight 633 in Oklahoma City, where we was facing criminal charges for fraud.

Fisher demanded $500,000 and a parachute. However, the airlines offered only $200,000, which he accepted and afterwards released the passengers. Then, he instructed the pilots to take-off and fly around the city, but for unknown reasons Fisher instructed them to land and he surrendered to the FBI. He was sentenced to a life in prison.

So, are these copycats a group? Is there any connection among them? For many of the copycats, their youthful recklessness is most apparent, along with psychological instability. Five copycats were obviously suffering from mental illness—Cini, Holt, Hurst, Spreck and Carre. Fisher and Goodell were most likely psychologically impaired also, judging from their impulsive decision making. Similarly, Robb Heady was suffering from a Vietnam War-based PTSD, and most likely LaPoint as well, and probably McCoy.

McNally is best characterized as a super goofball, so that leaves the two old guys, Hahneman and Cooper, with Lomas as an outlier.

Were the young and crazy influenced by MKULTRA? I have no concrete information to support that possibility. But DB Cooper seemed to be the best prepared and best able to execute his plan, and he is certainly the oldest—nearly twice the average age of most of the skyjackers. Richard McCoy is a close second, and as for Hahneman, he is definitely in their league but seems like a ghost and information on him is hard to obtain. As a group, I see no orchestration of the copycats, nor any substantive improvements in techniques—except for McCoy.

So, was there a relationship between DB Cooper and Richard McCoy? It remains a mystery.

Chapter 30

Interview with Copycat, Robb Heady

R obb Heady is the only skyjacker I have been able to interview. Again, Snowmman was instrumental in helping me find this taciturn hijacker. The following is a distillation of our phone conversations and emails in the spring of 2013, during which time Robb revealed many details of his hijacking, including his mindset and motivation.

In addition, Robb traveled to Tacoma in November 2013 for the DB Cooper Symposium, and told his story to the assembled audience members. Later, he attended the bash in Ariel, and over a few beers he expanded his narrative.

He also offered an apology.

On June 2, 1972, six months after he had returned home from Vietnam, Robb jumped over a three-foot high fence surrounding the tarmac at the Reno airport and ran towards an emptying United Airlines plane. It was Flight 239 from New York, a 727 bound for San Francisco.

It was sunset. Heady, 22, was wearing a small reserve parachute underneath his windbreaker, and carried a .357 Magnum that he had borrowed from a friend. He had a pillowcase over his head, with slits for his eyes. After he put the gun to the head of a stewardess the crew accepted his hijacking demands. However, they insisted on switching airplanes, claiming the original plane was low of fuel and had a bad engine.

Robb told me that he didn't consult with anyone about his intentions, nor did he study the Cooper case. "There wasn't a lot of planning," he told me, "but I knew it could be done."

Once aboard the second plane, Robb demanded that the door to the aft stairs be "cracked open," which probably alerted the crew to his imminent departure. After receiving $200,000 in hundred-dollar bills they took off, heading for San Francisco.

Unlike Cooper, Robb didn't give the pilots a lengthy list of instructions—only a series of radio frequencies to follow to San Francisco. He had planned to exit ten minutes after take-off when the plane banked towards the west.

Robb estimates the plane was traveling at about 300–350 miles per hour when he jumped, much faster than DB Cooper. According to official accounts, Robb exited at 12,000 feet.

Robb says he had intended to land near a highway on the southeast side of Lake Washoe, on the outskirts of Reno. However, the pilot had veered "too far to the right" and Robb was unable to correct his position even though he "tracked" through the night skies at speeds up to 220 mph in an effort to reach his target. As a result, he landed on the southwest side of the lake, and Robb could not easily reach the car he had parked. The delay sealed his fate. One-hundred and fifty law enforcement agents swarmed the area and he was trapped in Washoe Valley. "I underestimated how fast they could seal off the valley," Robb said.

Robb estimates that he jumped at about 10 or 11 pm, and a couple of hours later the cops found his car, festooned with a US Parachuting Association bumper sticker. Figuring the lone vehicle was the skyjacker's getaway wheels, the police put it under surveillance. When Robb approached at dawn, sheriff deputies arrested him. He surrendered without incident.

"What's it like to jump from a 727?" I asked.

"Yeah, I guess a lot of skydivers would want to know that, eh?" he said, laughing. "My body was whipped around pretty good."

At the time of his skyjacking Robb had over 160 skydives, but this was both his first jet and first night jump. He also said the reserve chute, which was a 24-foot round canopy, opened "really hard," even though he waited until deep in his decent and its heavier air before deploying.

Robb estimates that he opened about 1,000 feet above the ground. He wasn't wearing goggles, and even though it was dark he could see the ground as it rushed up at him—a phenomenon he said happens at about 1,000 feet and experienced skydivers really don't need an altimeter if they can see the ground.

I asked him if he was afraid.

"After Vietnam, nothing scared me," he replied.

"Were you cold?"

"It was May or something, so the air was cold—maybe about 45 degrees," he told me.

The actual jump was tricky due to the speed of the airplane, as Robb did not give them any instructions for airspeed, flaps, or landing gear. "I'm sure the pilot didn't show me any favors," he said with a laugh. "It seemed like a normal take-off, and I jumped about 20 miles from the airport as the crow flies."

Robb says he tumbled in the fierce slipstream for about fifteen seconds until he stabilized. "I held my arch (position)," he said, "and eventually I corrected."

Additionally, Robb had created a sleek profile by putting his ransom money into a fishing vest that had three large pockets, and protected the vest by wearing it under his windbreaker. "The bills didn't all fit in the vest so I had to leave some money behind, maybe $20,000," Robb said. "I also put some of the left-over bills in a stewardess' purse."

Nevertheless, the police reported that they found $45,000 on the plane two days after the skyjacking, but Robb was uncertain how that happened. "I thought I had left only about $20,000," he said wistfully.

"Did you land with the rest of the money?" I asked.

"Of course."

"But the police reported that you lost the money on the way down."

"Yeah, that's what I told the cops when they got me," he said. "But I buried it when I landed, and then I told my lawyer about it and we were able to make a deal. He went and got it."

Robb was sentenced to a 30-year prison term, but he was released after six years. He served his time in Lompoc federal prison, located in California. "It was a typical federal prison—lots of federal crimes like: bank robberies, drug cases, that kind of thing," he told me. "With all of my problems, I fit right in," he added, again with a laugh. "Prison was actually a good thing for me. It helped me being in a structured environment. I read a lot, and I began to feel better (regarding his Vietnam-sourced PTSD)."

Robb was released after his third parole review. One of the mitigating factors was the absence of any passengers on the plane he actually hijacked. When I asked him what happened to the San Francisco-bound passengers and if they stayed on their original plane, he didn't remember and had little energy for pursuing the question.

Continuing, I asked Robb why he stole the airplane, and the conversation reached a greater depth, one of earnest self-revelation. "I got really messed up in Vietnam," he said.

Robb described how he was drafted unexpectedly. "I ruptured my spleen playing football in high school," he said, "and had it removed. That usually keeps you out of the military because the spleen makes red blood cells, and without it you can get really sick, like with malaria, which I got in Vietnam." Robb said that the draft rules changed when the lottery was initiated in 1969 and his medical deferment was no longer accepted. Hence, he became 1-A and got drafted. Robb entered the army and was assigned to the infantry.

However, an opportunity arose for volunteering into an airborne unit, which Robb accepted since it would keep him out of Vietnam for another month while he received training. However, his plan for minimal exposure to combat back-fired because his new unit was staffed with several gung-ho officers, some fresh from West Point. "I had some good officers and some bad ones, but a lot wanted to see action."

These latter commanders were eager for the kind of fighting that resulted in promotions. "They pushed it, and it rubbed me the wrong way," Robb acknowledged. As a result, Robb was marginalized, and when his airborne unit rotated home he was forced to serve as a security grunt in Da Nang. Further, the army didn't want him and his adversarial attitudes stateside. So, like many others, the Army discharged him a few months shy of his two-year hitch. Ironically, he mustered out from Fort Lewis, smack dab in the middle of Cooper Country.

In Vietnam, Robb had served with the 173rd Airborne Brigade of the II Corps, a paratroop unit that functioned as infantry. He was stationed near Pleiku in the north-central part of the country, and it was a jungle environment ripe with combat. His first mission was to retrieve the bodies of a recon squad that had been wiped-out in an ambush, just one mile beyond the perimeter of their base camp.

Robb says that, on average, his own company was in the field about 16–20 days at a clip, and then would return to base camp for a few days. His longest trek was forty days. "Camp was the most dangerous place to be, though," he said. "At night, we'd get hit with rockets and mortars."

Besides enduring the traumas of war, Robb also suffered greatly from a bout of malaria, which he contracted in his fifth month in Vietnam. Without a spleen, he was racked with fevers. However, doctors had to test his blood at the height of a fever cycle to ascertain the exact type of parasite that had infected him, which took additional time.

Compounding his health issues was a harrowing chopper flight to a regional hospital at Qui Nhon (pronounced Quin yon). Racked with fever, Robb was medevac'd at night along with twenty-two soldiers wounded during the evening's rocket attack. He vividly described a pair of ARVN soldiers bleeding profusely next to him as they dusted off. "I just made it onto the chopper," Robb said. "As a medical evac, I was a low priority."

Robb recovered at Qui Nhon, but the doctors told him that he should never have been drafted, and certainly not sent to Vietnam. The doctors ordered him transferred out of combat, but his unit commander ignored Robb's medical condition and sent him back into the field. But, in turn, Robb refused to go back on patrol, so he was assigned to permanent guard duty. Despite this harsh treatment by the military, Robb fulfilled the remainder of his tour. He left Vietnam in December 1971, a couple of weeks after DB Cooper's hijacking.

The effects of Vietnam lingered, however, and Robb's return to civilian life was difficult. "I developed a severe case of PTSD," he told me. "I was feeling awful all the time when I got out of Vietnam. I thought I would feel better when I got home, but that didn't happen."

Robb spiraled downward to the point where he didn't care if he lived or died. From that state he decided to hijack an airplane. "Why? I didn't have a... ya know... a big reason," he said.

Robb expanded upon his state of mind. "I had been a normal, middle-class guy, and then two years later I'm hijacking an airplane. How does that happen?" he mused. Robb said that his father had been a physicist and a chemist, and Robb's pride in his dad is clearly evident.

When he returned to civilian life, Robb enrolled in school to become a CPA, but found he couldn't study or learn in the same way as he did prior to his military service. "I feel that I was brain damaged," he told me. "My IQ was about 145 when I went into the military. I know from when they tested me. Now, it's about 120."

Currently, Robb is still in treatment for his PTSD, and he also maintains contact with a few of his army buddies.

> A lot of guys have PTSD, but they don't think that they do. It's a quiet thing, and it just becomes a part of you. One of them—he can go off whenever the right combination of things happen. He's a ticking time bomb. Lots of guys are like that.

In Tacoma for the 2013 Symposium, Robb offered a more in-depth view of his psychological state of mind leading up to the skyjacking. Over beers, Robb told a group of us that his Vietnam experience warped his view of the world, and he believed that all wealth was created by committing some kind of crime. When the powerful have all the money they want, they make the laws that allow them to keep it. Then they form armies and invade countries to get even more.

"Back then, I believed that if you're not getting yours, then you're a loser," Robb told us. "So, I just wanted to get mine. $200,000 is better than robbing a bank and getting $8,000." Then Robb took a breath and said, "But I don't feel that way any more."

As for the possibility of a group effort in the Cooper hijacking, or some kind of orchestration of the copy cats, Robb accepts the former but doubts the latter. "Certainly having a ground team would help," he told me, referring to DB Cooper's getaway, "but I don't think there was any kind of group thing for the skyjackers."

Continuing, Robb clearly indicated to me that his actions were all of his own making, and he was not part of a mind-controlled or orchestrated group. As for learning about the technical requirements of the jump, Robb said that he had heard about Cooper while he was in Vietnam, but only in general terms so the exact details escaped him. However, Cooper's plane landed in Reno, Robb's hometown, and the FBI had talked to two of Robb's skydiving friends.

"I heard about it that way, I guess," he shared. "But I didn't do any research or study it."

Currently, Robb is considering writing an account of his experiences, and I hope he does. I have offered the *Mountain News* as a platform for his story, which may have planted the seed for his coming to Tacoma and Ariel. "I read your article in the *Mountain News* about Ariel. It looks like fun."

"You probably won't have to buy a beer all night long, ya know," I teased when we spoke about Ariel.

"I'll go, if you take me," he said. "But I don't want to answer questions all night long."

After I posted Robb's story on the *Mountain News,* he sent me the following denouement:

I do wish now that sometime in our two conversations I would have told you to tell people that I am sorry that I threatened people with a gun, put people at risk and hurt my family members, and I wish I could go back in time to change my mind. Thanks for telling my side of the story.
– Robb

Chapter 31

Recent Suspects 2013 to 2015

Although the DB Cooper case is over forty years old the suspects keep coming, and one of the enduring mysteries of this case is how many middle-aged Caucasian men didn't appear for Thanksgiving dinner in 1971.

One of the many gentlemen who missed out on his turkey was Jack Albert Collins, and family lore says he spent the holiday weekend with his younger brother, Romaine "Bud" Collins in unknown pursuits. Jack Collins' story as DB Cooper came to light in 2013 when his son, Bradley Scott Collins, published a narrative of his family: *My Father Was DB Cooper–$200,000 in ransom and a parachute jump to an uncertain fate.*

Bradley, who was fourteen in 1971, isn't sure where his father was on Thanksgiving Day, but remembers that he had departed from the family home in Everett, Washington on Wednesday, the day of the skyjacking. Jack Collins left early in the day and indicated that he was going to visit Bud, who lived near Battleground. Jack never called his wife or family during the holiday period, and returned on Sunday only to say that he "was tired."

Bradley says that initially he assumed that his father and uncle had gone skydiving, as both of them were experienced parachutists. In fact, they were both friends of Cooper suspect, Ted

Mayfield. Both brothers were also lifelong pilots, and further intrigue is added by Uncle Bud, who was a 727 pilot for Northwest Orient. However, Bradley doesn't prove what his father or uncle actually did that weekend, and only offers his "gut feelings" about the two men.

When the skyjacking was taking place, Bradley says that he heard Flight 305 circle overhead as he sold Seattle Times newspapers at the Everett ferry docks, and claims he instinctively knew that his father was performing the hijacking above him. However, Robert99 of the DB Cooper Forum has shown conclusively that the nearest Flight 305 came to Everett was 17 nautical miles south of town, and the cloud cover almost certainly muffled any sound from planes overhead, so Bradley's inner knowingness must be assumed to be of a mystical nature.

But, Bradley says his father was a risk-taker and would entice his younger brother to join in with his escapades, and casts the skyjacking as just their latest adventure.

As a result, Bradley feels his father performed the skyjacking and posits that Uncle Bud was the ground man. Bradley suggests further that Jack landed near the Merwin Dam in Ariel. As sketchy as this may be, Bradley's instincts were solidified in December 1971, when his father announced that the FBI had interviewed him and Uncle Bud in connection to the DB Cooper case. Apparently the local mayor, Harve Harrison, and his wife Jodi, strongly suspected Jack Collins of being the skyjacker, and had alerted the police.

Although Bradley offers no conclusive proof that his father was DB Cooper, he shares numerous tidbits about his father's questionable business practices, and intimates that his father engaged in business fraud and money laundering. In fact, Bradley's father was a kind of wheeler-dealer, and had the nickname of "Jumping Jack Cash."

In 2009, Bradley began researching his father's life and embraced his suspicions that "Jumping Jack Cash" was DB Cooper. As part of his process of discovery, Bradley contacted Curtis Eng at the Seattle FBI, who inquired about DNA samples. However, the results of Eng's investigation are unknown.

Then in a burst of the muse over a few days in 2012, Bradley penned his story. Besides the DB Cooper association, Bradley also delivered a dramatic account of finding the body of his Uncle Bud in their family home, deceased from a self-inflicted gunshot wound. Uncle Bud also left a suicide note, blaming his brother for "interfering in his life."

During the 2013 DB Cooper Symposium in Tacoma, I interviewed Bradley about his claims. The conversation became contentious, however, when I pushed Bradley for some proof beyond his own personal "gut feelings." He got angry and stormed away from our meeting. His wife, Robin, attempted unsuccessfully to soothe him, and later asked me to find a way to continue the interview. I told her I was available, but wasn't going to chase her husband. She lingered in my company hoping that Bradley would return, but he never did. In those few moments together, Robin had little to offer other than to say that Jack had been a very nice guy and had "always been very welcoming to the family."

Another fellow to miss Thanksgiving in 1971 was Robert Lepsy, of Grayling, Michigan. However, Lepsy missed more than a family gathering and vanished completely in 1969. The Lepsy story was brought to light in 2014 by Ross Richardson, an inquisitive scuba diver who loves exploring the sunken wrecks embedded in the Great Lakes surrounding his home (www.

michiganmysteries.com). In fact, Ross' moniker at the DB Cooper Forum is NMIWrecks, which stands for Northern Michigan Wrecks.

Nimi Wrecks, as he is belovedly known at the Forum, is our primary source of information on Lepsy, and he has included the Lespy-as-Cooper saga in his collection of secretive crimes from Michigan, titled: *Still Missing—Rethinking the DB Cooper Case and Other Mysterious Disappearances.* Nimi also told his story to Brent Ashcroft, a TV journalist at WZZM in Grand Rapids, Michigan. Ashcroft did a full treatment on the Lepsy story for the Cooper Anniversary in 2015 and the piece went viral, going nationwide within a week.

Here is what we know of Richard Lepsy: When he disappeared on October 29, 1969, he was 33 and the manager of Glen's Market, a small, rural grocery in Grayling, Michigan. That day he never returned from his lunch, and later that week his car was found abandoned sixty miles away at the Cherry Capital Airport in Traverse City, Michigan. The keys were in the ignition and the car was unlocked. A half-pack of cigarettes was found on the dashboard.

The Michigan State Police (MSP) and local police investigated, but discovered only a handful of clues, including $2,000 found missing from the grocery store safe. Also, some locals claimed that Lepsy had a girlfriend, and the MSP discovered that individuals resembling Lepsy and the girlfriend had been seen boarding a plane at the airport where the car was recovered. The pair were later rumored to have made their way to Mexico, and ultimately, the cops did not think Richard Lepsy was a "missing person," but had voluntarily left his life in Michigan for a romantic escapade south of the border.

As a result, the local media did not cover the story and never picked-up on the skyjacking angle two years later when DB Cooper made his jump. In fact, the official silence in 1969 was so complete that Ashcroft reported the original Lepsy files have vanished, which now adds an intriguing wrinkle to this mystery.

In 1986, Lepsy's family appeared on the Sally Jesse Raphael TV show and poignantly described their search for Richard. Lepsy's wife, Jackie, appeared to still be in shock, and as a result, the daughter, Lisa, did most of the talking. Currently, Lisa is advocating for the DB Cooper connection, and numerous news outlets carried her story as their 2015 DB Cooper Anniversary piece. However, there is no substantive reason to connect Richard Lepsy to the DB Cooper skyjacking. Lepsy had no known skydiving experience, nor any special awareness of 727s or flying. He was not a pilot. Additionally, he was only 35 years-old in 1971, and had only a passing resemblance to the sketches of DB Cooper.

But there are some similarities: Lepsy was six-foot tall and about 180 pounds. He had black, thinning hair and brown eyes, and as a native Midwesterner he spoke with no discernible accent. Like Barb Dayton and Dan Cooper, Richard Lepsy preferred wearing loafers.

In 2011, Lisa Lepsy entered her father's DNA in the NAMUS database, the **Na**tional **M**issing and **U**nidentified Person **S**ystem, but no leads have been forthcoming.

Further, Richardson says that he does not know if the FBI has explored Lepsy as a suspect. But as part of his 2015 story on Lespy-as-Cooper, Ashcroft contacted Ayn Dietrich-Williams at the FBI's Seattle office and asked her directly if Richard Lepsy was being investigated. Dietrich-Williams demurred, and would only say:

...it would not be appropriate to discuss whether or not we considered Lepsy as a subject... we are not still actively looking for information... when tips come into us, we assess each one, and if credible, pursue the lead accordingly.

But when I asked Dietrich-Williams, she was even more obtuse:

Unfortunately, I am unable to comment on the ongoing case, which includes disclosing whether or not someone has been considered a subject.

But there does seem to be possible federal involvement, even if the connection is a bizarre one. In 1993, Lisa Lepsy, now grown and living in Tennessee, was visited by two gentlemen dressed entirely in black. They said they were insurance agents, and barged their way into Lisa's home. They aggressively asked her about her father, and demanded to know if she had any knowledge of his whereabouts.

One man gave her his business card. His name was Charles J. Mitchell, and he claimed to be the "Director of Special Activities" of the John Hancock Insurance Company, based in Lisle, Illinois. But Lisa had no information to give them, and they left. Subsequently, Lisa called John Hancock and inquired about these "Men in Black." Lisa says the insurance company had no knowledge of any Charles Mitchell or a "Special Activities" division, and certainly did not authorized the visit.

As a result, researchers wonder if the intrusion was a heavy-handed interrogation by drug enforcement officials exploring a cold case, trying to establish a drug trafficking link to Dick Lepsy's disappearance twenty-four years earlier.

Another individual who has gone missing is the previously mentioned Melvin Luther Wilson, the father of DB Cooper researcher Vicki Wilson. Mel vanished from their Minneapolis home just a few weeks before the Cooper skyjacking, on September 15, 1971. Wilson was facing federal counterfeiting charges when he disappeared, and earlier had pulled stretches at San Quentin and Leavenworth in the 1950s and 1960s.

In addition, he had at least two separate wives and families. Further, when he left his first family in 1956, he also cut all ties to his mother, who was living in their family home in Oakland, California.

Vicki was a daughter of his second family, and was seven years old when Mel left her, a brother and sister, and her mother. Vicki has launched an intense campaign to understand her father's disappearance, and she and her sisters were featured on *Unsolved Mysteries*.

In 2011, Vicki entered her DNA into the NAMUS data bank on behalf of her father. However, a lack of a death certificate for her father has thwarted her attempts to enlist the help of the US Marshal's Service, the FBI, and the Secret Service in learning of his fate. Vicki is frustrated by their lack of assistance and says that she has received "zero cooperation." Ironically, calling attention to the possibility that Mel Wilson might be DB Cooper has raised his public profile and seems to be aiding her efforts, which echoes the experience of Lisa Lepsy.

Additionally, Vicki has been embraced by many DB Cooper sleuths, and actively posts at the DB Cooper Forum. In 2012, she spoke with DB Cooper case agent Curtis Eng, who simply asked: "So, why do *you* think *your* father is DB Cooper?"

Despite Eng's apparent cynicism, Vicki says that he has "not ruled out" Mel Wilson as a suspect.

Vicki is certainly an avid follower of the Norjak story, and besides her many pithy commentaries on the Forum, she attended the 2013 Symposium and shared the good times at Ariel. In fact, Vicki and her daughter Nicole were guests of Sailshaw at one of his Cooper salons in April 2013. In addition, Vicki Wilson is one of the few DB Cooper researchers who was hoping Marla Cooper's Uncle LD was the skyjacker. "Then, at least I'd know it wasn't my father," she told me.

As for being the skyjacker, Mel Wilson is a reasonable suspect. He was 44 years old in 1971, and was six-foot and 180. Additionally, Bill Mitchell, one of the primary witnesses to the Cooper hijacking, says that Wilson possesses a facial feature unique to the skyjacker—a fold of skin under the chin that Mitchell calls a "turkey gobble." However, Wilson has no known skydiving skills nor aviation experience, and few researchers consider him a strong candidate for DB Cooper.

Chapter 32

Cyber Attacks on Cooper Investigators

The murder of Earl Cossey is not the only crime to befall participants in the DB Cooper saga. Galen Cook and I have come under cyber attack, beginning in 2012. The intrusions are varied, and include document destruction, email blocking, and theft of email files. However, the most troubling has been the hijacking of selected Cooper emails between Galen and me and re-routing them to the FBI's main office in New York City.

The assault began in June 2012, hit a crescendo in August, and then went dormant until January 2013, when I began to write this book in earnest. The first evidence of the attack appeared when I discovered that some of my email files had been emptied. At first, I considered it trivial. The files were inconsequential, just old correspondence with colleagues of years past.

Somebody hacking I guess, one of the problems of being an open-sourced journalist, I told myself. Or someone was sending me a message? *You are not secure. We can hack into your files and take anything we want.*

That latter thought was unsettling, but still relatively minor as nothing substantial was affected. Besides, I was recovering from a 2012 heart attack so I had plenty of other things to think about, such as what new vegan concoction to cook for dinner.

However, the next cyber intrusion occurred in mid-August 2012, and was much more serious. While I was visiting family in New York, I checked my emails at a public library. In the midst of my perusing, nature called, so I shutdown the computer and headed to the restroom. When I returned, I fired up my library rig and reconnected to the emails. Surprisingly, about a dozen new emails had come in during my brief sojourn. They were all robo-type messages from the FBI headquarters in New York City, and were a response to somebody sending them a bunch of my emails. Oddly, all of the emails were ones that I had just deleted from my in-box.

The FBI emails said that they had received them on an account identified as "AGNY," and the message asked me to please remove the FBI from my "distribution list." In short, the FBI didn't want me to send them spam. Not realizing their importance, I deleted the robo emails.

I would have lost them anyway, because all of the emails I had read in New York were gone when I returned to Washington two days later. I was stunned. Over the years I had read my emails in New York using web mail access and never had a problem—they were always there when I returned to Washington.

I called the phone company that provides my email service. They told me they had downloaded all my new emails to the public library system and didn't save any copies. I don't know if that was a change in procedure, but I had no recourse. Further, the email tech said that he had never heard of any similar event and suggested that I change my password on my email account, which I did.

Next, I called the library in New York and asked them for advice. They had none, and added that they had never heard of a similar experience. I then called my computer security guy in Tacoma, a fellow who has an excellent reputation. He recommended that I call the FBI in New York and ask them for assistance. In the meantime, he would check my system and give it a good scrub.

During this time, Galen emailed me. **"I just got an email from the FBI office in New York! CALL ME—ASAP!"** Galen had received the same type of robo email that I had received a few days prior in New York, informing him that the FBI wanted to be taken off *his* distribution list. However, the email that had been sent to the AGNY address in New York was a snippet of four DB Cooper emails that Galen and I had exchanged two years prior. So, someone stole emails from my files and routed them to the FBI in New York City via Galen's computer. Hence, the FBI in New York thought they were coming from Galen.

Galen was furious, and impressed upon me the seriousness of the situation. Not only had my personal security been breached, but private correspondence between an attorney and a potential client—me—had been stolen and re-distributed publicly. Galen insisted that I take action, so I called the FBI.

The first FBI guy I spoke to in New York was polite and listened attentively to my story. He asked a question or two, and then announced that he was going to bump me to another agent who was more cyber savvy. The next agent listened again to my story, but with a much keener level of interest. Nevertheless, he didn't have any answers for me other than to suggest I change my email password. He also reassured me that he and the FBI were taking my issues seriously, and that the event seemed to be a "head-scratcher."

Further, he said he would ask others in his office what they thought was going on, and what I should do about it. Additionally, Galen sent me the email that the FBI had sent to him, and this is now the only evidence I have of the robo emails from the FBI.

From: AGNY0000@ic.fbi.gov
To: brucesmith; Galen
Date: Mon, 13 Aug 2012 16:06:27 -0400
Subject: RE: d b cooper

Federal Bureau of Investigation email is for official email only. We recommend that you remove the New York Field Office from your distribution list.

Federal Bureau of Investigation
New York Field Office
26 Federal Plaza
New York, NY 10258

Galen and I talked further and agreed to refrain from sending emails to each other that contained important information unless we are willing to have them hacked and misused. We have followed that scheme to this day, and fortunately we have not experienced any intrusions.

We also talked extensively about who would do this, and why. What could be gained by hacking my computer files when most of the information I have on DB Cooper is posted on the *Mountain News*? Galen posited that perhaps a wannabe Cooper writer was trying to get a jump-start on his research, but that possibility seemed spurious. *Is the FBI playing head games with us? Maybe, but why?* If someone really wanted to mess up my investigation, why not just clean out my hard drive? Why send old emails to 26 Federal Plaza?

Was someone was sending me a warning? Letting me know I was stepping on some very large toes?

Regardless, the issue that arose in New York faded as I stopped writing in the face of additional health issues that emerged in early

September 2012. After another cardiac adventure, I entered heart rehab and trudged through the fall of 2012. In January 2013, I returned to my writing with determination. The hacker returned as well.

A literary agent, who had requested the first three chapters of this book in December 2011, told me that even though my email had arrived, the attachment containing the Cooper material hadn't. That kind of glitch happens from time-to-time with emails, but I suspected the hacker was active again and snatching attachments.

Undaunted, I sent the chapters off to the agent, again. However, in the process my computer speeds dropped dramatically, and I had to wait ten seconds for every change in function. It was maddening. *"I've got to call my tech guy and get rid of those damn cookies!*

Then, on Sunday January 13, the hacker struck hard. I had created a new word document for a revision of Chapter 3. However, the word doc disappeared during the time I had initially saved it and left my desk to make a cup of tea. By the time I returned it was gone. *Damn, I thought I had saved it. Maybe not?*

Fortunately, all I had done was create the new document and hadn't started writing. So, I merely reformed it and began writing. I was inspired and wrote for two hours. Then my mouse began to act funky, and I was unable to scroll down my page. I popped the cover plate off the mouse and began cleaning out the accumulated gunk on the wheels. By the time I finished, the whole document was gone, again. I could find no trace of it. I searched my computer using every function I could think of, but was unable to retrieve anything.

Two poofed documents in one night? Ug. Oh, well, I'll deal with it tomorrow and save everything to hard disks. I went to bed.

The next day, I decided to file a formal complaint, and composed a document describing these events. As I began writing, my mouse lost its ability to scroll. Sensing trouble, I shutdown my rig, then fired it back up and finished—using my computer as a word processor only, without any Internet connections. My mouse worked perfectly. I got angry realizing I was under direct attack.

I made a number of phone calls, first to my security guy, who promised to launch an additional "deep clean" from his office. When I told him the whole story he replied, "Bruce, you're scaring me."

Through the course of the ensuing week he ran a couple of scans—first, a malware search—and then another form of deep cleaning that included a scan for keystroke loggers, a nefarious tool of serious hackers and Intel agencies. Then I called Galen and strategized. He advised me to contact Curtis Eng, the Cooper case agent.

I sought Eng through the main switchboard at the Seattle FO, and followed up with an email. I heard nothing back. I contacted the Seattle PIO, Ayn Dietrich-Williams. We had a lengthy chat and she was sympathetic in a federal sort of way. She advised me to file a formal complaint at a website known as IC-3. Simply, IC-3 is a federal acronym for "Internet Crime Complaint Center."

The online IC-3 complaint process was relatively straightforward and easy to complete. Nevertheless, I was taken back when I read in a follow-up robo email from the IC-3 announcing they receive thousands of complaints every day and could not guarantee when or if any investigators would be able to respond to me. Ms. Dietrich had already spoken to that issue, and had told me that due to the volume of complaints it could take time.

In addition, she said the current nature of federal law enforcement was changing, and the FBI might not be the lead agency in this investigation. Surprisingly, the Secret Service is taking a major role in cyber security these days, and the FBI is playing a reduced role. Ayn also told me that a third agency might get involved, a new division of Homeland Security called the *Homeland Security Investigations Department,* or HSID.

Ms. Dietrich also requested that I send her my cyber attack document so that she could keep track of the specifics. I did so, and she called me the next day. Moments later, I received an email from Curtis Eng, my first and only from the Cooper case agent despite my many requests for an interview. Agent Eng was very formal with me, and I include his response because it is informative of both his demeanor and the FBI's position in this matter:

Mr. Smith:

I do not have any further suggestions to add to what Ayn suggested to you. Filing a complaint with IC3 is definitely the best course of action. What is happening to you is no different than somebody breaking into your house and stealing personal papers or your work on the Norjak case. You would of course, call the police and report that you were burglarized. Hence, that is what you are doing now by reporting these incidents to IC3. Although you believe that you have been specifically targeted because of your work on Norjak, the intrusion will not be pursued by the FBI with more urgency or priority because your Norjak data is not government property. I apologize that I cannot offer you more suggestions or assistance beyond what you have already done. I hope you are able to implement technical safeguards to prevent future intrusions because it sounds like you are definitely the victim of being hacked. Thank you for contacting me about this since it concerns Norjak. Take care.

- SA Curtis J. Eng

Following receipt of Agent Eng's email I specifically requested an interview with him to discuss the case. I haven't heard back.

Still unsettled, I checked with my computer security guy. He assured me that my rig was clean and operating in a safe manner. "Have you ever encountered anything like this before?" I asked.

"No, not really."

We chatted about why somebody would perform this kind of intrusion. His final words were chilling:

"Whoever it was, it seems like they got in and then left, leaving nothing behind them. We know the FBI can do this kind of thing," he said.

"Yes, that is my perspective as well, but it could be bigger than just the FBI—like any intelligence outfit, the NSA, or rogue guys at any of those agencies?" I asked.

He had no answer.

But for me, the bottom line is this: In our world never assume that any correspondence is secure. In fact, it is the guiding principle of open-source sleuthing—act as if everything is being written across the sky in big letters for the whole world to read.

As such, I have received numerous suggestions on how to protect this work. Some took their advice a little further, and one correspondent asked succinctly: "If the FBI hacked you, why would they let you know? Why would they care what you are doing? Are you digging up some stuff that could embarrass or damage them?"

In response, I wrote: "I see three possibilities why I was hacked:

1. Somebody in the FBI wigged-out about what I am writing and went nuts. Or,

2. Somebody in the FBI knows why the DB Cooper case has not been solved and feels that my book will bring more attention to this issue, thus causing problems for the Bureau. Hence, they are trying to scare me off. Or,

3. They are not FBI, but knowledgeable of the case and are trying to warn me that I am about to step into deep doo-doo. They want to protect me in a back-handed manner.

However, there are other possibilities, and Snowmman has offered a few that have nothing to do with the FBI or spooks. First, Snow feels that my effort to clean my mouse while a document file was open was ill-advised, and most likely caused the document to be deleted. Secondly, public libraries are notorious places these days for cyber surveillance by law enforcement, and my personal emails were not safe while I was reading them at my NY library. Lastly, hackers lurk in public libraries. Did a library-based hacker have a field day with my files?

Nevertheless, the hack was serious. My email correspondences with Galen were hacked and sent to the FBI in New York. Plus, some of my email files were wiped-out. Even Eng seems to agree that my IC-3 claim is legitimate. Fortunately, since filing my IC-3 complaint in January 2013, I have not experienced any further computer difficulties.

Until 2015. Then, in early August, I began receiving an email correspondence from a "Lars Skoland," who told me that he was acting as an intermediary for a DB Cooper forum poster named Moriarty. Shutter, who moderates the Forum, told me that Moriarty is the moniker of a guy named Reichenbach, who posted on the DZ briefly in 2014, and Shutter said this identity was probably a group name for several individuals.

The gist of the Lars Skoland/Moriarty/Reichenbach exchange of emails was that the group wanted my help to uncover the identity of Al Di. Specifically, they wanted me to intercede with Galen and encourage him to send Al Di's email server information to the triumvirate of LS/M/R.

Galen refused, and Lars got nasty. He sent me veiled threats of a personal nature:

> Moriarty says to tell Galen he's not interested in his email or the contents. Says he's disappointed.

> Thought they might be friends, especially since M had a brother born on Valentines Day!

> Bruce, it's not advised to disappoint M

Other emails claimed Moriarty/Reichenbach would post my e-book on DB Cooper on the Internet and block the *Mountain News.* In addition, a few of my files appeared to be hacked, with content missing. As a result, I filed an IC3 report on Lars Skoland-Moriarty-Reichenbach on September 8, 2015.

I have not been bothered further.

Chapter 33

Why Can't The FBI Find DB Cooper?

Is there a cover-up?

In the preceding chapters I have cited numerous instances of sloppy police work, systemic deficiencies within the FBI, and problematic decision-making. But does this mean there is an actual attempt to prevent us from knowing the truth of DB Cooper?

Simply, I don't know. I have no direct evidence that supports a cover up. All I have is circumstantial evidence that suggests Norjak has been compromised. At the very least, I have a long list of facts, decisions, and behaviors that the FBI needs to explain. Here is my top ten questions for the Bureau:

Top Ten Questions for the FBI

1. Cigarette Butts
- Where are they?
- If lost, is anyone looking for them?
- Were they used for DNA analysis, as alleged by Pat Forman from a NBC-News broadcast?
- If so, where is the paperwork?

2. Ground Search
- Why was the initial ground search outsourced only to Sheriff Departments?
- Why weren't there checkpoints and roadblocks established once LZ-A was determined, understood to be approximately 11 pm, November 24, 1971?
- Why was the ground search called off on Monday, November 29, 1971?
- Why did Seattle FO tell FBI HQ that there was too much snow on the ground to continue, when there was no snow reported in the LZ-A by local officials.

3. Clip-on Tie
- Why did it enter the Seattle evidence cache four days after the hijacking?
- Where was it for that time?
- Was the chain of custody broken?

4. Reno, *fingerprints*
- Who conducted the fingerprint search aboard 305?
- What was obtained in that search?
- Why weren't the "In-flight" magazines gathered into evidence?

5. Reno, *behaviors of FBI agents*
- What happened to cause the memories of the agents on evidence retrieval to be forgetful, fuzzy or in conflict with each other?
- Were these agents "victims of some strange post-hypnotic suggestion," as Bernie Rhodes has written?
- Did MKULTRA play a part in Norjak?

6. SOG and 727s

- What was the nature of the investigation of SOG troopers regarding Norjak?
- What was the role of 727s in the Vietnam War?
- Were they used to deploy soldiers into combat?
- Did any units utilize techniques similar to those of DB Cooper, ie: jumping from a 727 with flaps at 15, gear down and locked, etc.?

7. Money Retrieval

- How many shards of money were found at Tina Bar?
- Where are they, currently?
- Did the FBI find part of DB Cooper's briefcase at Tina Bar, as reported by PIO Dorwin Schreuder?
- Why was the money found in a highly compressed state?
- What kinds of follow-up were done along the Columbia River, i.e.: fishermen interviewed, other sites dug-up, etc.?

8. Richard McCoy

- What was he doing in Las Vegas on November 24–25, 1971?
- What was he doing there on November 2–3, 1971?
- How did he learn the details of hijacking an airplane?
- What was his relationship with "Dan Cooper?"
- Why does the Seattle FO accept McCoy's alibi that he was home with family on Thanksgiving, refuting the findings from Salt Lake City FBI agents?

9. Radar Findings

- What did SAGE radar record the night of November 24, 1971?
- Can the public view any records of its findings?

- Did the F-106s following Flight 305 have any radar findings of Cooper or his jump? If not, why not?
- Why did NORAD tell Major Dawson to "back off" the F-106s?

10. Earl Cossey
- What was the role of Earl Cossey in the Norjak investigation?
- Did he own the "back" parachutes delivered to the hijacker?
- Did Cossey influence the FBI's perspective that Cooper was an inexperienced skydiver?
- Why did the FBI flip-flop on their assessment of Cooper's skills?
- Why was Cossey murdered?

Besides these specific concerns, there is a more compelling, overarching dynamic that has impacted the case in every dimension, and that is the failure of leadership. At times, no one seems to be in charge of Norjak—certainly in the early stages of the investigation. Farrell was in charge of Seattle-based activities, Manning on the ground near Ariel, Mattson in Portland and later Himmelsbach, and the Las Vegas-based Campbell in Reno.

Why didn't Charlie Farrell jump on a plane and fly to Reno to insure a proper retrieval of evidence, thus minimizing the predictable bureaucratic turf battles that followed?

Additionally, Farrell and his team worked in secrecy and still reside there, apparently. Farrell is reported to have penned a 300-page account of his experiences in Norjak, and Geoffrey Gray says he has read it. But my efforts to obtain access to a copy have been met by resistance from the Farrell family, Geoffrey, and the other

FBI agents from the Seattle office that I've asked to intercede in my behalf.

Similarly, the Norjak case agent at the time of the money find, Ron Nichols, remains silent on the money find, shards, and documentation. Coupled with the stonewalling by Himmelsbach on these controversies, I find the whole situation unacceptable.

Another example of poor supervision is the care given to the evidence that is stored in Seattle. The main pieces are stored loosely in a cardboard box that looks like it once held knickknacks in my grandmother's attic. Concerns over the chain of custody pepper Norjak as well, such as the clip-on tie being torn apart by the Citizen Sleuths. It appears they were able to review physical evidence without *any* FBI agent present, although Alan Stone refutes that assumption.

Nevertheless, these breaks in the chain of custody are serious concerns. The DZ's 377, an attorney in the Bay Area, offers a cogent view of the matter:

> The FBI has been amazingly cavalier about the handling of physical evidence (in Norjak). It's not normal practice. As a defense lawyer, when I had my experts examine physical evidence or run lab tests the prosecution enforced strict protocols so that the custody chain was unbroken and fully documented and that contamination or alteration of evidence was prevented.
>
> Even in minor cases this was how things were handled. I represented a ghetto bar owner who the cops hated. He was arrested for serving alcohol to a minor. It was a major hassle just to get a sample of the drink which was

preserved. My lab had to sign for the sample and document its handling at every step. The prosecution wisely only gave my lab a portion of the sample so that they had a control if my findings were later to be disputed. My client got really lucky. My lab tested zero alcohol. When the police lab repeated their test they found the same thing. Case dismissed.

It might be that the FBI has some undisclosed evidence that has been very carefully handled and that is highly probative in identifying Cooper, enough so that a conviction could be secured without any other evidence. Cigarette butts might fit this description. It just makes no sense that they would be 'lost.'

Peterson, a highly qualified suspect, was ruled out on DNA. Maybe it wasn't tie DNA but cigarette DNA which would be more confidently linked to DB Cooper.

In addition, there has been an uncanny passivity to the FBI's work at times. Ralph Himmelsbach never interviewed Tina even though she moved to Portland after the skyjacking, nor when she received medical treatment. Is this a proper handling of a primary witness in a major case? More troubling, Himmelsbach's book reveals—and Dorwin Schreuder confirms—that for much of the Norjak era, the Portland FO had a reactionary stance to the investigation, and only responded to leads as they came in to the office. Similarly, Seattle agents, such as Bob Sale and Sid Rubin, have also indicated that the Cooper case was near-dormant in the Seattle FO between the money find in 1980 and the resurgence in the late 1990s.

Further, does silence on the details of the case really serve the investigation? Why didn't a single FBI agent attend the DB Cooper Symposium in 2011 or 2013? What did that avoidance achieve? What kind of investigatory integrity did that maintain?

At times, it appears that FBI agents don't talk with one another, either, even when working on the same case. Galen has a telling story on this subject:

> Seems like the NORJAK agents die by the vine, but DB Cooper lives on. The Bureau must hate that. No one ever hears from Carr since he left. He e-mailed me about 6 months after I started talking with Eng, but Eng wasn't too enthused that I was still talking with Carr about the case. Led me to believe that the agents aren't necessarily on the same page, and rather territorial of their own turf (even among other agents).

Part of this *non-sharing* with fellow agents was fostered by J Edgar Hoover. As discussed previously, Hoover awarded cash bonuses to agents who busted tough cases, so field agents had an incentive *not* to share, as it could cost them money. Plus, we have the pressures seeping from the mundane area of internal politics, promotions based upon performance, and professional status within the office.

As for my relationship with FBI agents, when I ask questions beyond their initial set story, they balk. I call it the "One and Done" scenario. I get one good interview—usually a recitation of their well-rehearsed narrative—then, nothing. Follow-up phone calls and emails go unanswered. Sadly, even Russ Calame seems to be avoiding my calls at this point. Thus, I strongly suspect that what I was told initially was a spin job and they don't want me to scratch beneath the surface.

Currently, formal communications with the FBI have become strained. In 2015, I was told the official policy of the FBI was to not say anything about Norjak to anyone in the media unless the contact is specifically authorized. After years of exchanging increasingly opaque emails with PIO Ayn Dietrich-Williams, she finally stated the obvious on December 7, 2015:

> The FBI's media policy prohibits discussing ongoing investigations unless a release is specifically thought to have potential benefit to the investigation.

> ...I understand your continued interest in our investigation and apologize that I will not be able to share additional information to answer your questions.

Nevertheless, I have not abandoned all hope in the FBI, and I will be providing them with a "Special Edition" of this book, complete with phone numbers and contact information for all of the major figures of the case. At least then, the Bureau will have a comprehensive overview of the case for future investigators to consult.

Of course, they can call me anytime for assistance.

Chapter 34

New Forensic Tool—
Remote Viewing

Although controversial, a bold and innovative forensic tool has entered the Norjak case, a process called "remote viewing." Some might call it psychic sleuthing or Extra-Sensory Perception (ESP), and despite the uncertainty over its reliability, the scientific proof of remote viewing is significant.

Dr. Hal Putoff of the Stanford Research Institute organized the first large-scale investigation of ESP in the 1970s, and eventually his research attracted the interest of the CIA. By the 1980s the agency had placed Putoff in charge of their remote viewing research, and several years later that effort coalesced into the US Army's Stargate Program. Several of the early Stargate "RV'ers," as they are called, have written extensively about their work, especially David Morehouse in *Psychic Warrior,* and Joe McMoneagle in *Mind Trek: Exploring Consciousness, Time and Space, Through Remote Viewing.*

On a personal level, I have spent over twenty years studying the methodology of remote viewing at Ramtha's School of Enlightenment (RSE), in Yelm, Washington. Additionally, I have integrated those teachings with my undergraduate studies in biology at Hofstra University, and my current research on the New Physics.

According to my understanding, remote viewing is a part of the New Physics, which is an expanding field of study that explores how consciousness influences physical reality. In effect, the New Physics is the "old physics" with one additional twist: it asks, *how do your thoughts affect your life?* This research suggests that thoughts interact with physical reality in a dynamic manner, even changing it materially. Simply, this science of mind-over-matter is the underpinning of remote viewing. Specifically, the New Physics says that with the proper training our thoughts can transcend the usual boundaries of time and space. As a result, a successful remote viewer would be able to re-visit November 24, 1971 and observe Norjak unfolding in person.

Here is my understanding of how this radical science works: The customary five senses of perception: sight, smell, hearing, touch and taste, involve the higher brain functions of the neocortex, frontal lobes and the complex part of the brain known as the cerebrum.

However, there is another part of the brain that is much different and its capacities are very unusual, according to recent neuro-physiological research. This unique section is called the limbic system and is located deep within the center of the brain. It is filled with glands and tissues that specialize in emotions and feelings, and combined they have the capacity for a deeper level of perception—one that is often characterized as psychic awareness. Thus, it is hypothesized that the limbic system gives us access to expanded realms of consciousness.

But what exactly is consciousness, and how can the limbic system overcome the barriers of time and space? That in turn begs the question: what exactly is time and space? Einstein's Theory of Special relativity shows us that time and space are not static or concrete. Time changes as one moves differently through space, and the 2014 movie "Interstellar" portrays the phenomena exquisitely. PBS' Dr. Brian Greene offered a concrete example of how time changes relative to movement through space in a recent Town Hall meeting in Seattle.

Greene said that if two people had absolutely synchronized watches and sat together on a couch watching TV, when one of them went over to the television set and changed the dial, their watch would read a different time than the person still sitting. Continuing, Greene said the concept has been proven many times by flying clocks around the world nonstop. When they get back to their airport of origin, the clocks aboard the aircraft read differently than those at their home base. Similarly, the clocks on the International Space Station have to be re-calibrated periodically to get back into sync with their earth-surfaced bases.

As for consciousness, it seems to be a vast awareness that spreads beyond what we usually consider to be time and space, even if those concepts are mutable. Specifically, as I understand Ramtha the Enlightened One, *thoughts* are created by *consciousness* interacting in our *brain.* Similarly, *mind,* and a concept Ramtha calls "deeper mind," seem to be various levels of consciousness. Together, all of reality exists in a kind of eternal, endless "Now."

With that model it is possible to envision consciousness moving through the Eternal Now. In particular, being consciously aware of another time and space via a focused, meditative thought. Simply, we shift our conscious awareness and relocate to a different position within the Eternal Now. Thus, with a precise, focused change of consciousness we could travel back to the skyjacking and visit Flight 305 for ourselves.

I have attempted to do just that. Additionally, I have undergone hypnosis several times with a hypnotherapist named Gloria Peach to further explore Norjak.

I have also contacted RV'ers Morehouse and McMoneagle and asked them if their programs investigated Norjak, or if they would like to join my efforts. Unfortunately, they have not replied. I have also been unsuccessful in enlisting other professional remote viewers to apply their skills towards Norjak.

I leave it to you to judge the validity of my experiences. To me, they are earnest, initial steps in penetrating the veils that surround Norjak. However, I am ever-mindful that the Stargate guys considered their best work to be only 20 percent accurate. I suppose the big question is: how does one know which remote view falls into the 20 percent. As a result, I consider all of my experiences as possibilities, and use them as a starting place from which to conduct more conventional investigations.

In March 2010, I began my remote viewing sessions. Despite its fancy name, my sessions would appear to most folks as a typical meditation routine—I sat crossed legged in a comfortable position, closed my eyes, and breathed slowly and deeply. As I entered my meditative trance, I envisioned Flight 305 flying through the clouds. I felt excited. Soon, I saw the red tail of a Northwest Orient 727 in my mind's eye.

Next, I heard the roar of the engines. Then, the smell of jet fuel. At that point, I focused on the sketch of DB Cooper's face and I felt myself inside the cabin of Flight 305. I was immediately enveloped into an environment that I can only describe as a "70s vibe." Specifically, I looked around and saw men with long sideburns and 1970s dress—polyester clothing and bell-bottomed trousers. Oddly, I felt oppressed by these sensations and began getting nauseous. To counter that experience, I refocused on DB Cooper's face. I sensed him sitting next to Tina and I tried to envision what they were doing and saying, but little came from it. I kept trying to drill into the focus but I only got more nauseous. After a couple more attempts, I stopped. I was surprised how difficult the experience was and how awful I felt.

Something powerful must have transpired, though, because I needed more time than usual to return to my normal state of mind, or even open my eyes. When I did, I became dizzy if I moved too quickly. Later, I found it very difficult to write any notes. At best, I scribbled cursory notes before the memory faded, somewhat like recording a dream.

I repeated these meditative efforts several more times, through March 2010, but received little new information. Oddly, to this day I can re-visit these "in-flight" scenes easily, but I can't get any more detail. It always makes me nauseous, too. As a result, in subsequent meditative sessions I have shifted my approach slightly and focused only on the sketch of DB Cooper. Within a few moments I saw a face. Then I asked questions, and the first was obvious: "Who are you?"

"I am Charles!... Bar... ka... ley... clay," I heard the face say, pronouncing his first name quite loudly. But his last name was garbled to me, and I heard variations of Bar-Clay, Bark-Lee and Berkley. I wondered if I was superimposing my memory of the famous basketball player over what I was receiving through my limbic system. This confusion persisted, but I returned to the meditation several times over the next few days. Finally I heard him say, "Barclay, like the bank in Great Britain."

Clear, I proceeded and asked, "Where are you?"

Spontaneously, in a little squeaky voice like a child, I heard, "I'm in heaven."

A couple weeks later, I re-visited Charles. He confirmed he was Charles Barclay, and was now out of his body and in a place he called "heaven." I continued with my questions, "Where did you land?"

"In a field," he replied.

I saw an image of a flat, open terrain with a small stand of older saplings thick along the perimeter to the east. I heard road noises nearby. The scene felt rural, but not wilderness. Seeking more detail I asked again, "Can you tell me where you landed exactly? What state or area?"

I heard no reply, so I offered a prompt. "Washington or Oregon?"

Again, I received no response, but the visualization of the field came back into my mind. After a long pause, I received a thought from Charles. "I'm protecting someone who is still alive," I heard him say, and I sensed the person he was shielding was a woman.

I thought of the character, "Clara," in the book, *DB Cooper—What Really Happened,* by Max Gunther. In Gunther's novel, "Clara" was house-sitting a cabin in the Cooper's LZ and met the skyjacker in the woods shortly after he landed. He had a sprained ankle and Clara took him home to nurse his injury. Eventually, they fell in love and moved to New York, spending the ransom money after laundering it in Atlantic City casinos.

Whether my remote view of Charles Barclay had anything to do with a "Clara" or Gunther's book, I don't know. However, I continued my focus on the face of DB Cooper, but no other information came forward. I felt like I was interviewing a very reluctant witness, and I wondered how reliable any of this was.

Several months later, a hypnotherapist named Gloria Peach volunteered to help me search for DB Cooper. I heartedly agreed.

Over the next few weeks, we had six sessions. Gloria put me into a trance-like state reminiscent to my solo work, and then used guided-imagery techniques to lead me through successive levels of consciousness. Eventually, I was able to interact with DB Cooper and others in the case, such as Tina Mucklow and Ted Braden.

Our first session was September 19, 2011, and Gloria guided me back to the plane in flight. I found it very helpful to have a guide. Here is my report:

"The smoke! UG! The cigarette smoke!" I shouted to Gloria. I lingered and observed the cabin, especially Cooper and Tina. I saw that Tina was in control of the situation even though Cooper had the bomb on his lap. She looked and acted confident, smooth but not flirty.

Gloria put me a little deeper into trance. "I can't get a good read on his face," I wrote later in my notes. "He's leaning into her. Tina jokes with Cooper, they light cigarettes. She is comfortable. He seems comfortable, or 'not tense.' He's tall and lean."

I asked Cooper why he hijacked the plane.

"Airline safety improved didn't it!" he said emphatically, following a line that is espoused by Bob Knoss, a Cooper gadfly who claims Norjak was a rogue Governmental operation to build political support for increased airline security.

I asked about the hijacking and got the following tidbits: I was told Cooper boarded in Pittsburgh and got off in Chicago, but this was not the actual itinerary of Flight 305.

I asked him his name again, and I was surprised when he said "Richard." I have no idea what happened to the Charles Barclay persona. "Richard" confirmed that the hijacking was a quasi-military operation, with a "General Sherman" in charge.

"But, he was a major at the time," Richard added.

Richard told me about his upbringing and background. He said that his father was in WW II as an intelligence officer, a "General Brack" or "Brock." Again, it came across garbled.

For Norjak, Richard was "part of a team."

Richard said that he had died in 1986 and that he was in heaven. I asked him to describe it. "You can say that I'm on a cloud," he said, smirking and chuckling.

My second session with Gloria occurred a week later. I was able to go more deeply into "absolute elsewhere," as Ramtha describes the experience, and we covered a range of topics pertaining to Norjak.

First, I visited Ralph Himmelsbach. I saw a basement filled with lots of file cabinets. It was dark, and file cabinets surrounded a conference table. I opened a cabinet drawer and was surprised to see it was mostly empty. The files themselves were skinny.

Not much in here, I said.

Gloria told me to "see something new," and I left Himmelsbach. Within moments I encountered a dark haired woman who told me her name was Doris. She was an older woman and seemed like she was a WAC in WWII, or she looked like a picture of a WAC pilot—short curled hair, styled. But I knew she was something else.

"Are you a flight attendant?" I asked.

"Yes," she answered. I heard her last name as "Berdanke," or Bern-Danks."

She said she knew DB Cooper from the composite drawings, and she was part of 305's originating crew from Washington, DC. Doris told me she had served Cooper drinks as they flew into Chicago from Pittsburgh, and said the skyjacker had a bag in the overhead compartment. She said she remembered Cooper getting off in Chicago, and has never told anyone this information. She said she was never questioned by the FBI.

Gloria told me to move on. I encountered Richard, again, and looked him in the eye. "Can I talk with you?" I asked.

Richard didn't answer; then he shrugged.

"Why?" I asked. The following is what I received:

"It was a job. It was an operation. Our identities were totally protected. We never talked about it. We never talked about the job. To talk is like deciding not to breathe—it's just not done. It's not a problem. I don't need to talk and never have. It's how things are, in my world. Lots of us are like this. Keeping quiet is part of the job, part of who we are. It's like looking in a mirror and seeing that we are physically fit—that our workouts keep our bodies in tip-top shape. Our training is top-notch, too. Keeping your mouth shut and not needing to talk, is all part of the conditioning, the makeup of who we are. Nobody is flabby and gabby. Nobody. Nobody ever talks about any job. Nobody would think to do that. If they did, they'd never be here."

I asked Richard where "here" is. He launched into another soliloquy on his professional life. He told me his "world" is an isolated, hidden one, cloaked by the rural geography of military bases and veiled by the culture of military life. He said he has "minimal interaction with the world," meaning life outside the military. He continued and said the military world is so separate from the civilian world that it's easy to stay silent.

"No one ever asks, so no one ever has to say anything," he told me.

"Why?" I ask.

"It's a warrior's code," he tells me. "It's what we do. Why did I do it? (the skyjacking). Because that's what we do, that's what I do.

I had a job to do and I did it. It's like counting coup. Am I prepared enough? Is my gear good enough? Is my team organized and smart enough? Am I tough enough? It's a personal challenge.

"You (reporters) will never find us," he added. "The only way is to do what you're doing now (remote viewing)."

He continued. "It was a military job. We ate the FBI's lunch. They'll never know. It was an operation. Purpose? I don't know. Could have been a lot of reasons—test the SAGE radar? Improve airlines safety? Check out the radios? Test law enforcement on the ground? Who knows? It could have been a lot of reasons depending on who was involved. It's a game, a test of one's skills. It's all a game—our dreams, our jobs, whatever we do."

Richard continued and told me he has no particular pride in being DB Cooper.

"Why did you pick the name, Dan Cooper?" I asked.

Richard laughed loudly. "I liked the name," he said, and laughed again. "But it got changed right away! *DB* Cooper—who the fuck is that? Unless others changed the name on purpose." Richard then appeared very somber and serious, even a little anxious. *Is the game still afoot?* I wondered.

I asked Richard if he will re-incarnate. He shrugged.

"I might be an intelligence operative," he says. I'd always have a job, always have a paycheck—that's how the world is. If the world doesn't want you, they don't pay you."

Richard told me about his father, again, and said, "Military intelligence is a father-son thing. It's like passing down a trade. You know how it is." He told me his brother was also in military intelligence.

He said his unit was part of the army, but that his particular outfit was not SOG. "It's deeper than that," he said, meaning that it was more covert and hidden. However, he acknowledged that his unit was under the same command as SOG.

I asked Richard how he died. He shrugged. I asked again. He hesitated, but realized I was going to be insistent. "I was drinking. I got tired of living and died."

"Can we talk again?" I asked.

"If you can find me," he said smiling.

A few days later, I went looking for Ted Braden. It was a very difficult session, even with Gloria's help. I went into a very deep trance and was very groggy afterwards. I believe one of the reasons for the difficulty is that I sought more specific information, not just general impressions. I wanted facts that could be verified.

After Glory put me into a trance, I focused on an image of Ted in a Vietnamese field. Here is what I received in response: Ted said he was dead, having passed away in 2006. "2007 was a mistake," he told me, apparently correcting some clerical error that still haunted him. He added that he died of a heart attack.

I asked him if he drove a truck in the second half of his life. "Yeah, I needed a job," he told me.

Continuing, I asked him if he was DB Cooper, and he denied it. Ted told me that the skyjacker was a covert CIA operative named "John Romano." Ted also said that he wanted to be part of John's group but was denied. He also said that John is still alive.

At this point something unusual happened—a silvery hue enveloped the figure I knew to be Ted Braden. He was back-lit, and I saw an opening that appeared to be a staircase. *The aft stairs to a 727? The Stairway to Heaven?*

Then, the scene shifted back to Vietnam. Ted was on bivouac and seemed aware of how I was communicating with him. "You would have learned a lot in Vietnam," he told me. "That's how we stayed alive here—we had to *focus!*"

After a long hiatus from remote viewing caused by family visits, financial difficulties and my heart attack, I resumed my sessions with Gloria in June 2012. I re-visited DB Cooper, and received my fourth name-change. Now, Cooper said he was "Richard Bengstrom," and stated that he died in 1986.

We spoke at length about his team. He called it "The Group." He said they had all served in covert ops in Vietnam together, and had been stationed at Fort Lewis before deploying. Richard told me that The Group had three members, and they acted as his ground retrieval team. He identified them as Ralph Munce, a second soldier named Jim—whose last name I never got—and a third trooper, Pete Stupinski. According to this Richard, Munce found him in a field and took him to PDX, where Richard flew home to Fort Bragg.

Richard said that The Group buried the money and chutes in a field just south of Ariel, near a line of trees. He said that they communicated with radios.

Richard also said that he didn't know either Sheridan Peterson or Ted Braden. Richard characterized the skyjacking as a "private job done on military time." He added that most of the preparation for the skyjacking was done as part of their normal covert training in the military. "The taxpayers paid for it," he said simply.

After these sessions, I decided to stop the remote viewing. Frankly, the information seemed too chaotic for me to corroborate. Nevertheless, I needed to start somewhere on this remote viewing business, as it has the potential to circumvent all of the people and events that have thwarted the hunt for DB Cooper.

Afterwards, I had a delightfully lucid dream that touched upon this work. I was walking down the aisle of Flight 305 and approached seat 18-E.

"Excuse me, Mr. Cooper," I said, "my name is Bruce Smith, and I'm a reporter with the *Mountain News*. Do you mind if I sit down and talk to you about what is going on?"

He looked at me in a nonplussed manner, and nodded to his left. *Sure, sit down,* he indicated with his chin. He looked me over a bit and eyed my lanyard and credentials, my short hair and polar fleece jacket.

"You're from the future, aren't you," he asked.

"Yes, I am," I replied.

DB Cooper sat back in his seat and smiled.

"Then kid, you're my ticket out of here."

Chapter 35

What I Think Happened to DB Cooper

Since nothing substantial has ever been found from the skyjacking other than the three bundles of twenties, there are a lot of blank spaces to fill in the DB Cooper case. I am asked routinely what I think happened, and here is my view:

I think DB Cooper made it. I say that because the jump wasn't too tough and all the copycats made it. Further, I think DB Cooper was trained to do the jump since he had top-secret level information.

Specifically, I think DB Cooper was special ops, possibly SOG or some subset of SOG, or even Delta Force or a Navy Seal. I say this because that's what commandos have told me.

"DB Cooper was one of our guys," a SOG trooper told me. "It looked like one of our operations—it had all the hallmarks of how we do things. It was well-planned and well-executed—and clearly Cooper was well-trained. So like they say, if it looks like a duck and quacks like a duck, it's a duck."

Since DB Cooper had top-secret information, it is possible that he also had relationships with top-secret types of people, such as commandos who could comprise an extraction team. They could have possessed state-of-the-art radios and tracking devices to retrieve all the gear, and able to obtain a variety of vehicles replete with medical supplies, clothing, and disguises to conduct a successful getaway.

Added to that, DB Cooper and his extraction team had at least an 11-hour head start before anyone flew over LZ-A, and no one on the ground was looking for the skyjacker for at least 40 hours. That would give the team plenty of time to make contact with Cooper, grab all the gear, pull any parachutes out of the trees, and vacate the area before anyone could spot them.

In addition, I believe the FBI, or certain elements within the Bureau, have perpetrated a cover-up for all the reasons speculated throughout this book, most likely to minimize the exposure of clandestine combat operations in Southeast Asia. I further believe that MKULTRA-like techniques were used to control principals involved in Norjak, such as the FBI agents in Reno who now can't remember anything. Also, I think it possible that Tina Mucklow is affected by these types of processes.

Lastly, I strongly believe that Earl Cossey was murdered because of his knowledge of unsavory actions in the Norjak case, such as orchestrating a campaign against the image of DB Cooper as "The Man who beat Da Man."

Who's Who of Norjak

The FBI

Although the skyjacking began in Portland, Oregon, overall case management was given to the Seattle office because it had the most interaction with Cooper. First, they had to procure the parachutes and ransom money. Then they had to secure the passengers and the airport. Subsequently, they helped organize the effort to track the plane, and later launched the ground and aerial search. To accomplish those tasks they mobilized their entire office, about thirty agents.

As a result, Seattle is the "Office of Origin." However, no one from the Seattle office has ever written a public account of the investigation, and it is difficult to know who did what. Nevertheless, here is what I have been able to ascertain, starting with the basics: organizationally, the FBI has different levels of leadership.

At the primary level are "special agents." This term is given to all certified FBI field agents, and besides their specialized FBI training, special agents also have strong academic backgrounds. During the Hoover era most special agents had law degrees, and during the 1970s that requirement was expanded to include other specialties, such as accounting.

Leading a field office, called a "FO," is the Special Agent in Charge, the "SAC." Special agents who lead the investigation into a particular crime, such as Norjak, are called "case agents."

Groups of agents can be assembled for specific tasks and are called "squads."

DB Cooper Case Agents

From the early days of the investigation to his retirement in 1977, Special Agent **Charlie Farrell** was the head of the FBI's Norjak investigation. At the 2011 Symposium, Geoffrey Gray gave an extensive examination of Farrell's role and announced that Farrell had penned a 300-page commentary on his Cooper investigation. However, Farrell passed away in 2005, and all my efforts to contact his family have been unsuccessful. Nor have I seen Farrell's case history despite my requests to Mr. Gray.

J. Earl Milne has been recently identified as the agent in charge of the FBI operations at Sea-Tac airport during the skyjacking. In the years that followed, Milne continued with Norjak in a senior role. Many other agents in the Seattle office were active in the Norjak investigation beyond the initial blanket effort, especially **John Detlor** and **Don Steele**. During the first few years, these agents joined with Charlie Farrell and Milne to form the backbone of the Bureau's DB Cooper investigation.

In addition, Farrell and his team were assisted by senior staff at the Seattle FO by handling administrative details. This included assignments of ancillary squads, which were groups of agents involved in special projects, such as interviewing groups of suspects or maintaining the perimeter defense at Sea-Tac on the night of the skyjacking.

Special Agent **Sid Rubin** was one such investigator assigned to the security detail out on the runway. Sid also joined Norjak researcher Bob Sailshaw and me at one of Sail's DB Cooper Luncheons held at the Seattle Yacht Club, and gave us a clearer picture of the inner workings of the Seattle FO.

Ron Nichols was the Cooper case agent following Farrell's retirement in 1977. Nichols is reported to have been a brilliant agent, and he graduated second in his class at the Naval Academy. He reportedly served with distinction in the Bureau until his retirement. However, he has resisted all of my efforts to speak with him.

Don Glasser, a former Navy Seal, joined the FBI in 1978 and reportedly formed a dynamic investigatory partnership with Nichols.

Nichols is also reported to have had a contentious relationship with Ralph Himmelsbach, the FBI agent in the Portland office leading Norjak efforts there. Allegedly, Himmelsbach did not alert the Seattle office to the Cooper money find at Tina Bar in 1980, and as a result Nichols learned about it by reading the Seattle newspapers.

Other Norjak Principals

Ralph Himmelsbach, the above mentioned agent, was stationed in the FBI's Portland, Oregon field office and designated to handle all skyjackings involving that jurisdiction. He says he received this role because he was an accomplished pilot and owned an airplane. In fact, Mr. Himmelsbach was an aviator in WW II and flew P-51s. As mentioned earlier, he scouted the Ariel area from the air immediately after the skyjacking. Further, Himmelsbach claims that he was the "naming agent" for the Cooper case, now known as "Norjak." Himmelsbach is also co-author of *NORJAK: The Investigation of DB Cooper*, which is an account of his work. His co-author is a professional writer named **Thomas Worcester.**

In the course of the investigation Ralph became good friends with **Bill Rataczak**, the pilot of Flight 305. In fact, Bill telephoned Ralph during my interview with Agent Himmelsbach.

However, Himmelsbach did not play a major role in the early days of the investigation. Over the Thanksgiving Day weekend, field operations in Portland were clearly under the direction of **Julius Mattson**, the SAC of the Portland FO. Further, Himmelsbach did not play a prominent role in Norjak until he presented the FBI's evidence against Cooper to a federal grand jury in Portland in 1975.

Nevertheless, Himmelsbach was the leader of the evidence retrieval at Tina Bar in February 1980 when $5,800 of the ransom money was found. Ever since, Himmelsbach has been the public face of the FBI's DB Cooper investigation, and he has appeared in numerous documentaries and news broadcasts. Ralph has repeatedly told me that he expects payment for his interviews, and according to British newspaper reporter Alex Hannaford, Himmelsbach asks for $600 from print journalists. Author Robert Blevins reports further that Ralph charges $2,100 for a video filming. Lacking those kinds of funds, I have offered to take Ralph and his wife out to lunch. So far, he has not agreed to a formal interview, and only spoke with me when I stopped at his house unexpectedly. Nevertheless, he graciously spoke with me for about twenty minutes in 2011.

Himmelsbach also has a remarkable relationship with Cooper sleuth **Jerry Thomas**, and the latter calls Ralph a "second father." It appears the affection is mutual. The relationship between

Himmelsbach and Thomas is so extraordinary that I felt I had to ask Ralph about his associate. "How well do you know Jerry Thomas?" I asked.

"Very well, "Ralph replied. "He was my primary source for investigating the topographical area of where Cooper jumped. Jerry grew up there, and he knows the area very well. Plus, he was an Army Special Forces instructor. He's got a great background and I knew I could rely absolutely on the accuracy of his reports." After a pause he continued, "I knew we were getting good information from him on the area." Ralph paused again, and then added, "I've searched the area many times myself, from the air and on the ground."

"Are we talking the Washougal watershed area?"

"Yes," Ralph said.

"How long have you known Jerry?" I continued.

"Oh, we, ah, go way back," Ralph replied.

"Did you know him at the beginning of the Cooper investigation, then?"

"Oh, no. I guess I've known Jerry for about ten years."

"How did he come to join your investigation?"

"He volunteered. He initially contacted me and offered to 'help in any way,' particularly with any ground searches in the area.

"Ralph, it is my understanding that Jerry has posted on the DropZone website that he knew Cooper suspects Richard McCoy and Sheridan Peterson in Vietnam. Is that true?"

"We've never discussed that."

Due to mandatory age retirement policies, Himmelsbach was compelled to retire from the FBI just two weeks after the money find in 1980. His retirement home in Woodburn is so extraordinary that I was compelled to ask retired Special Agent **Bob Sale** if the Bureau is particularly generous with its pension benefits.

Sale told me that he knows Mr. Himmelsbach, and claims Ralph is good friends with Phil Knight, the founder of Nike, which is based near Portland. Bob suggested that Ralph's' apparent wealth may have come from timely investments in Nike during the early days. Further, Sale told me that a typical special agent has a pay grade of GS 13, earning about $70,000–80,000 a year. After a full career in the FBI, an agent would retire with a pension of 75 percent of their salary, or about $60K per year. Sale also said that the FBI has a special "availability" status for retired agents, who would earn an additional 25 percent.

Special Agent in Charge (SAC) Russ Calame

Russ Calame was the SAC in Salt Lake City and led the team that captured Richard McCoy in one of the first so-called "Cooper copycat" skyjackings. In April 1972, McCoy hijacked a 727 out of Denver flying to San Francisco, and bailed into the evening skies over his home of Provo, Utah.

Calame later partnered with federal sentencing official **Bernie Rhodes** to write *DB Cooper—the Real McCoy*. To this day, Calame believes that Richard McCoy was DB Cooper. Further, Calame and Rhodes believe that McCoy perfected his second skyjacking by demanding $500,000. Calame also says that many in the Seattle FO agreed with him in the early 1970s. Calame presents compelling information that McCoy might have been involved in the Cooper skyjacking, and proves that McCoy was in Las Vegas, Nevada the day after the Cooper hijacking—shattering McCoy's alibi that he was at home for Thanksgiving dinner. Oddly, the Seattle FO accepts McCoy's alibi. After capture, McCoy escaped twice from federal custody and was finally killed in a gun battle with FBI agents in Virginia Beach, Virginia. The Special Agent in charge of that team was **Nick O'Hara**, and Bernie Rhodes states that O'Hara proclaimed: "When I shot Richard McCoy I killed DB Cooper."

In 2012, O'Hara, now retired from the FBI, told me that he has become a good friend of Mr. Rhodes and they regularly vacation together at the latter's Florida home. Despite the cordial conversation I had with Agent O'Hara, he declined my request for help in making contact with Bernie. Although I have Mr. Rhodes' phone number and address from Russ, Bernie declines all requests for an interview. Whenever I call his phone, it rings into infinity.

I also asked Nick about McCoy's wife. One of the mysteries of the Richard McCoy story is how the FBI knew to find him in Virginia Beach. It is widely believed that McCoy's wife became the FBI's informant. Such happenstance makes sense because it is also believed that she was in cahoots with her husband as his getaway driver. Hence, the FBI had leverage with the wife, and this scenario is inferred in the Calame-Rhodes book. Also, it is rumored that the wife successfully sued the authors over this issue, causing Calame and Rhodes to forfeit movie rights to their story.

Nevertheless, I asked O'Hara directly if the wife was his source of information. He laughed when I posed the question. "I'm not going to tell you that!" he roared. "I've never revealed that information in all these years, even though Bernie keeps bugging me to!" O'Hara also confirmed that many within the FBI feel that McCoy-was-Cooper, especially in Salt Lake City.

Calame and Rhodes also infer that FBI chief **J. Edgar Hoover** sabotaged the Cooper investigation. Calame suggests that when he was forced to retired shortly after McCoy's arrest due to mandatory age requirements, Hoover placed a dud in charge of the Salt Lake City office, causing the McCoy-Cooper investigation to wither.

Special Agent in Charge (SAC) Red Campbell

Harold "Red" Campbell was the SAC of the Las Vegas, Nevada FBI office, and was in charge of the evidence retrieval and crew debrief in Reno on the night of the skyjacking. His actions and those of his team are considered highly problematic, and allegedly they botched the fingerprint retrieval, failed to recover the glossy "in-flight" magazines that the skyjacker fingered, and hid the clip-on-tie for four days. In addition, Campbell apparently carried the eight cigarette butts to Las Vegas and never transferred them to Seattle. Later, the butts were lost from the Las Vegas depository.

More troubling, Campbell didn't remember much from that evening when questioned by federal official Bernie Rhodes in preparation for the latter's book, *DB Cooper—The Real McCoy*. In addition, neither Campbell nor any of his staff have offered explanation for any of their actions or egregious memory losses.

Special Agent Richard Tosaw

Richard Tosaw's participation in the Cooper case is unusual. Even though he is a former FBI agent, he was not involved in the official investigation and only joined DB Cooper saga when he provided the legal services necessary for Brian Ingram's family to get some of the ransom money returned. After aiding the Ingrams, Tosaw became a zealous private investigator in the Cooper case. His *DB Cooper—Dead or Alive?* was one of the first significant books written on the skyjacking.

As for the money, the FBI claimed they needed it for evidence when they took it from the Ingrams. However, a Seattle court awarded the Ingram family about half the bills and the Bureau received a dozen or so. The remaining bills went to Global

Indemnity, the insurance company that had underwritten the NWO plane.

Surprisingly, Tosaw's brother, **Michael Tosaw**, was a special agent serving in Seattle during the 1970s.

Richard investigated Norjak extensively, spending summers on the Columbia dredging the river bottom looking for Cooper's remains and artifacts until his death from cancer in 2009. Richard Tosaw is also the last journalist to interview Tina Mucklow before her 30-year silence took hold, speaking with her during the early stages of her residency in the Maria Regina Carmelite monastery in Eugene, Oregon.

Although I had spoken on the phone with this kindly old gent before his death in 2009 from cancer, I had never met him.

Special Agent Larry Carr

Larry Carr is perhaps the best known DB Cooper case agent in the history of Norjak, and he handled the investigation from 2007 until late 2009.

Carr is unique in his efforts to forge a partnership with the public and he shared never-before-released evidence and information on the skyjacking, such as the presence of the clip-on tie that Cooper purportedly left aboard the aircraft. He also allowed selected members of the public to review the evidence and review files, such as the Citizen Sleuth team. In addition, he allowed author Geoffrey Gray to have unprecedented access to the Norjak files.

During his tenure as case agent, he was fiercely involved in Norjak. One night at 4 am when I couldn't sleep, I went to the DZ and found Carr making a post. *Can't sleep either, eh, Larry?* I said to myself.

Sadly, his tremendous visibility in the public eye may have back-fired. His commentary in the 2009 National Geographic documentary on Cooper: *The Skyjacker Who Got Away*, placed Carr in an unfavorable light for presenting the "Propeller Theory"—the notion that the bundle of $5,800 found at Tina Bar arrived there after being temporarily wrapped around the drive shaft of an inbound freighter heading up the Columbia River. Such an implausible scenario was made even weaker by Carr's lack of any concrete evidence to support his theory. Shortly afterwards, Larry was taken off the case. Reportedly, he was promoted and re-assigned to FBI headquarters in Washington, DC. At that time, researcher Galen Cook told me that Larry had informed him that the FBI was "shutting down the case." In addition, Carr stopped posting on the DZ and he has not returned any of my phone calls or emails.

Special Agent Curtis Eng

Curtis Eng is the current DB Cooper case agent, and he is as different from Larry Carr as night is from day. Eng is circumspect and virtually silent on the case. He has declined all my requests for an interview and has only contacted me once, responding to an email when I alerted him to an Internet hacking episode that involved the FBI and my Norjak files. Nevertheless, Eng seems to be very busy on the case, and during his tenure we have had the Marla Cooper flap, the release of Letter #3, the arrival of the mysterious "Al Di" to the investigation, and the extension of permission to Geoffrey Gray to peruse FBI files that began under Larry Carr, along with continuing the presence of the Citizen Sleuths.

This latter happenstance resulted in Gray's account of the early hours of the skyjacking and many others heretofore unknown aspects of the investigation, such as the true owner of the parachutes, Norman Hayden.

An FBI official that works closely with Eng in Seattle is the PIO, **Ayn Dietrich-Williams**. Although she is quite young and her knowledge of the case appears at times to be rudimentary, she is a solid professional. She returns all my phone calls and emails.

Other Case Agents

Ralph Hope was the Cooper case agent around 2001, according to Jo Weber, who had extensive dealings with the Seattle office at this time regarding her deceased husband and Cooper confessee, Duane Weber.

Afterwards, **Eric Mueller** was the Cooper case agent until he retired in about 2007 and Larry Carr took over, according to attorney Galen Cook, who sued the FBI for access to the Cooper files during Mueller's tenure. Galen describes Mueller as a soft-spoken man and a "nice guy."

Other Norjak Agents

Tom Manning was the nominal head of the Norjak investigation for the first few days, as he busily organized the federal and local law enforcement teams conducting their air and ground search throughout southeast Washington. He was based in the "Resident Agency" of the FBI's Longview, Washington office, an administrative satellite of the Seattle FO. Manning concentrated his ground searches in the Ariel area, both in the days immediately after the skyjacking and then later in the spring of 1972 when the massive Army effort was launched.

Dorwin Schreuder took over Norjak duties in Portland after Himmelsbach retired in 1980. In addition, Dorwin was the PIO for the money retrieval at Tina Bar.

Also, Dorwin has a Master's Degree in Behavioral Sciences and became an expert hostage negotiator, especially with skyjackings. After DB Cooper, Schreuder was involved in the second hijacking attempt by the notorious Glenn Tripp. Previously, Tripp had attempted to snatch an airplane in 1980, and during his second effort three years later, which occurred at Sea-Tac airport, Dorwin was selected one of the FBI's negotiators.

Dorwin told me he was on the phone with the skyjacker at the moment other agents stormed the airplane and fatally shot Tripp. "Over the phone I heard the guns fire. I asked Tripp what was happening, but all I heard was silence... it was very disturbing," Dorwin told me.

Years later Dorwin was summoned again, this time to the Portland airport to negotiate the surrender of one of his neighbors who had hijacked a TWA flight over a beef with officials at the Portland Police Department. It was successfully concluded without injury. Dorwin's fourth skyjacking was to negotiate a hijacking in Eugene, Oregon, on small local flight headed for Hillsboro, Oregon, a suburb of Portland. Again, Dorwin engineered a successful conclusion. "He was a very depressed guy, and an alcoholic," Schreuder told me.

I found Agent Schreuder to be a kindly old gent. Currently, he lives in Montana where he skis daily. He has invited me to visit him any time I'm in the area, and I plan to do so when I get a few extra dollars.

Mike McPheters participated in the money retrieval at Tina Bar, looking for fragments at the tide line. McPheters claims he found about a dozen pieces at a depth of one to two feet. Earlier, McPheters had handled skyjackings when he was stationed in Miami. After McPheters left the Bureau he became a Mormon bishop, and he has written an account of his remarkable life, titled: *Agent Bishop—True Stories of a FBI Agent Moonlighting as a Mormon Bishop*. I spoke with him in 2009.

Lee Dormuth is the brother-in-law of Tina Mucklow, the flight attendant that Cooper kept on board as a hostage. Dormuth is a 32-year vet of the FBI, and was a special agent in the San Diego office at the time of the skyjacking. Dormuth told me that he and his wife, Tina's sister Jane, flew to Reno to be with Tina the night of the skyjacking.

I have visited with Lee briefly on two occasions, and he has been civil but tightly guarded when we spoke on his front stoop. He ended both conversations by walking back inside his home and shutting the front door. He says he wants "no part of it," meaning his sister-in-law and the Norjak case.

Yet, he is deceitful for unknown reasons, as he tells me that Tina is fine when she clearly is not. Further, I strongly believe that he has regular dealings with Tina despite his disclaimer; and he also told me his wife spoke at length with researcher Jo Weber the night before my last visit to their humble double-wide, located in a bucolic setting in the Puget Sound area.

Dormuth currently works as a private investigator.

The FBI's "Vault"

At the FBI's website there is a special DB Cooper section and it features the "Vault." Within this file are volumes of old documents, giving researchers a tangible feel for the early days of Norjak. Sadly, the files do not appear to be updated or even well-organized, so finding meaningful information can be daunting. Nevertheless, it is a valuable depository of raw data, newspaper clippings, and court testimonies. In addition, the FBI site has a slew of video clips, most notably those featuring case agent Larry Carr. Although uneven, The Vault is of value to the serious researcher.

Authors, Investigators, and Luminaries

Galen Cook is one of the leading figures in the Norjak investigation. He has been digging into the case for at least twenty years, and probably more than that. He is an attorney, licensed in both Washington and Alaska, and currently lives in Fairbanks. Galen is arguably the most knowledgeable investigator on the case and has invested tens of thousands of dollars in his research. As an attorney, he has access to many networks of law enforcement personnel, and he is a superb sleuth. His knowledge of the law has also been of critical importance to me at numerous points in my research. Galen is the leading advocate for William Wolfgang Gossett, but I have never found Galen hamstrung by that perspective.

Galen is also the only reseacher to have sued the FBI for access to the Bureau's files on DB Cooper. In 2004, he filed a lawsuit with the US Department of Justice but did not win his case. Although dismissed, Galen did prevail on a motion for an "in camera" review of the files, granted by the Chief US District Court judge in Seattle. Over time, Galen says his welcome at the Seattle FO became established through the courtesies of the Seattle SAC. In general, Cook enjoys the greatest amount of access to the FBI of any private investigator. He has actively worked with Norjak case agents, in particular Eric Mueller (2004–2006), Larry Carr (2007–2009) and the current Cooper case agent, Curtis Eng. Galen has told me that he has exchanged at least 60 emails with Eng, and they have reviewed physical evidence together as well.

Cook is currently writing a book on his findings. Lastly, I am proud to call Galen my friend.

Geoffrey Gray is a top-notch writer for *New York* magazine and the author of *Skyjack–The Hunt for DB Cooper*, published in 2011. Geoffrey spent several years of research on his book, traveling repeatedly across the country to investigate virtually every lead and suspect. When I asked him how he could afford to bounce between New York and Sea-Tac so frequently—and also go to California to see the Dayton family, Florida to speak with Jo Weber, South Carolina to speak with Florence, and Minnesota to meet with the conspiratorial gadfly Bob Knoss—Geoff replied: "Plastic. I go where I want to go and I put it all on plastic."

As an "A" list journalist, Geoffrey also seems to have extensive contacts within the government and military. Geoffrey is also the author of the term, "The Cooper Curse," the notion that when an investigator closes in on a kernel of truth concerning Norjak, something out of left field derails the attempt. Perhaps the grandest example of the Cooper Curse was the discovery of the money in 1980, which seems only to further complicate the case. Further, Geoffrey organized the 40th Anniversary Symposium on DB Cooper, a monumental and important undertaking.

Even though his book was released in 2011, he is still actively involved in the case. To wit: Geoff was a major architect of the 2013 Symposium in Tacoma.

My relationship with Geoffrey is also mysterious. Although our collegial interactions are usually warm and he invited me to sit on the Tacoma symposium panel, Geoffrey, nevertheless, drives me crazy—especially when I attempt to understand his involvement with the FBI.

Robert Blevins and his co-author **Skipp Porteous** have written the 2009 book, *Into the Blast—The True Story of DB Cooper.* Despite its title, the work is actually a compilation of circumstantial evidence that places a Northwest Orient Airlines purser by the name of Kenny Christiansen on the list of Cooper suspects. A key element of their argument focuses on unusual amounts of cash at Kenny's disposal, both immediately after the skyjacking and later throughout his life. A shorter version of the essential story was written by Geoffrey Gray in 2007 for *New York* magazine, titled "Unmasking DB Cooper." In this work Gray reveals that Christiansen was probably gay and had troubling relationships with teenage runaway boys, allowing them to stay in his Bonney Lake, Washington home.

Blevins and Porteous do not investigate this dimension of Christiansen's life nor his continued work at NWO for twenty years after the skyjacking. Further, they do not explore what Christiansen's activities were in Asia and if Kenny had any independent business activities there, as he flew routes to the Orient exclusively throughout his career.

Blevins lives in Auburn, Washington and is the head of Adventure Books of Seattle, a small independent publishing house. In addition, he cleans houses to pay bills. Porteous was a private investigator in New York City and the former owner of Sherlock Investigations. He sold his PI business in 2013, and reportedly moved to Morro Bay, California.

Dona Elliott was a major figure in the cultural appeal of DB Cooper. She bought the Ariel Store in 1990 and continued to host the annual DB Cooper Day Festival, a rousing bash that celebrated the notorious skyjacker. The upper floor of her store was her residence, while she maintained a pub and souvenir stand on the ground level—giving the establishment a luscious, homey feel.

Dona also maintained a section of the store as an *ad hoc* museum of the DB Cooper case, including the 1972 ground search that swarmed all around her as hundreds of soldiers and FBI agents conducted a second, unsuccessful effort to discover evidence.

Dona was always ready to talk "DB Cooper," and she enthralled the numerous tourists that visited her tavern with stories about the skyjacking—many of them not supported by facts, as far as can be determined. But her effervescence transcended all concerns for factuality, and her death on October 13, 2015 from long-standing health issues stunned Cooper World. It also triggered a temporary halt to the DB Cooper Festival for the first time since 1974, when former Ariel Store owner **Jermaine Tricolor** initiated the festivities.

George Nuttall is a retired captain from the California Highway Patrol and the author of the *DB Cooper Case Exposed—J. Edgar Hoover Cover Up?* Nuttall entered The Hunt as a tag-along buddy to his law enforcement friend, **Harry L. Grady**. The pair stumbled into Norjak when Grady retired to southwestern Washington after a career in military intelligence and the San Diego Police Department. Once he started digging into Norjak, Grady realized that everything was not kosher, so he summoned his old friend Nuttall to assist him and together they began a foray into the mysteries of Norjak.

They concluded that the Cooper case was sabotaged by FBI boss J. Edgar Hoover in order to cover up his involvement with Mafia-based gambling activities. Nuttall also charges that Ralph Himmelsbach acted irresponsibly with Grady, regarding Grady's privacy and safety. Specifically, Grady was an investigator for the San Diego DA's office in organized crime and he had received death threats from some of the wise-guys he had incarcerated. As a result, Grady lived *incognito when he* moved to the Portland area for his retirement.

However, as his interest in Norjak deepened he called upon Himmelsbach to confer on the case. Surprisingly, Nuttall says Himmelsbach gave Grady's contact information to Jerry Thomas, and the latter telephoned Grady. According to Nuttall, Thomas berated Grady for his Cooper investigation and even threatened him. Mr. Thomas completely refutes this charge, however, and told me that Harry Grady had called him directly when the two San Diego cops began their Cooper investigation.

Grady died in 2009, but his co-researcher Nuttall published their work in 2010. George continues to live in San Diego and is always willing to talk about Cooper. He picks up on the first ring.

Ron and Pat Forman are the co-authors of *The Legend of DB Cooper—Death by Natural Causes,* published in 2008. As described previously, they entered the hunt for DB Cooper after their friend, Barb Dayton, confessed to being DB Cooper. Not fully believing her, the Formans surreptitiously kept notes on Barb's pronouncements until her death in 2002. Then, the Formans launched a solid investigation into the many claims of their friend, including her sex-change operation in 1969.

Bob "Sailshaw" has a unique position in the pantheon of investigators—he buys lunch for Cooper sleuths at the Seattle Yacht Club and invites interesting people to talk about the skyjacking. In effect, he runs a Salon of Cooper Inquiry, and as a former commodore of the SYC Sail knows a surprising number of folks who have ties to the Norjak story—retired FBI agents, former Boeing engineers, skydivers and pilots. In fact, Bob's own connections are extraordinary—he once rented a room to prime suspect, Sheridan Peterson.

Sluggo, aka Wayne Walker, has developed the quintessential depository of Norjak fact and has unmatched amounts of files, details and facts about Norjak, including copies of the flight transcripts. In addition, he has profiles on all the crew members, and has compiled a laudable array of composite drawings of Cooper, including aged-advanced sketches that portray what Cooper may look like today.

In 1971, **Bruce Thun** was a jump plane pilot at his family's air field in Puyallup, WA and knew Earl Cossey, who was widely known as a skilled skydiver. In his later duties as the manager of Thun Field, Bruce was part of the DB Cooper documentary filmed by the National Geographic that featured local authors Ron and Pat Forman, and focused on the Barb Dayton angle. During the shoot, Earl Cossey was on site and Bruce met him again.

In addition, Norman Hayden rented a hangar at Thun Field during the 1980s, as did **Stan Gilliam**, a Boeing engineer involved in the secret testing of the 727 aft stairway system.

Participants

Norman G Hayden provided the back chutes the skyjacker used, and as a result he is now immersed in a major controversy. The parachutes have become central to understanding DB Cooper's skills, and thus Norman's perspectives on the chutes are invaluable. In another strange twist of fate so common in the Cooper case, Norman's "Hayden Manufacturing Company" built serrated pitch adjustment parts used by Boeing in the fabrication of the 727 aft stairs. "DB Cooper jumped from stairs that I helped build, wearing my parachute!" crowed Norman when he told me the story.

As for DB Cooper, Norman's eyes twinkled when I asked him his thoughts on the famed skyjacker. "I think he was a cool guy," answered Mr. Hayden.

Hayden's claim of ownership challenges the pronouncements from another principal, **Earl J Cossey**, who emphatically claimed he owned the chutes. Cossey also functioned as a kind of "de facto" technical expert for the FBI on the matter of the parachutes.

The Hijacked
Crew of Flight 305

Bill Rataczak was the first officer of DB Cooper's plane and was at the controls when the skyjacker jumped. He was a career pilot for Northwest Orient and has lived in Minnesota with his family. I spoke with him in 2009, and he was both gracious and generous with his time. However, as we concluded, he asked to see what I was writing, "to get a feel for who you are and where you're going with this." In response, I sent him a 32-page overview of my findings, but ever since then he has not returned any of my calls or emails.

In a surprise twist, Ralph Himmelsbach says that he and Bill have become good friends ever since they met for the first time at Ralph's retirement party in 1982. Ralph also told me that he was very touched that Bill and Scotty flew in for the celebration.

Nevertheless, Himmelsbach misspelled Bill's surname in his *NORJAK: The Investigation into DB Cooper,* and wrote his name as Ra**d**aczak.

William Scott, "Scotty," was the senior officer and the captain of the flight. After the skyjacking, he continued to fly for Northwest Orient and died in the mid-1990s. In YouTube clips Scotty appears to be a solid and dependable company man, deferring most media questions to others or stonewalling them in a civil-but-firm manner. This has given credence to the belief that Northwest Orient kept 305's crew on a short leash after the incident.

Harold "Andy" Anderson was the flight engineer. His responsibilities included monitoring the weather, navigational issues, and mechanical operations. After the skyjacking, Anderson also continued to fly for NWO, eventually becoming a full captain. Andy has also stayed out of the limelight, and he has spoken only to Galen Cook of all the journalists on The Hunt.

Alice Hancock was 24 years old at the time of the skyjacking, and was the senior flight attendant and purser—the individual who handled the team of stewardesses and had primary responsibility for the passengers. She is also someone who has not spoken publicly about the skyjacking to any great degree. I called her in 2015 and she hung up on me—but not before saying, "I've been asked so many times to talk about it, but it's just too time consuming." Nevertheless, she has been interviewed recently by Galen Cook and attempted to intercede with Tina on Galen's behalf.

Florence Schaffner worked the economy cabin with Tina Mucklow. Flo has assisted many researchers in exploring the case and played a key role in the 1980s to develop a better sketch of DB Cooper. Flo has been claiming since 1971 that the FBI's initial drawings were not accurate. Further, Ms. Schaffner has spoken extensively with Geoffrey Gray and others including Galen Cook, but she has apparently clammed-up in 2007. She has not returned any of my phone calls or letters since I started investigating the case in 2008, nor has she spoken with any other journalists since that time.

Tina Mucklow joined NWO about a year before the skyjacking and often roomed with Florence during lay-overs. Tina is a highly religious woman and reportedly had a bible with her aboard Flight 305. Galen says that Florence told him that Tina would often proselytize excessively in the stew quarters. Tina left NWO a couple of years after the skyjacking and married, but was soon divorced. Currently, she is believed to be working in the social services field in central Oregon.

The Passengers

Most investigators have decided to protect the privacy of the passengers of Flight 305 unless they individually choose to make public statements, and I do the same. One of the few passengers to speak publicly in recent years is **Jack Almstad**, and I include his generous conversation with me in these writings.

In October 2013, Flight 305 passenger **Bill Mitchell** was interviewed by researchers from the Washington State Historical Museum for inclusion in their "COOPER" exhibit. Mitchell confirmed that he was 20 years old at the time of the skyjacking, and that he sat in seat 18 B directly across from DB Cooper. As such, he is considered to be the best eyewitness to the hijacking outside of Florence and Tina. In fact, Bill stated that he was interviewed by the FBI "two to three times a day" in the period immediately after the hijacking.

Mitchell also says that the WSHM exhibit was "100 percent accurate." Over time, I was able to contact Bill directly and found him to be a charming and funny guy.

Reference B

What if DB Cooper Didn't Jump?

No one actually saw DB Cooper leave the plane, so we do not know with absolute certainty that he parachuted away. So, is it possible that DB Cooper didn't jump? Did he crawl into a space above the lavatory or burrow his way into the cargo hold, re-appearing after all the commotion dissipated or joining the hub-bub dressed as a worker or FBI agent and then escaping? Many people ask that question, so let's explore the possibilities:

First, there is no known concrete evidence to support this hypothesis, but let's not stop because of that.

Secondly, exactly where did he stash himself? How big was the spot? Was it big enough for his body and all of his stuff? How did he pull the panels back into place and re-secure them? People familiar with the 727, such as Don Burnworth, say he could have hid behind a door panel. One aficionado said Cooper could have hidden in the luggage compartment beneath the passenger cabin, as the two are connected on some versions of the aircraft. Others speculate Cooper hid in the compartments above the lavatory.

But his getaway would still be problematic. Reno was filled with cops and FBI—at least two hundred—and then a ton o' media, so the chaos was great, lending some credence to the notion that Cooper could have blended into the mix and slithered away.

But: It was 11 pm, rainy, and temperatures were in the 30s when the plane landed at Reno, so Cooper would need to be dressed for the weather to blend in. Also, if DBC sneaked out, how did he get away from the airport? It's unlikely that he rented a car. Take a bus? Was he picked up by an accomplice? How would the accomplice know the pick-up was in Reno?

Or: Did Cooper stay on the plane until it went to its next destination, which is unclear and no definitive statement about the immediate disposition of the airplane is publicly known, but is thought to be either Boeing Field for repairs or Quantico, VA—the HQ for the FBI's test facilities—for more forensics. How did he deal with the cold and de-pressurization issues? Plus, the walk-away scenario gets dicier the longer he stays with the plane.

And: If Cooper walked away somewhere, did he take any money with him? In what? Even more problematically, if Cooper stayed on the plane, how did three bundles of his money land at Tina Bar?

How about the rest of the evidence? Did Cooper take that, too, when he escaped at Boeing, or did he leave it all on the plane in his hidey-hole? Was it ever discovered? If not, why not? How big is the cover-up, then? How come the bomb-sniffing dogs never discovered Cooper or the bomb? Was it because the bomb was composed of road flares and there weren't any explosive chemicals to detect? Or did Cooper compromise their nostrils by filling the pilots' Styrofoam dinner containers with hot sauce, ruining the canines' sense of smell? Plus, how did Cooper stash the coveralls and work coat that he would have needed later to blend into a crowd of workers at Reno?

But there is an *Out-of-the-Box* idea related to the above hypotheses, only reversed.

Did DB Cooper start his day in Washington, DC, and pre-load his gear on the East Coast? Did he stash boots and a jump suit, radios and a reliable parachute in the overhead compartments, and then depart at the next stop and take a direct flight to Portland, arriving well before 305? Then, did he re-board 305 at PDX knowing that all the stuff he needed was already in place, and had the added good fortune to arrive undetected in Portland? So, as a result, Cooper had lots of warm clothes, the exact parachutes he wanted free of detection devices, radio gear for his ground crew and maybe a thermos of hot coffee.

Skyjack anyone?

Why National Geographic Dumped Barb Dayton

The Barb Dayton story is so compelling that National Geographic cable TV filmed a documentary of her and slated it to be half of a larger treatment on DB Cooper. The show was titled, "The Skyjacker Who Got Away," and was scheduled to air in 2009.

However, the 20-minute section on Barb was cut entirely a few days before the national broadcast. Here is the story of how and why that happened.

In November 2008, Ron and Pat Forman were contacted by Edge West Productions, who said they were under contract with National Geographic and wanted to use the Formans' book on Barb Dayton as a template for their DB Cooper documentary. Specifically, Edge West said they would like to interview them in Ariel during the upcoming DB Cooper festival, and then conduct in-flight reenactments a few months later.

At the time, I was writing for the Pierce County *Dispatch* and my editors were enthralled—*local authors getting filmed for a National Geographic special!* So, as long as I didn't "go overboard on the sex-change thing," they were good for copy, and I headed down to Ariel with the Formans.

In an Ariel residence, Edge West interviewed Ron and Pat, Barb Dayton's daughter Rena Ruddell, and a couple of Thun Field pilots who had known Barb. Later, they all came down to the Ariel Tavern and kibitzed in a side room that is ideal for quiet chats and beer.

In my role as a reporter I interviewed all of these folks, plus Phil Day, the executive producer of Edge West. In addition, I had a lengthy conversation with Phil's teen-aged daughter, who was tagging along and had plenty of time to listen to me spiel about the FBI. The young girl must have talked to her dad because in the midst of my drinking a beer, Phil turned the camera in my direction and began asking questions. Thus, I became part of the documentary, being the red-faced guy emphatically proclaiming: "DB Cooper was one tough-assed dude."

After Ariel, Edge West came up to Tacoma on a fiercely cold day in January 2009, and conducted several days of filming at Thun Field, the air strip in Puyallup where the Formans had first met Barb. I covered the shoot, and also learned that the manager of the airport, Bruce Thun, was an avid DB Cooper aficionado.

The documentary was scheduled to air in July, but all of the material on Barb was deleted a few days before broadcast. I called Phil Day in Los Angeles to learn what happened. Phil was beyond grumpy when I spoke with him, sounding both exhausted and exasperated.

He told me that prior to the excoriation, the Barb Dayton story had gone through several script reviews by National Geographic and had been approved at all levels. But days before broadcast it hit an additional round of review at the highest levels of corporate management, and was axed. With only a few days until showing, Edge West had to scramble to fill twenty minutes of air time to replace the excised Dayton-Forman material. In a rush, Edge West hired an actor, grabbed a parachute, and headed to a Hollywood pool to film a back-up scenario first speculated by Larry Carr and Tom Kaye—their so-called Propeller Theory. Edge West filmed a Lewis River "splashdown" in the pool, and used voice-overs from Carr and Kaye to sop up the excess screen time. Cinemagraphically, it was a disaster.

With all these frustrations, Day told me that he never wanted to touch the DB Cooper story again. Nevertheless, he told me the reasons he was given by the Nat Geo executives on why they nixed the Barb Dayton angle:

1. The sex-change topic was too spicy for nationwide consumption, and was too complex to present adequately in a one-hour broadcast.

2. The Formans had no concrete evidence Barb was DB Cooper.

3. The FBI did not support the theory

However, good things came from this drama. The 2008 Ariel shoot was the time that I first met Geoffrey Gray, and I asked him if he thought Kenny Christiansen was DB Cooper. Geoffrey said simply, "No," but that position faded in his 2011 book, *Skyjack—The Hunt for DB Cooper*. Additionally, a journalistic bond was formed with Geoffrey that exists to this day. Geoffrey also reassured me that he did not feel threatened by my research, and that "The Cooper story is big enough for both of us to write about."

Meeting Bruce Thun was also a plus. Bruce revealed that the Bureau's agents swarmed over Thun Field in the days of the holiday weekend, and in particular asked about one young skydiver who had a girlfriend in Oregon. Apparently, the skydiver was not at home in Puyallup or at his girlfriend's place for Thanksgiving as planned. *Did Bruce, or anyone at Thun Field, know where he was?*

Bruce told the feds that he didn't know what had happened to the skydiver, and was greatly perturbed at the FBI agents. "How did they know that kind of stuff?" he asked me. "How did they know that some kid who skydived at a small field in Pierce County has a girlfriend in Oregon and that he didn't make it there for Thanksgiving? How do they know this much stuff about people?"

Of course I didn't have an answer for him, and I just speculated that Thun Field may have attracted both "tree-top flyers" and accompanying scrutiny from the feds.

Through his life-long association with aviation and aviators, Bruce has many contacts with people connected to the case. Besides Barb, Bruce had also met Earl Cossey at Thun Field, along with Stan Gilliam, a Boeing engineer heavily involved in the development of the 727's aft stair system. Yet, even Bruce didn't know that a 727 could be jumped until Cooper. "The day after DB Cooper jumped, everybody around here (Thun Field) was saying, 'Why didn't I think of that!'" he told me laughing.

Odd Facts from the 2013 Symposium

The Washington State Historical Museum presented an exhibit on DB Cooper in 2013, and as part of the festivities the WSMH also hosted a DB Cooper Symposium. All events were held in Tacoma, Washington and the highlights can be viewed here: www.collections.washingtonhistory.org.

In building their exhibit, the WSHM uncovered some wonderful factoids, such as the price of jet fuel was 11¢ a gallon and the total bill to refuel Flight 305 was $116.27. Additionally, Flight 305 flew back to Sea-Tac on Thanksgiving Day "with crew," presumably Tina, Bill, Scotty and Andy, who then went home to MSP via NWO Flight 70.

The WSHM also addressed the little things of life, such as the mail on board 305 was delivered to the Reno Post Office. Surprisingly, the passengers had to return to Sea-Tac to retrieve their luggage. Also, damage to the aft stairs was listed as "minor," according to NWO reports.

More importantly, though, a memo from NWO operations chief, George E Harrison to JA Rigby, Director of NWO flight services, confirmed that Norman Hayden owned the back parachutes, and they went sent directly to NWO Air Freight Services, as has been recounted by Norman.

In addition, J. Earl Milnes was the agent in charge of the FBI crew at Sea-Tac and worked directly with George Harrison. Milne was a veteran agent and continued in the Norjak case as one of Charlie Farrell's primary investigators.

The WSHM also presented original notes and documents from the family of George Harrison. The WSHM made the following post on the DZ about their exhibit and archives:

> ...Harrison coordinated the hijacker's demands with the FBI and local law enforcement. The archives from Mr. Harrison include documents never before seen by the public, including twenty-three pages of handwritten notes with a timeline of the hijacking as it unfolded; a refueling receipt for the Northwest aircraft; copy of the check made out to Seafirst National Bank, for the $200,000 ransom amount paid to the hijacker; and an original copy of the teletype transcript of communications, between the crew of flight 305 and Sea-Tac Airport.

These documents can be viewed at: collections.washingtonhistory.org/details.

Harrison also wrote that initial reports put DB Cooper at 60 years old.

Acknowledgments

With profound gratitude I thank Galen Cook, Mark Metzler, and Ron and Pat Forman for their assistance in writing this book. They have given me invaluable information on the facts of the case, and along with Bob Sailshaw they reviewed every chapter as it was "hot off the press" between November 2012 and May 2013. That's a lot of reading, and they have been steadfast in this work and in our friendship.

But, most of all I am grateful to Sue Leonard at Rose Island Bookworks for getting *DB Cooper and the FBI* to the finish line. She did the interior designs and book covers for both the E-Book and hard copy editions. Hers was the guiding hand of a skilled editor who took *DB Cooper and the FBI* to all the places a book has to go to become real. But most of all, she held my hand when I was freaking.

And I offer special thanks to Marty Andrade, who in the bottom of the 9th inning volunteered to do extensive compositional and line editing of this book. Hence, Marty became a major architect of the 2nd Edition. Similarly, Kristina Meister came in to do major mop-up work.

Another Literary Angel is Lisa Twinning, who helped with the initial formatting of the POD edition. She got me going when I was feeling stuck.

Literary agent Liz Kracht deserves special attention for not giving up on me as she waded through four versions of this manuscript, while Meyer Louie deserves special thanks for delivering the first round of line editing.

As for copy and compositional editing that took me from the initial stages to this version, I am indebted to the award-winning word queen, Barbara Smith-Vargo.

Similarly, my friend and fellow writer, Cate Montana, gave me many useful suggestions and tons of morale support. She helped me restructure the book to get it nearer to completion, and even re-wrote Chapter One *in toto* to show me what she meant in her critiques!

I also extend my deepest thanks to all those who grace these pages. You gifted me with your stories and time, even though many of you may appear in a light less appealing than you had originally hoped.

Plus, where would I be without my ex? Thanks, Peachy, for everything.

Gloria Peach is another individual who provided both professional assistance in the realm of remote viewing and the comfort of friendship.

As for remote viewing, I want to deeply thank Ramtha and his staff at Ramtha's School of Enlightenment for helping me develop an appreciation of the "long view."

My family and circle of friends also deserve heaps of credit for keeping a roof over my head, helping get to a dentist, and all the other little aspects of life—like a heart attack. Thanks, Mom, Sis, Dave and Jo, and especially Barbara Jean. Also, Medicare, Medicaid, Good Sam Hospital, and the crew in blue from the South Pierce Fire and Rescue. Multi-care, too. And Trista Mortenson for helping me remain sane. Eric Lundstrom, too.

The many readers of the *Mountain News* and the DZ have earned my appreciation and thanks. Please know that your support is treasured.

Sail, special thanks for all the luncheons.

I also want to thank Kourtney Scudder, a young barista at the Volcano Coffee Shop in South Hill, WA. When the writing was a thick slog in the winter of 2013, Kourtney listened attentively to my ramblings while making a great Americano. Kourtney also suggested that I call the book, "Sky Thief," which was the working title for several years.

Snowmman—whoever and wherever you are, thanks for all those phone numbers and ideas.

Biography of
Bruce A. Smith

Before writing *DB Cooper and the FBI—A Case Study of America's only Unsolved Skyjacking*, I was an investigative reporter at *The Dispatch* in Eatonville, Washington. From 2006–2010, I wrote five stories a week on local crime, Pierce County politics, and the cultural happenings of life in the country.

After a change in ownership, I left the *Dispatch* to form my own online news magazine, *Mountain News-WA,* which is based in Eatonville. I cover stories of interest to the folks who "live close to Mount Rainier, either in body or spirit," and since DB Cooper flew right over our heads, Norjak is a major topic of conversation around Eatonville, even after these many decades.

Before becoming a journalist I had been a professional storyteller, and was the 1997 National Storyteller of the Year, 2nd runner-up, and the 1998 National Storytelling Champion, runner-up. Additionally, I had spent fifteen months in Nashville polishing my performing career. From those adventures came my first writings: *Campfire Tales—True Stories Not Everyone Believes; Stories from the Journey,* and *Stories from Backstage.*

But most importantly, I moved to Washington State in 1990 to study with Ramtha the Enlightened One, and my experiences of the mystical life are sprinkled throughout this work.

Prior to Ramtha, I had been a recreation therapist in several psychiatric settings in New York, including the Northport VA

Medical Center and the Nassau County Medical Center. In addition, I was a commercial beachcleaner from 1982-1990, owning and managing Sandsifter, an outfit that used modified potato-pickers to sift the beach sands of New York and keep them free of debris. I have also worked in foster care programs, and from those experiences I wrote my first novel, *The Men of Honor of Unity House.*

Currently, I reside in the foothills of the Cascades, and one day soon I plan on walking The Camino de Santiago de Compostella.

Tina Mucklow, crew member of Flight 305

This photo of Tina was taken by Galen Cook in 2010, and is used with his permission.

DB Cooper's ticket to Seattle

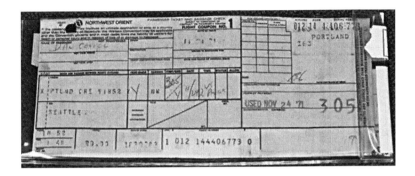

This is a picture of "Dan Cooper's" original plane ticket for Flight 305, Portland to Seattle, November 24, 1971. This picture has been published in many publications and is ubiquitous in all DB Cooper research. Picture provided courtesy of the FBI.

DB Cooper's tie and pin

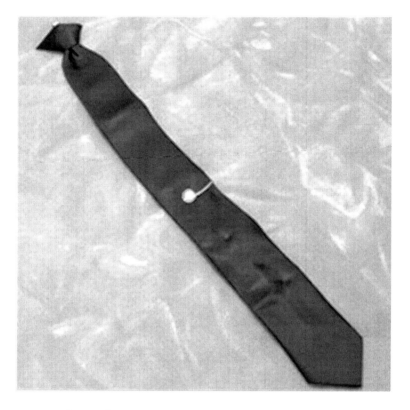

DB Cooper inexplicably left this tie and pin on seat 18-E. It allegedly contains DNA samples on the clasp, and unexplained titanium fragments have been found on the cloth. Photo is from the FBI "Vault" at its DB Cooper website.

Money found at Tina Bar

This "high-resolution" picture of several $20 bills found at Tina Bar shows some of the mysterious holes that are not completely understood. In addition, a few are blackened, which was reportedly caused by the FBI's use of silver oxide when dusting for fingerprints. Picture is provided courtesy of Galen Cook.

Tina Bar, where the money was found in 1980

Note the steeply sloped beach behind the famous sign. In 1980, this beach was less eroded and the money was discovered just below the far trees, about 40-feet from the water's edge. Photo taken by author.

Brian Ingram

The 8-year old boy who found some of DB Cooper's ransom money is now a grown man. Brian Ingram, shown here, attended the 2011 DB Cooper Symposium in Portland, Oregon and spoke at length to reporters. He claimed that after finding the three bundles of twenties buried in a few inches of sand, his family continued looking for more money on the beach but didn't find any. This refutes later claims by the FBI. Photo taken by author.

Richard and Al Fazio, owners of Tina Bar

As owner of the property where $5,800 in twenties from DB Cooper's ransom was found, Richard (l), and Al (r), were central to the money retrieval in February 1980, and the many documentaries and books which followed. Photo taken by author.

Norman Hayden, owner of the "back" chutes

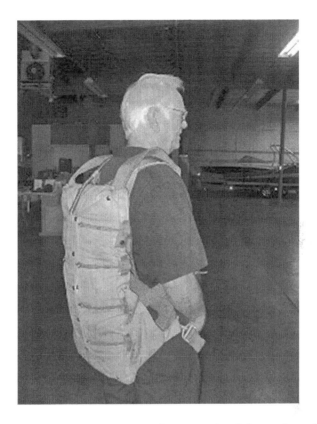

This picture shows Norman Hayden wearing his 26-foot Steinthal canopy, housed inside a Pioneer container. According to Hayden, this is the "not-used chute" that went aboard Flight 305, and Norman says this parachute is identical to the one that DB Cooper used. It was returned to Hayden from FBI custody in 1981. Photo taken by the author.

Duane Weber

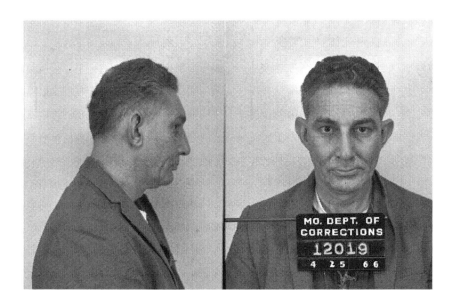

This picture of Duane Weber was taken in the late 1960s upon his incarceration at the penitentiary in Jefferson, Missouri. It has been widely circulated on the Internet, especially at the DZ, and was originally obtained by Dave Shutter via a FOIA request.

Barb Dayton

Pictures of Barb, post-surgery, with her hair pulled-back. This composite was made by Ron and Pat Forman to re-create the photo that was taken in 1979, just after her confession to her friends. Used with permission.

Wolfgang Gossett

This picture of Wolfgang Gossett is circa 1970, and is provided by Galen Cook and used with permission. It originated with Mr. Gossett's family.

Kenny Christiansen

This picture shows Kenny in his purser uniform, circa 1970s. Picture is provided by Kenny's brother, Lyle Christiansen, and used with permission.

Sheridan Peterson

This picture of Sheridan Peterson was taken in the late 1960s as part of a Boeing Employees Skydiving promotion. Photo proved courtesy of Bob Sailshaw.

Marla Cooper and Dale Miller

This picture was taken during the 2011 Annual DB Cooper Days Festival, held at the Ariel Tavern. Marla and "Santa" arrived immediately after Marla's presentation at the Portland Symposium. Photo taken by author.

DB Cooper as Cultural Hero

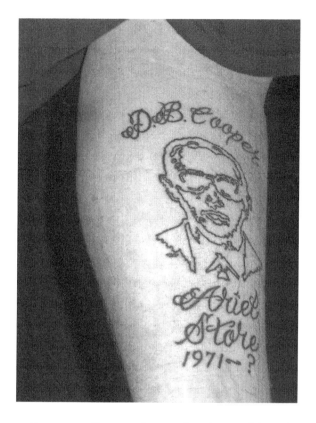

A tattoo on the arm of a reveler at the Annual DB Cooper Days festival in Ariel shows the degree of affection for The Man Who Beat Da Man. Photo taken by author

DB Cooper Days Festival in Ariel

One of the highlights of the annual DB Cooper Festival is the "Look-a-Like" contest. Shown is one of the contestants from the 2008 competition. Photo taken by author.

Geoffrey Gray

This picture was taken in 2013 at the DB Cooper Symposium at the Washington Historical Museum. Geoffrey is the author of "Skyjack— The Hunt for DB Cooper," and was speaking as part of their exhibit on DB Cooper. In addition, Geoffrey was the organizer of the 2011 DB Cooper Symposium in Portland, Oregon. Photo taken by author.

Bruce A. Smith and Galen Cook

This picture was taken in the spring of 2010 during the height of our investigation into Tina Mucklow. Galen (right) and the author (left) met at their favorite DB Cooper rendezvous spot—Fish Tales Pub in Olympia, Washington, just west of Victor-23. Photo taken by author.

DB Cooper researchers

Pictured left to right: Robb Heady, Vicki Wilson, Ron and Pat Forman. This picture was taken in 2013 at the Lewis River Bed and Breakfast, a favorite respite for Cooper aficionados attending the Annual DB Cooper Days festival at the nearby Ariel Tavern. Photo taken by author.

Index

431

Made in the USA
Lexington, KY
01 August 2016